T0361305

Assess and Analyze

Lean is about building and improving stable and predictable systems and processes to deliver to customers high-quality products/services on time by engaging everyone in the organization. Combined with this, organizations need to create an environment of respect for people and continuous learning. It's all about people. People create the product or service, drive innovation, and create systems and processes, and with leadership buy-in and accountability to ensure sustainment with this philosophy, employees will be committed to the organization as they learn and grow personally and professionally.

Lean is a term that describes a way of thinking about and managing companies as an enterprise. Becoming Lean requires the following: the continual pursuit to identify and eliminate waste; the establishment of efficient flow of both information and process; and an unwavering top-level commitment. The concept of continuous improvement applies to any process in any industry.

Based on the contents of *The Lean Practitioner's Field Book*, the purpose of this series is to show, in detail, how any process can be improved by utilizing a combination of tasks and people tools and introduces the BASICS Lean® concept. The books are designed for all levels of Lean practitioners and introduce proven tools for analysis and implementation that go beyond the traditional point kaizen event. Each book can be used as a stand-alone volume or used in combination with other titles based on specific needs.

Each book is chock-full of case studies and stories from the authors' own experiences in training organizations who have started or are continuing their Lean journey of continuous improvement. Contents include valuable lessons learned and each chapter concludes with questions pertaining to the focus of the chapter. Numerous photographs enrich and illustrate specific tools used in Lean methodology.

Assess and Analyze: Discovering the Waste Consuming Your Profits explores the tools used to assess and analyze the process. It starts off with Learning to See waste and follows with the three analysis tools: mapping the product flow, documenting the full work of the operator, and implementing SMED or changeover reduction and closes with exploring Lean and change management.

BASICS Lean® Implementation Series

Baseline: Confronting Reality & Planning the Path for Success
By Charles Protzman, Fred Whiton & Joyce Kerpchar

Assess and Analyze: Discovering the Waste Consuming Your Profits
By Charles Protzman, Fred Whiton & Joyce Kerpchar

Suggesting Solutions: Brainstorming Creative Ideas to Maximize Productivity
By Charles Protzman, Fred Whiton & Joyce Kerpchar

Implementing Lean: Converting Waste to Profit
By Charles Protzman, Fred Whiton & Joyce Kerpchar

Check: Identifying Gaps on the Path to Success
By Charles Protzman, Fred Whiton & Joyce Kerpchar

Sustaining Lean: Creating a Culture of Continuous Improvement
By Charles Protzman, Fred Whiton & Joyce Kerpchar

Assess and Analyze
Discovering the Waste Consuming Your Profits

Charles Protzman, Fred Whiton, and Joyce Kerpchar

Routledge
Taylor & Francis Group

A PRODUCTIVITY PRESS BOOK

First published 2023
by Routledge
605 Third Avenue, New York, NY 10158

and by Routledge
4 Park Square, Milton Park, Abingdon, Oxon, OX14 4RN

Routledge is an imprint of the Taylor & Francis Group, an informa business

ISBN: 978-1-032-02914-6 (hbk)
ISBN: 978-1-032-02913-9 (pbk)
ISBN: 978-1-003-18578-9 (ebk)

DOI: 10.4324/9781003185789

Typeset in Garamond
by KnowledgeWorks Global Ltd.

This book series is dedicated to all the Lean practitioners in the world and to two of the earliest, my friend Kenneth Hopper and my grandfather Charles W. Protzman Sr. Kenneth was a close friend of Charles Sr. and is coauthor with his brother William of a book that describes Charles Sr. and his work for General MacArthur in the Occupation of Japan in some detail: *The Puritan Gift: Reclaiming the American Dream amidst Global Financial Chaos.*

Charles W. Protzman Sr.

Kenneth Hopper

Contents

Acknowledgments

There are many individuals who have contributed to this book, both directly and indirectly, and many others over the years, too many to list here, who have shared their knowledge and experiences with us. We would like to thank all of those who have worked with us on Lean teams in the past and the senior leadership whose support made them successful. This book would not have been possible without your hard work, perseverance, and courage during our Lean journey together. We hope you see this book as the culmination of our respect and appreciation. We apologize if we have overlooked anyone in the following acknowledgments. We would like to thank the following for their contributions to coauthor or contribute to the chapters in this book:

- Special thanks to our Productivity Press editor, Kris Mednansky, who has been terrific at guiding us through our writing project. Kris has been a great source of encouragement and kept us on track as we worked through what became an ever-expanding six-year project.
- Special thanks to all our clients. Without you, this book would not have been possible.
- Russ Scaffede for his insight into the Toyota system and for his valuable contributions through numerous e-mail correspondence and edits with various parts of the book.
- Joel Barker for his permission in referencing the paradigm material so important and integral to Lean implementations and change management.
- Many thanks to the "Hats" team (you know who you are).
- I would like to acknowledge Mark Jamrog of SMC Group. Mark was my first Sensei and introduced me to this Kaikaku-style Lean System Implementation approach based on the Ohno and Shingo teachings.
- Various chapter contributions by Joe and Ed Markiewicz of Ancon Gear.

For the complete list of acknowledgments, testimonials, dedication, etc. please see The Lean Practitioner's Field Book. The purpose of this series was to break down and enhance the original Lean Practitioner's Field Book into six books that are aligned with the BASICS® model.

Authors' Note: Every attempt was made to source materials back to the original authors. In the event we missed someone, please feel free to let us know so we may correct it in any future edition. Many of the spreadsheets depicted were originally hand drawn by Mark Jamrog, SMC Group, put into Excel by Dave O'Koren and Charlie Protzman, and since modified significantly. Most of the base formatting for these spreadsheets can be found in the Shingo, Ohno, Monden, or other industrial engineering handbooks.

About the Authors

Charles Protzman, MBA, CPM, formed Business Improvement Group (B.I.G.), LLC, in November 1997. B.I.G. is in Sarasota Florida. Charlie and his son, Dan along with Mike Meyers, specialize in implementing and training Lean thinking principles and the BASICS® Lean business delivery system (LBDS) in small to fortune 50 companies involved in Manufacturing, Healthcare, Government, and Service Industries.

Charles has written 12 books to date and is the coauthor of Leveraging Lean in Healthcare: Transforming Your Enterprise into a High-Quality Patient Care Delivery System series and is a two-time recipient of the Shingo Research and Professional Publication Award. He has since published *The BASICS® Lean Implementation Model* and *Lean Leadership BASICS®*. Charles has over 38 years of experience in materials and operations management. He spent almost 14 years with AlliedSignal, now Honeywell, where he was an Aerospace Strategic Operations Manager and the first AlliedSignal Lean master. He has received numerous special-recognition and cost-reduction awards. Charles was an external consultant for the Department of Business and Economic Development's (DBED's) Maryland Consortium during and after his tenure with AlliedSignal. With the help of Joyce LaPadula and others, he had input into the resulting DBED world-class criteria document and assisted in the first three initial DBED world-class company assessments. B.I.G. was a Strategic Partner of ValuMetrix Services, a division of Ortho-Clinical Diagnostics, Inc., a Johnson & Johnson company. He is an international Lean consultant and has taught beginner to advanced students' courses in Lean principles and total quality all over the world.

Charlie Protzman states, "My grandfather started me down this path and has influenced my life to this day. My grandfather made four trips to Japan from 1948 to the 1960s. He loved the Japanese people and culture and was passionate and determined to see Japanese manufacturing recover from World War II."

Charles spent the last 24 years with Business Improvement Group, LLC, implementing successful Lean product line conversions, kaizen events, and administrative business system improvements (transactional Lean) worldwide. He is following in the footsteps of his grandfather, who was part of the Civil Communications Section (CCS) of the American Occupation. Prior to recommending Dr. Deming's 1950 visit to Japan, C.W. Protzman Sr. surveyed over 70 Japanese companies in 1948. Starting in late 1948, Homer Sarasohn and C.W. Protzman Sr. taught top executives of prominent Japanese communications companies an eight-week course in American participative management and quality techniques in Osaka and Tokyo. Over 5,100 top Japanese executives had taken the course by 1956. The course continued until 1993. Many of the lessons we taught the Japanese in 1948 are now being taught to Americans as "Lean principles." The Lean principles had their roots in the United States and date back to the early 1700s and later to Taylor, Gilbreth, and Henry Ford. The principles were refined by Taiichi Ohno and expanded by Dr. Shigeo Shingo. Modern-day champions were Norman Bodek (the Grandfather of Lean), Jim Womack, and Dan Jones.

Charles participated in numerous benchmarking and site visits, including a two-week trip to Japan in June 1996 and 2017. He is a master facilitator and trainer in TQM, total quality speed, facilitation, career development, change management, benchmarking, leadership, systems thinking, high-performance work teams, team building, Myers-Briggs® Styles, Lean thinking, and supply chain management. He also participated in Baldrige Examiner and Six Sigma management courses. He was an assistant program manager during "Desert Storm" for the Patriot missile-to-missile fuse development and production program. Charles is a past member of SME, AME, IIE, IEEE, APT, and the International Performance Alliance Group (IPAG), an international team of expert Lean Practitioners (http://www.ipag-consulting.com).

Fred Whiton, MBA, PMP, PE, has 30 years of experience in the aerospace and defense industry, which includes engineering, operations, program and portfolio management, and strategy development. He is employed as a Chief Engineer within Raytheon Intelligence & Space at the time of this book's publication.

Fred has both domestic and international expertise within homeland security, communications command and control intelligence surveillance and reconnaissance sensors and services, military and commercial aerospace systems, and defense systems supporting the US Navy, US Air Force, US Army, US Department of Homeland Security, and the US Intelligence Community across a full range of functions from marketing, concept development, engineering, and production into life cycle sustainment and logistics. Fred began his career as a design engineer at General Dynamics, was promoted to a group engineer at Lockheed Martin, and was a director at Northrop Grumman within the Homeland Defense Government Systems team. As vice president of engineering and operations at Smiths Aerospace, he was the Lean champion for a Lean enterprise journey, working closely with Protzman as the Lean consultant, for a very successful Lean implementation within a union plant, including a new plant designed using Lean principles. Prior to joining Raytheon, Fred was a senior vice president within C4ISR business unit at CACI International and prior to joining CACI was the vice president and general manager of the Tactical Communications and Network Solutions Line of Business within DRS Technologies.

Fred has a BS in mechanical engineering from the University of Maryland, an MS in mechanical engineering from Rensselaer Polytechnic Institute, a master's in engineering administration from The George Washington University, and an MBA from The University of Chicago. He is a professional engineer (PE) in Maryland, a certified project management professional (PMP), served as a commissioner on the Maryland Commission for Manufacturing Competitiveness under Governor Ehrlich, as a commissioner on the Maryland Commission on Autism under Governor O'Malley, and as a member of the boards of directors for the Regional Manufacturing Institute headquartered in Maryland and the First Maryland Disability Trust.

Joyce Kerpchar has over 35 years of experience in the healthcare industry that includes key leadership roles in healthcare operations, IT, health plan management, and innovative program development and strategy. As a Lean champion, mentor, and Six Sigma black belt, she is experienced in organizational lean strategy and leading large-scale healthcare lean initiatives, change management, and IT implementations. Joyce is a coauthor of Leveraging Lean in Healthcare: Transforming Your Enterprise into a High-Quality Patient Care Delivery System, Recipient of the Shingo Research and Professional Publication Award.

She began her career as a board-certified physician's assistant in cardiovascular and thoracic surgery and primary care medicine and received her master's degree in Management. Joyce is passionate about leveraging Lean in healthcare processes to eliminate waste and reduce errors, improve overall quality, and reduce the cost of providing healthcare.

Introduction

This book is part of the BASICS Lean® Implementation Series and was adapted from The Lean Practitioner's Field Book: Proven, Practical, Profitable and Powerful Techniques for Making Lean Really Work. In Book 2, we begin with discussing waste versus efficiency. Then we perform a detailed walk-through of how to conduct the ASSESS and ANALYZE steps in the BASICS Lean® Implementation Model. These steps include analyzing the product process flow, the workflow of the operator, and changeovers. These are the same teachings of Shigeo Shingo from his famous P-course in Japan. We end with exploring the change management required to implement Lean. This is the most difficult part of any implementation.

The books in this BASICS Lean® Implementation Series take the reader on a journey beginning with an overview of Lean principles, culminating with employees developing professionally through the BASICS Lean® Leadership Development Path. Each book has something for everyone from the novice to the seasoned Lean Practitioner. A refresher for some at times, it provides soul-searching and thought-provoking questions with examples that will stimulate learning opportunities. Many of us take advantage of these learning opportunities daily. We, the authors, as Lean practitioners, are students still thirsting for knowledge and experiences to assist organizations in their transformations.

This series is designed to be a guide and resource to help you with the ongoing struggle to improve manufacturing, government, and service industries throughout the world. This series embodies true stories, results, and lessons, which we and others have learned during our Lean journeys. The concept of continuous improvement applies to any process in any industry.

The purpose of this series is to show, in detail, how any process can be improved by utilizing a combination of tasks and people tools. We will introduce proven tools for analysis and implementation that go far beyond the traditional point kaizen event training. Several CEOs have shared with us; had they not implemented Lean, they would not have survived the Recession in 2008 and subsequent downturns.

Many companies prefer we not use their names in this book as they consider Lean a strategic competitive advantage in their industry, and some of these companies have now moved into a leadership position in their respective markets; thus, we may refer to them as Company X throughout the series. We explain to companies that Lean is a 5-year commitment that never ends. Eighty to ninety percent of the companies with whom we have worked have sustained their Lean journeys based on implementing our BASICS® Lean approach that we will share with you in this book.

The BASICS Lean® Implementation Series discusses the principles and tools in detail as well as the components of the House of Lean. It is a "how to" book that presents an integrated, structured approach identified by the acronym BASICS®, which when combined with an effective business strategy can help ensure the successful transformation of an organization. The Lean concepts described in each book are supported by a plethora of examples drawn from the personal experiences of its many well-known and respected contributors, which range from very small machine shops to Fortune 50 companies.

The BASICS Lean® Implementation Series has both practical applications as well as applications in academia. It can be used for motivating students to learn many of the Lean concepts and at the end of each chapter there are thought-provoking questions for the reader to help digest the material. The investment in people in terms of training, engagement, empowerment, and personal and professional growth is the key to sustaining Lean and an organization's success. For more on this topic, please see our book Lean Leadership BASICS®. Lean practitioners follow a natural flow, building continually on previous information and experiences. There is a bit of the Lean practitioner in all of us. Hopefully, as you read these books to pursue additional knowledge, as a refresher or for reference, or for academia, it can help expand your knowledge, skills, and abilities on your never-ending Lean journey.

Chapter 1

Waste versus Efficiency

Lean Production should be changed to Easy Production—constantly ask yourself, how do we continually make everyone's job easier?

Mauro Chiodo

Barge, Italy

How Do We Define Waste?

According to Dr. Shingo, "Waste is any activity which does not contribute to operations. There are two types of operations: value-added work and non–value-added work. Some non–value-added work is necessary but is still non–value-added work. Work advances a process and adds value while an operator merely moving quickly and efficiently may not accomplish anything."[1] We define waste as any activity increasing cost with no corresponding value added to the product or customer. When your organization becomes literally obsessed with the total elimination of waste in everything it does and is never satisfied with the current state, then your organization will be well on its way down the Lean maturity path.

Lesson Learned: When you think you have improved enough, it is time to quit! Every organization should view Lean as an integral part of the organization's competitive business strategy combined with a strategy to grow the business. We are never done improving! There is always a better way… you just must find it.

Waste Characteristics

Waste is like a virus because it hides and then incubates. If we do not treat it or eradicate it, it festers, mutates, grows, and multiplies all around us. Waste creates workarounds to our processes, creating poor staff and customer satisfaction as we are constantly searching for things, which delay our products and services. Ultimately, waste decreases our ability to compete in the marketplace. Waste can deter us from working on key initiatives that would help drive innovation and future growth. Waste causes variation and imperfection in our processes. The big question is… Do we have enough dissatisfaction with the

DOI: 10.4324/9781003185789-1

1

waste to create a compelling need to change the system and rid ourselves of the waste? The Lean tools in this book will help you to find waste in your organization. Shop floors, offices, government, healthcare, homebuilders, the military, banks, insurance companies, landscapers, even PTA (Parent Teachers Association) volunteers, moms, and dads at home, all have applied Lean tools.

Lesson Learned: If utilized properly, Lean tools will expose waste but does not guarantee the elimination of waste. That job will be up to you! Customers and "fresh eyes" can provide valuable input on the quest to eliminate waste. They can help us identify waste we do not see or do not want to see. You just need to ask for the feedback.

Lean Case Study: Live Green Landscape Associates, by Michael Martin, President

As a recent startup and now a major landscape contracting company in the Baltimore Maryland region, we were looking to save money and increase our bottom line and continue to grow in a very competitive market. We reached a point where we just couldn't figure out a way to cut costs any further, which impacted our ability to maintain competitive prices in the market. The landscape company has three main cost areas:

1. Labor
2. Materials
3. Overhead

We determined we could not squeeze any further monies from materials or overhead. We saw some opportunity in the labor area, but people were already working as hard as they could. We felt if we could save an hour here and there then we could start growing the bottom line and generate more cash flow. As with any small business, cash flow management is our top priority and concern. Then I heard about Lean. I was not sure Lean was going to be a good fit or could even work in the contracting world as I thought it was mostly used in manufacturing. We decided to give it a shot and hired a Lean consultant to show us the way. In the beginning, there was plenty of opposition from different people on our staff. "This is going to be more work for us," they said. As time passed and different events showed results, the people in the company began to come around. Let me share with you two examples of how we embraced Lean to reduce waste.

Live Green's First Kaizen

Problem:

Every morning for years I would come in at 6:00 a.m. and watch crew after crew load their trucks with the materials and equipment they needed for the day. Day after day, there would be a line at the mulch bin or at the diesel fuel tank and 50 guys would be standing around waiting. This process took up to 1 hour each day. This was 50-man hours a day we were losing and 250-man hours per week of unbillable hours. However, for years this is how we had always done it, no one ever thought about it. I know now this is called the boiled frog syndrome.

We put together a kaizen group to watch and map out the event and followed the BASICS® model. First, we baselined the metrics and then analyzed and documented the current conditions.

We identified the waste and then developed solutions. We took several days to pilot some ideas and make changes. Once we saw the improvements, we standardized and documented the process. The best thing we did was build the team with both office and field personnel. It was surprising to realize some of the group had never seen the loading process in the morning. The ideas they came back with were unbelievable. I say that because I cannot believe we did not think of any of this before doing kaizen.

Lean Solutions:
Some of the ideas they developed and implemented:

- Load the trucks on the way in at night.
- Have the crew leader call the manager and see how much mulch was needed for the next day's work, which eliminated the mulch line. How each crew comes into the yard at a different time in the evening? This created a natural lag time between trucks and thus there was no stacked mulch. Essentially, we level loaded (Heijunka) the process.
- The second change was the location of the diesel fuel tank. The tank was now located near the mulch bin to allow trucks to fuel up on their way into the yard in the evening.

Results:
These two simple changes saved the company thousands of unbillable hours. Not only in the yard, but also in the morning, they were out of the yard quickly and far ahead of the morning rush hour traffic, saving thousands of hours of unbillable time. Multiply thousands of hours in a year times an employee's hourly rate and you can figure how this helped our company's bottom line.

Live Green's Second Kaizen: Lean Is Iterations of Improvement

Problem:
This kaizen addressed the follow up to the trucks loading mulch and diesel at night instead of in the morning. A new kaizen group was formed, comprising a variety of different employees within the company. This time they looked at how to get the crews out in the morning even faster. We followed the same BASICS® model as before:

- This time they found the daily work sheets were not posted in the evening and the crew leaders were not receiving them in the morning and thus the necessary tools and equipment, such as tillers and saws, were not being loaded until the next morning.
- The second process they documented was that the production manager was fielding a long line of questions from each crew leader.

Solution:
- Their solution was to have the production manager write all the daily work sheets and have them posted by 3 p.m.
- The crew leaders now returned from their day's work with their sheet in hand for the next day. They could ask the manager any questions at that time, which allowed them to load the necessary tools and equipment for the next day.
- Again, the crews returned from their jobs at different times in the afternoon (level loading) so there was no longer a line at the production manager's door.

Results:
The results were the following:

- The crews saved another 10–20 minutes in the morning searching and loading out their trucks.
- There was more organization and less chaos in the morning.
- The result of this process was that few tools and equipment were forgotten and left at the shop. This was an unexpected increase in efficiency!
- The crews were more efficient on the job equipped with all the correct tools.

Summary:
All the aforementioned events were ways Live Green was able to use a kaizen to get out of our yard and into our customer's yard quicker in the morning and be more efficient and Leaner. These changes created more money to the bottom line enabling us to continue growing our business and provide more jobs in very difficult economic times. Isn't this what all businesses are trying to achieve?

Obsession with Waste

The Japanese are literally obsessed with waste. They must import virtually everything since they have no natural raw materials. Property in Japan is a valuable commodity. Either land has a building on it, or it is growing something. One sees this obsession with waste everywhere in their culture… even their television newscasts mention the word kaizen repeatedly.[2] Lean principles are evident everywhere in Japan: for example, the Lean principle of zero defects or mistake proofing (poka yoke) seen in Figure 1.1. One cannot cross a major intersection in a big city. Pedestrians must go either over it or under it in tunnels. The Lean principle of flexibility is very evident in Japan. Trucks in Japan do not unload from the back (see Figure 1.2). They open on both sides so they can be unloaded simultaneously and more quickly. Their trucks have panels underneath so cars cannot inadvertently be trapped. These are now appearing on US trucks.

Mistake Proofing in the Hotel[3,4]

I had a problem with my hotel room. I could not figure out how to turn on the lights. The electricity did not seem to work in the room. I had to get the interpreter to go with me to the front desk to ask them what the problem was with my room. The front desk clerk told me there was a panel on the wall next to the door (see Figure 1.3). The panel controls the electricity in the room. You must put in your hotel key and turn it clockwise to turn the electricity on in the room. Then to leave the room what do you have to do? You must turn the key counterclockwise and remove it to leave the room. This turns off the electricity and makes sure you do not forget your key. Therefore, it combines energy efficiency with mistake proofing.

Next, look at the picture in Figure 1.4. Look closely. After taking a shower, the mirror usually steams up, right? However, notice there is a section that did not steam. Every hotel we stayed in had this feature. I have not seen this in an American or European hotel to date. The only way I

Figure 1.1 Over and underpass in Japan on major intersections.

Figure 1.2 Commercial trucking in Japan—unloaded from sides. Twice as fast.

Figure 1.3 Must remove the key to leave the room which turns off the lights. Now pretty much standard in Europe.

have been able to duplicate it is by rubbing shaving cream onto the mirror. Therefore, this idea of waste elimination seems to be easier for the Japanese because it is built into their culture. They eat, live, and breathe this stuff! It is much more difficult for Westerners to get rid of the waste paradigm!

Seven (Eight) Wastes

There are seven primary wastes: overproduction, time on hand (idle time/waiting), transportation/travel, overprocessing, inventory (overstocking), movement/motion, defects/rework, and, an eighth waste we added almost 20 years ago, the waste of talent. The following are definitions and examples of all eight primary wastes. The identification and elimination of waste is a critical component of Lean.

Figure 1.4 Mirror is not fogged in middle.

Waste of Overproduction

This is the number one waste in the Toyota production system (TPS), the one Ohno worked on the most, and we find it is the hardest to remove. This is what drives the conversion from batch to flow production. This waste focuses on the following:

- Making only the customer driven amount of product
- Making it only when needed

If (for any reason) we make more than we need or we make it before we need, it must be stored, which is waste. What are some characteristics of overproduction? By characteristics, if you were walking around the plant, what would overproduction look like?

What would you physically be able to see?

- Inventory stockpiles
- Problems with on-time delivery
- Extra equipment/oversized equipment
- Unbalanced material flow
- Extra racks/dunnage[5]
- Extra manpower
- Complex inventory
- Management of excessive capacity/investment of additional floor space/outside storage
- Hidden problems
- Creates unsafe work environment
- Excessive obsolescence
- Large lot sizes
- Pre-building product ahead

Things you might not see:

- Constant rescheduling of suppliers
- Ongoing expediting at all levels of the organization
- Hours spent tracking variances
- Reduced morale
- Reduced cash flow

Some causes of overproduction:

- Batch processes
- Incapable processes
- Just in case (JIC) reward system
- Lack of communication
- Local optimization
- Scrap and rework
- Automation in the wrong places
- Long die changes
- Printing out extra reports or copies

- Cost accounting practices
- Low uptimes/insufficient preventative maintenance
- Lack of stable/consistent schedules
- Focus on expectation (forecasted sales) versus customer demand (consumption)

Waste of Time on Hand (Idle)

What would you physically be able to see?

- Anyone who is idle when they should be working
- People trying to look busy
- Waiting at a machine or copier
- Operator waiting for machine
- Machine waiting for supervisor or team leader
- Operator waiting for an operator

Things you might not see:

- Lack of operator concern for equipment breakdowns
- Unplanned equipment downtime
- Machines not in use (indicates excess capacity; find work for the machine or sell it)

Some causes of idle time:

- Poor layouts
- Poor management systems
- Unbalanced operations (work)
- Poor work habits
- Lack of discipline
- Lack of motivation
- Batch processes
- Part shortages
- Poor order scheduling, planning, or production control
- Lack of pride in the workplace

Waste in Transportation

What would you physically be able to see?

- Parts or paperwork being transported from one place to another by people
- Hitting the send button on email or text
- Forklifts, hand trucks, cranes, and other material handling devices
- Inventory waiting for transport
- Conveyors moving inventory
- Multiple storage locations
- Extra racks/dunnage
- Complex inventory management
- Extra facility space

- Opportunity for damage/floor loss
- Drivers having unbalanced work schedules
- Heavy duty barriers and protection devices
- Costly, inflexible conveyors and automated guided vehicle (AGV) systems
- Repair lines and rework stations

Things you might not see:

- Someone idle waiting for materials or tools to be moved to them
- Incorrect inventory counts
- Injuries due to forklift accidents
- Lost time due to operators getting their own materials

Some causes of waste in transportation:

- Layouts: sometimes producing in different buildings
- Distance between machines or processes
- Batch processes: leaving room for inventory
- Poor scheduling
- Physical size or weight of materials

Waste of (Too Much) Processing

We define this as doing more to a part or paperwork (electronic or paper) than necessary to meet the customer-defined specifications or perceived quality needs. We find this waste when an organization or individual does not really know what the customer needs, so they do tasks/activities based upon what they believe the customer needs.

What would you physically be able to see?

- Inspection: including source inspection or 100% human inspection
- Inventory queuing up
- Paper in inboxes: physical or electronic
- Rework or scrap
- Sometimes arguments over what is required
- Process bottlenecks

Things you might not see:

- The cost of excess labor
- Negative impact on on-time delivery
- Excess paperwork
- Reduced employee morale
- Reduced customer satisfaction

Some causes of waste of (too much) processing:

- Incapable processes
- Government or industry regulations

- Poor interpretation of customer specs
- Part is over engineered
- Computers: unnecessary excel sheets created
- Testing machines that fail good parts
- Finance: cost accounting variances, budgeting processes, etc.
- Too many approval levels
- Poor interpretation of ISO or other government regulations
- Operators' perception that without it they are not producing high-quality parts or paperwork
- Machines with more functions (bells and whistles) than required (e.g., lab machines in a hospital which produce a standard set of results regardless of what is ordered)
- Financial: additional revenue (e.g., cost plus contracts, auto repair shops)
- Waste, fraud, and abuse
- Lack of boundary samples or clear customer specifications
- Endless refinement
- Redundant approvals
- Extra copies/excessive information

Waste of Stock on Hand (Inventory)

This includes not only excess stock, which is nonproductive inventory (excess and obsolete— E&O) or which we will never use, but also the following.

What would you physically be able to see?

- Warehouse, stockrooms, closets, drawers, and shelves
- Inventory stockpiles
- E&O tooling and parts
- Office supply cabinets
- Salvage areas
- Old machines kept for parts
- Stock kept around in case it can be reworked
- Stock or paperwork kept because we just do not want to throw it out
- File cabinets, inventory records
- Material review board (MRB) cages
- Extra space on the receiving dock
- Work in process (WIP) between processes hide problems
- First in still here (FISH) instead of first in first out (FIFO)
- Massive rework campaigns when problems surface
- Requirement of additional material handling resources (men, equipment, racks, storage space/systems)

Things you might not see:

- Slow response to change in customer demands
- Stagnated material flow
- Long lead time for engineering changes

Some causes of waste of stock on hand (inventory):

■ Batch processes
■ Incapable processes
■ Engineering change to new rev level
■ Customer requirements change or misinterpreted
■ Setups
■ Parts shortages
■ Complete dependence on material requirement planning (MRP) systems
■ Poor scheduling
■ Waste of overproduction
■ Over shipment by suppliers
■ Unauthorized shipments
■ Excess stationery and crib stores

Waste of (Worker) Movement

We define this waste as follows: whenever someone must reach outside their normal path of motion while sitting or standing, including having to get their own supplies. This includes getting up and down from a chair.

What would you physically be able to see?

■ Parts delivered to a cell for workers to put away
■ Workers walking anywhere to get parts or paperwork
■ Walking to the centralized Xerox® machine or printer
■ Reaching for parts or paperwork
■ Bending over to pick up parts or paperwork
■ Workers getting their own tooling
■ Centralized tool cribs or stockrooms
■ Excessive walk time—station too big—tools not in easy reach
■ The walk between headquarters and engineering buildings
■ Over cycle (movement) of machine

Lesson Learned: Caution! Do not confuse motion for work!
Things you might not see:

■ Unpacking or rearrangement of parts by the operator
■ Future employee ergonomic issues
■ Employee lost time and/or increase in personal days
■ Safety issues—lost workday incidents

Some causes of waste of (worker) movement:

■ Batch processes
■ Layouts
■ Poor workstation design
■ Offices with higher than 4-ft partitions

- Production areas with walls
- Centralized stockrooms and kitting
- Lack of point of use philosophy
- Stocking subassemblies (WIP)
- MRP bill of material (BOM) levels
- Looking to find tools
- Excessive reaching/bending
- Machines/material too far apart (excessive walk time)
- Shuttle conveyors between equipment to carry parts
- Extra busy movements while waiting
- Part presentation method

Waste of Making Defective Products

- This is making products which do not meet the customer's specifications or perceived quality characteristics. In the words of Yoshio Kondo,
- Keep in mind for Total Company Wide Quality Control, products have two specifications[5]:
  - Specification quality. i.e., Do the parts meet the specification?
  - Customer quality i.e., does the part meet parameters of what the customer is looking for that might not be in the specification?

In the words of Dr. Joseph M. Juran, there are two definitions of quality critical to managers:

1. It is oriented to income
   Quality in this context is designing in the features resulting in customers willing to buy your product instead of a competitor's. This definition is cost oriented; the more trouble there is the more it costs. If the trouble occurs in your organization, it costs only you. If it occurs when the product is used in a customer's organization, it also costs the customer, which intersects with your income as it makes the customer less willing to buy that same product in the future, despite its great features.
2. It is high quality
   This definition means more products sold and thus more income for your company:
   - Freedom from trouble
   - Freedom from errors
   - Freedom from defects
   - Freedom from redoing
   - Freedom from field failures

Many managers debate whether higher quality costs more or less. Very often they literally do not know what the other person is talking about because one of them is thinking of the first definition of quality and the other of the second. As a result, they are going to reach different conclusions. Before beginning a quality initiative, companies must be sure the word "quality" is well defined and understood within the organization. There are enormous differences between the two.

Most companies are set up for the first one. By contrast, Quality in the sense of eliminating defects and product failures has no established method: we don't find it in the business plan and most of the time there is no infrastructure for it. Responsibility for this type of quality is vague and improvement voluntary, despite the fact wastes are huge. Corporations need to concentrate on improving the process needed to increase this second type of quality. The dollar amounts at stake here are just as large as the amounts at stake when we attempt to increase sales by developing new products.[6]

Waste of defects: What would you physically be able to see?

■ Rework and scrap areas
■ Idle time
■ Human inspection
■ Warranty department
■ Large MRB areas
■ Repairmen or servicemen
■ Temperature or humidity-controlled areas
■ Red colored scrap bins
■ Material piled up next to a test machine
■ Extra floor space/tools/equipment
■ Specific inventory stockpiles
■ Complex product flow
■ Questionable quality
■ Poor customer/supplier relations
■ Lower profits due to scrap, premium freight costs
■ Organization becomes reactive (firefighting, expediting vs. prevention orientation)

Things you might not see:

■ Extra time required by our workforce to inspect, rework, and repair
■ Impacts on on-time delivery and reduced customer satisfaction
■ Supplier rescheduling
■ Increase in expediting time
■ Increase in freight

Some causes of waste of making defective products:

■ Incapable processes
■ Engineering: product life cycles, trial and error designs requiring tweaking
■ Sales taking orders which cannot meet specifications
■ Batch processing: material damaged during transport and storage
■ Measurement systems evaluation (MSE): testing machines pass bad parts or are incapable of measuring to the required tolerance—processes not capable
■ Wastes of transport, overprocessing, and overproduction

Waste of Talent (an Organization's Most Valuable Asset)

We see this waste when organizations do not tap their employees' brainpower, ideas, and experience. The engagement of an organization's talent is critical in making Lean initiatives successful.

The talent in your organization will drive innovation and change by identifying and eliminating all waste.

Batch processes.

- The other seven wastes
- Dictators
- People always provide solutions to people's questions
- Everyone does it differently on the floor or in the office
- Indifference: lack of motivation

Things you might not see:

- Idea boards
- Lack of visual controls, mistake proofing, standard work
- Standard problem-solving models
- No QC circles
- No daily huddles
- Poor HR systems, orientation, and hiring processes

Some causes of overproduction:

- Lack of leadership
- Lack of people development and respect for people
- Lack of company values
- Lack of feedback systems
- Lack of standard work
- Lack of pride in the workplace
- Lack of capable processes
- Lack of communication
- Long die changes
- Low uptimes/insufficient preventative maintenance
- Lack of stable/consistent schedules

There are many more wastes than these eight; however, these provide a good foundation to begin your quest.

Banana Example

Dr. Shingo's books use the banana story as an example of waste. When you go to the register, you pay for the banana by weight, but Dr. Shingo points out most of the weight is in the peel, which you discard.

Other examples of waste include the following:

- Walking waste
- Watching waste
- Searching waste
- Waste due to large machines

- Waste embedded in conveyors, which store versus transport
- Waste caused by poor layouts
- Waste due to meetings
- Operators are famous for this waste—picking it up and then setting down without using it
- Waste of not knowing what to do next—structure absent
- Waste of finding others to make decisions—absence of escalation protocols
- Lack of direction from leadership

Where Does Waste Come from?[7] What Are the Overarching Root Causes of the Eight Wastes?

We need to look at waste in a much different way and at a much higher level of detail:

- What is waste?
- If you take some time and really think about it, where does waste come from?
- What are some of the root causes of waste?

Listed below are some of the primary drivers of waste we see in organizations:

Waste You Tend to be Able to See

1. The batching system in general. Batch processing needs inventory to survive. Indiscriminately reducing inventory without implementing the Lean principles of just in time (JIT), single-minute exchange of dies (SMED), one-touch exchange of dies (OTED), mistake proofing, visual controls, etc. will result in missed production or service schedules. As a former materials manager, it was not unusual to order the same materials two or three times for the same job. Batch processing characteristics are as follows:

   - Lack of process and workflow
   - Everything is pushed until something ships out the door
   - Excess inventory everywhere as the batch is pushed through the process.
   - Excess floor space/resources/equipment utilized as the product moves through the shop.
   - Idle time.
   - All operators are sitting down.

2. Lack of standardization throughout the company:

   - Undocumented, poorly documented, or outdated methods and processes
   - Poor engineering designs which require tweaking, tuning, etc.
   - Poor equipment designs and maintenance
   - Lack of proper training

3. Waste due to inefficient layouts:

   - Does the workflow or is the movement of work product erratic caused by facility challenges such as equipment located in a particular area, for instance, because it was the closest power outlet or just putting equipment where it fits versus in the proper flow?

- How workstations or work areas are designed in terms of flow, fixed versus flexible, sitting versus standing and walking, extra table, or shelf space where it is not required.
- Poor or wrong equipment (lack of Jidoka, if an abnormal situation arises does the activity stop to allow for correction of the problem)—analog gauges.

4. Complacency—no compelling need to improve, need paradigm shift: Tends to occur in highly profitable companies. The question to these organizations should be, "Why would you not want to make more profit?"

Things You Might Not See

1. Centralization: is a huge creator of waste and most of it is hidden. Centralizing is paramount to and synonymous with batching!
2. Once you centralize something, it needs to be scheduled, which then requires a manager. Everything now must be scheduled through that manager, and immediately many departments become dependent on that centralized area and manager. If the managers are not local or familiar with the area, they can't possibly know all the problems and they are not in touch with all the customers, etc. Very quickly, the centralized area becomes a cost center! We lose all accountability now in the other areas because whenever there is a problem, they blame the centralized area. Normally the first things to blame are the processes or departments we have no control over. As a result, not only, the centralized processes become very inefficient but the processes dependent on them become less efficient. Ironically, the centralization proposal probably had a big return on investment (ROI) behind it.
3. A good example is hospitals. Transport, for example, is often centralized. We were standing outside a patient's room in the ED who needed to be moved and called transport. A transporter was right outside the room. We could see him! We were told we would have to wait 15 minutes to send a transporter to us. When we asked the transporter outside the room (who was not busy by the way) he said he could not help us, we needed to contact transport. Their manager boasted on how good their response time was. He convinced management that a response time within 15 minutes to any request was good! When we dissected the measurement, we found that the 15 minutes he used to measure himself was to the time he told the department he would have someone there and was not calculated from the time the department called for the transporter.
4. We see this time and time again, in offices, maintenance departments, and throughout the companies. Some things make sense to centralize (e.g., payroll and billing, generally processes that are automated). However, we have seen some companies almost destroyed by it.
5. Lack of company loyalty. When employees have no loyalty, there is no incentive for them to suggest ideas. Some companies encourage employees to leave if they can make themselves more marketable. This creates waste when employees leave, and their knowledge goes with them. In addition, we then must hire and train their replacements.
6. Lack of standards and standardization at the work instruction level (I do it my way as my area is different). However, it is exacerbated by training methodologies and lack of leadership accountability to ensure compliance.
7. Poor hiring practices—many companies just look to get a body in to do the job. Toyota and many other organizations have extensive screening processes and assessments to get the right person for the job, that is, get the person on the bus in the right seat paradigm.
8. Results only driven metrics creating shoot from the hip solutions and variation—this reactive approach is driven by making the numbers, not improving their processes.

9. Lack of voice of the customer (VOC): working to people's interpretations or opinions of what is desired needs to clearly understand and document the customer's expectations—not only from the end user but also from the customer in the next process downstream.
10. Lack of leadership—inflexible—no constancy of purpose—fear-based environments—lack of clear ownership, responsibilities, discipline, and accountability.
11. Lack of pride in one's work or one's workplace—I use the example of installing a seat belt into the vehicle. What if this car were to be purchased by your wife, children, parents, grandparents, good friends, etc. How would you install this seat belt? Would you make sure the belt was installed perfectly every time?—Would you take pride in the job you performed? Would you emphasize the need for every process to be performed to the standard to guarantee the customer receives product/service to the highest quality, on time, in the right quantity? So, what does this say when we don't take pride in our work or our workplace?

Levels of Waste

We have categorized waste into six different levels[8]:

1. The first level is obvious waste: low-hanging fruit (or walking on it).
2. 5S wastes: the easiest wastes to see.
3. The seven (eight) wastes: discussed earlier.
4. Boiled frog waste: the waste that is hard to notice because it is old, and we pass by it every day.
5. Tribal waste or sacred cows: untouchable waste in our culture and systems.
6. Hidden unseen waste: waste we don't typically see, as it is hidden behind or masked by other wastes; you really must hunt for it! The hardest waste to find and yet the most dangerous, impacting an organization's ability to innovate, grow, and prosper.

Obvious Waste: Low-Hanging Fruit

The easiest waste referred to as low-hanging fruit as it is easy to see and obvious to anyone in the area. It could be trash/parts on the floor, a long waiting line at a register, someone searching for an office supply, standing at the printer, or waiting at the store while someone checks for a price on an unmarked item. They could be part of another waste level, but they are so obvious they should just be dealt with right away and are things you just can't miss.

5S Wastes

These are the wastes which have to do with housekeeping and discipline. These wastes include items not labeled, tools not put back where they belong, or operators having to go get their parts or tools or running out of parts or product. The 5Ss translated in English are sort, store (straighten, set in order), shine (sweep, clean), standardize, and sustain.

The Boiled Frog Syndrome

The most difficult waste to see is the waste which occurs in processes we have created or already improved ourselves. When these wastes are pointed out, we tend to be defensive. After all, this puts the blame on us. This is normal behavior and justified as it shows our ownership over the process. We should take pride in everything we do; however, it is because we take pride in our areas, we should be willing to expose the waste or be grateful when others point it out to us.

Sometimes, outsiders help to show us the waste we don't see, or we intentionally or unintentionally refuse to see. A fresh set of eyes look at and see things we don't because we are so close to it. We all tend to be boiled frogs. The key is not to be defensive when it is presented. Being defensive hurts us in the long run because it discourages others from telling us when they see a problem or when they find waste in our area. We should recognize the waste that exists, thank those who tell us, and work to eliminate it. Waste exits in all work and at all levels of an organization. We must all work together to first identify waste and then eliminate it.

How Do You Find Waste? The Five Whys

In a Lean culture, we need to know there is always a better way to perform a process and continuously pursue improvements. We may not always know how to do it better, so sometimes we just need to figure it out or solicit help from others to figure it out. The best way to figure it out is to constantly ask "why?," asking Why five times allows the opportunity to start searching for root causes and begin to identify waste and opportunities for improvement. The following is a five-why example.

A part was installed in reverse position:

1. Why?—the worker is not sure of the correct part orientation?
2. Why?—the part is not marked properly?
3. Why?—engineering ordered it that way from the vendor?
4. Why?—the process didn't account for possible manufacturing assembly issues (root cause)?
5. Why?—engineering is not trained in design for assembly (DFA) and doesn't consider assembly in its design considerations. If they can do it at their bench, they assume it can be repeated on the shop floor. This is the problem which needs to be resolved.

Lesson Learned: Never get too attached to your solutions and encourage anyone who tours your area to provide feedback in a list of good things and bad things they witnessed. Thank them when you receive it. Whenever you come up with what you think is the best way, start figuring out the next best way to do it. Ask the daily challenge question "What can I improve today in my area?"[9]

Three A's

To find waste, you must go out and look for it, and then recognize it for what it is. Honda does this with an exercise they call the three A's,[10] which are to go to the actual place and see the actual part in the actual situation (Table 4.1).

In our Lean training classes, we ask our students to go out to the floor and write down examples of waste wherever they see it. Many come back with 30–50 examples to share. When we ask the supervisors what would have happened in the past if someone had come to them with a similar list, they tell us they would have been very upset, shut down to what they were saying, been defensive, and continued to do what they always did. When we ask them what they think now, once their eyes are opened, they say, "We see all this opportunity to improve!"

Exercise: Go into your workplace or office and look for waste. See how many examples you can identify.

Five Best Practices of Honda

Honda has a different production and management system than Toyota.[11] While Toyota and Honda are neck-to-neck in their dedication to car making, their management styles are polar opposites. Honda's three As led to their Five P[12] program that targets five strategic improvement areas:

1. Best Position: improve global competitiveness
2. Best Productivity: improve the process
3. Best Product: improve quality and delivery
4. Best Price: decrease cost
5. Best Partners: improve Honda/supplier relationship

Homework: Can Honda's five Ps work for your company? Think about it and write down how it could work for you.

Toyota's Values

1. Customer first
2. Respect for people
3. International focus with all stakeholders
4. Continuous improvement and innovation
5. Long-term focus

There are some similarities between Honda and Toyota approaches. At Toyota and Honda, going to the Gemba, Genchi Genbutsu (go and see at the) actual place, seeing the actual thing gives us a deeper understanding and stresses the importance of understanding what is occurring through first-hand experience. All levels of employees are expected to go and see the problems for themselves rather than calling a meeting or receiving a report on the problem.[13]

30-30-30 Exercise

Taiichi Ohno was known for drawing a chalk circle around managers and making them stand in the circle until they had seen and documented all the problems in a particular area (sometimes an entire shift or longer) (Figure 1.5). Today the stand in a circle exercise is known as a 30-30-30 and is a great first step to train someone's eyes to see waste and to provide structure for the group leader/supervisor or manager to carry out daily improvement or for the busy executive with limited time to go to the Gemba and see what is really happening. The exercise entails telling the person to stand in a circle for 30 minutes or more and just watch and look around to capture at least 30 wastes and then spend 30 minutes fixing one of them. When one spends time in the Gemba (the area where the work is being done) standing in the Ohno circle, you will see the gap between the target condition, if it even exists, and the actual condition.

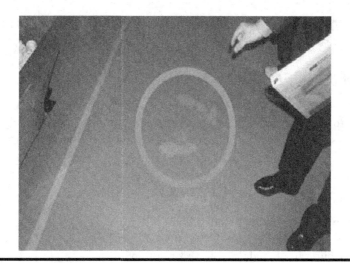

Figure 1.5   Ohno circle.

Homework: Go and walk through your area or someone else's area. Answer the following questions regarding People, Equipment, Communication, Visual Controls and Leadership (see Figure 1.6).

People

- What are people doing (or not doing)?
- Are we tapping their brains? Getting them thinking?
- Is there an idea board in the area?
- Is there a flurry of motion?
- Are people searching? If so for what? How to eliminate?

Equipment

- What is the equipment doing or not doing?
- How smart is the equipment?
- Where is the high-volume equipment?
- Does the equipment drive batch or single-piece flow?
- Is there a pre shift startup checklist? If so, is it up to date?
- Are the machines being maintained? If so, by whom and at what frequency?

Communication

- How is information communicated? Are the areas linked together? Is the area on plan or on schedule? Can you visually determine what is going on?
- Is there a mechanism to make suggestions or recommendations?
- Daily communications—standup pre shift meeting as well as interaction with employees during the shift.
- After communication, are metrics and information accessible to all employees?

Key Observation Work Sheet—Fill in Each Observation—1 per Page and Summarize Findings on Key Waste Summary Sheet									
Overview									
Waste Observation Number	Process Owner	What is the Root Cause	Action to be Taken	Date Due	Date Completed	Standard Work Updated (If Applicable)	All Employees Trained (If Applicable)	Reaudit Date	
Detailed findings									
Waste discovered—enter text here					Waste discovered—enter drawing or				
Enter causes and highlight root cause									
Enter improvement ideas (if applicable - fill in improvement idea cards and post on idea board)									
Enter action(s) to be taken, responsibilities, due date and follow up date							After picture		
Action to be taken	Responsibility	Due date	Follow up date	Status	Reaudit date	Is this a counter measure or containment action			

Figure 1.6 Key waste observation sheet.

Visual Controls

- How do we know if there is a problem?
- What are escalation protocols? Are they visible? Is everyone aware of them and how to use these protocols?
- Is the area 5S'd? Is the area neat and organized?
- Are there stockpiles of inventory?
- Are there visual controls in place?
- Are there any metrics posted?

- Action items from metrics?
- Is standard work posted?
- What are improvement activities being worked on?
- What are the capabilities of workers in this area—cross training/versatility matrix? Do you see muda, mura, or muri?

Leadership

Leaders must have the following[14]:

- An unrelenting hunger to eliminate waste
- A dream (vision and shared goals)
- Strength of will and tenacity of purpose
- Ability to win the support of followers
- Ability to do more than their followers, without interfering when they can do it alone
- Successes
- Ability to give the right advice
- Ability to teach, coach, mentor, and facilitate individually or in a team environment
- Respect from peer and teams under them
- Ability to walk the talk
- What behaviors does the leadership drive? Is it obvious in the area?
- Are there audits in place?
- Did you ask people what they are measured on?
- Do people feel comfortable stopping the line?
- Are people afraid of their leaders?
- How many suggestions are implemented?
- How is leadership monitored (held accountable) for management of an area?
- How approachable are the leaders?
- Is daily interaction with the team evident?
- Levels of leadership on the shop floor daily interacting with employees.

When we assess companies, we do the same exercise. We look to answer these questions and more. For example, do leaders' roles model the behaviors they desire? In a Lean environment there is no place for egos and arrogance.

Homework: Try the 30-30-30 exercise. A good time for this exercise is at the end of the day, shift change, or right after lunch. Go spend 30–60 minutes (depending on time available) standing in one place (Ohno circle).

Lesson Learned: Now that you have completed your homework, what did you find? Did you find some waste? What level was it? If you were to tell the process owner about the waste you found, how do you think it would be received? If someone were to come into your area and tell you what they saw, how would you receive it now? How would you have reacted prior to this exercise? The key is not to be defensive; instead, to recognize the waste, and work to get rid of it. Generally, outsiders will see wastes insiders do not see. Was it easier to identify wastes in an area belonging to someone else? If it was your area to manage, supervise, or work, would you have found as many wasted activities as possible? How would it have felt if you were the supervisor, and the wastes were reported to you? How would you have reacted prior to this exercise?

Exercise: What can you see wrong in the pictures in Figures 1.7–1.13? How much do you think productivity could be improved?

Visible wastes:

- Sit down station
- Cluttered
- Blocked so no flexing by the operator
- Open drawers—what's in them? Why not labeled? Are they needed?
- Batching at station (WIP is on marble table)

Lean improvement estimate—40% or more productivity improvement!

Figures 1.7–1.13   Can you see the waste?

Visible wastes:

- Sign says it is a cell but is it really?
- Sit down stations
- Workstations cluttered
- Operators missing
- Batching between stations and shelves set up for batching
- No 5S—It's a mess

Estimate 40% or more productivity improvement!

Figures 1.7–1.13   *(Continued)*

Four to nine wastes:
• Sit down stations
• Workstations cluttered
• Batching everywhere between stations
• No 5S—It's a mess
Estimate 60% or more productivity improvement!

Figures 1.7–1.13 *(Continued)*

Visible wastes:
• Sit down stations
• No flow
• Workstations cluttered
• Batching everywhere between stations
• No 5S—It's a mess
• No visual controls
Estimate 60% or more productivity improvement

Figures 1.7–1.13 *(Continued)*

Visible wastes:
• Sit down stations
• No flow
• Workstations cluttered
• Batching everywhere between stations
• No visual controls
• No 5S—It's a mess
Estimate 60% or more productivity improvement!

Figures 1.7–1.13 *(Continued)*

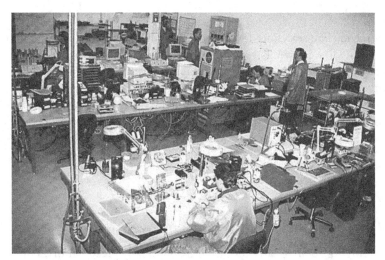

Visible wastes:
• Sit down stations
• No flow
• Workstations cluttered
• Batching everywhere between stations
• No 5S—It's a mess
• No visual controls
Estimate 60% or more productivity improvement!

Figures 1.7–1.13 *(Continued)*

Visible wastes:
These are our favorite type of pictures! We look for these
wherever we go.

Figures 1.7–1.13 *(Continued)*

Cost of Waste

Each time you spend time searching for something, or if you are idle, who pays for the searching or idle time? The first answer is your company, and the second answer is your customer or, we all pay through higher prices. Consider the impact of waste on your customer, time, product quality, and experience. Imagine if your products could talk, what would they be saying to you? In healthcare, government, and service industries, many times the product can talk because the products are each of us.

Table 4.2 is a Machine Idle Time Log[15] dating back to the late 1940s.

Efficiency

Concept of Strenuousness versus Efficiency

Strenuousness bringing about greater results with abnormally greater effort. For example, piece rates that are paying workers based on the number of pieces they produce per hour or per day are based on the theory of strenuousness. A destructively offensive company is based on strenuousness. An organization based on efficiency is diametrically opposed to strenuousness. Efficiency brings about greater results with lessened effort. Standard times and bonuses are based on the theory of efficiency. Piece rates are a reversion to historical standards, whereas standard times are a step into the future. The differences between the two types of companies are both philosophical and physiological.

Twelve Principles of Efficiency[16]

Many of the fundamental concepts of Lean as well as the cultural considerations can be found in the 12 principles of efficiency which were published in 1911 by Harrington Emerson (see Figure 1.14). Emerson begins by defining two types of companies:

1. The destructively offensive
2. The constructively defensive

He notes that the two types of organizations are radically different leveraging primitive examples to show the differences. He describes the constructively defensive as a plant and the destructively offensive as a mammal. The constructive defensive type or plant trusts the generous, often enthusiastic, cooperation of forces outside of itself and it therefore draws strength of a wide and unlimited range. Plants trust all nature and draw help from everywhere and see the view from 400 ft. The destructively offensive or "mammal" trusts the occasional, often grudging, cooperation of powers identical in kind; animals trust none but their own kind and grow through destruction and have a view of the tallest animal, the elephant which stands at 12 ft.

Contrasting the two reveals the difference in spirit, effectiveness, and methods. Most organizations choose to operate as mammals, limiting their ability to apply the efficiency principles effectively, rather than operating as constructively defensive. We know the constructively defensive up building company is a better choice and suited to the processes of productive up building.[17] Listed and detailed are Emerson's 12 principles and some direct quotations from his book. We have found Emerson's definitions of companies, and these 12 principles still apply today:

1. Clearly defined ideals
2. Common sense
3. Competent counsel
4. Discipline

Figure 1.14   Harrington Emerson.

5. The fair deal
6. Reliable, immediate, and adequate records
7. Despatching
8. Standards and schedules
9. Standardized conditions
10. Standardized operations
11. Written standard-practice instructions
12. Efficiency-reward

Principle 1: Clearly Defined Ideals

Organizations must have clearly defined "high ideals" with very specific targets. At present time, in large plants men succeed to authority by transfer or by promotion. They are without definite conceptions of the purposes for which the plant is working. Workers and foremen at the lower end of line organizations are so far from the "Little Father" or from the "Big Stick" who dictates all policies, who alone is responsible for organization, for delegation of power, and for supervision, they are driven to create minor ideals and inspirations of their own, these being often at odds with the ideals of those above them.

If all the ideals from top to bottom could be lined up to push in the same straight line, the resultant would be a very powerful effort. But when those ideals pull in diverse directions, the resultant force may be insignificantly positive or may be negative. This condition of…conflicting ideals is very common in all American plants, as well as great vagueness and uncertainty as to the major ideal, even among the higher officials.

Note: This idea of alignment is behind what is known today as Hoshin planning or policy deployment.

Principle 2: Common Sense

Emerson discusses the difference between near common sense and supernal common sense, which looks at every problem from a lofty versus a near point of view.

Note: Common sense in Emerson's terms today is how we view the process. Emerson favored the lofty common sense postulated as viewing processes from a systems thinking point of view and in contrast would equate to myopic or short-term and reactive thinking. Lean requires a systems thinking view to fully realize the benefits of a Lean business delivery system.

Principle 3: Competent Counsel

Emerson suggests that we all need competent counsel. For example, most companies have a vice president (VP) of legal, finance, materials, operations, or engineering… "Yet where is the counsel (Executive i.e., Vice President) on efficiency? If it exists at all it is in a minor position" (i.e., The Lean team or Master Blackbelt). Emerson argues "every company if it wishes to be constructively defensive should have a chief efficiency counselor to install and develop an efficiency organization from top to bottom with each minor official having his staff of efficiency experts but all subject to the direction of the chief efficiency counselor whose main duty would be to standardize and organize operations." "Competent counsel must permeate every efficient organization, and if competent counsel cannot be carried into the organization…it is because the organization is defective…," Emerson goes on to say.

Even if he (the Chief Efficiency Counselor) is in the position of highest authority at the top, this is not easy as he must run counter to most of the ideals and life-long practices of an extended line of subordinates. If he finds himself many steps below the top, he is indeed caught between the upper and lower levels. Those above him will treat his suggestions with impatience and skepticism while those below him will meet them with rebellion... If a manager has succeeded in modifying the organization (to one that is constructively defensive) and if he has succeeded in emphasizing the governing ideals so that all may understand it and work for it, he suddenly meets new difficulties from both customers and government, who will make the occasion of his efforts to eliminate waste (i.e., To make better use of materials, of labor, of equipment) an excuse to demand a higher physical valuation of his material property, which will result in higher freight rates and other charges, thus imposing a direct penalty on his efforts to improve efficiency.

Note: Today we might consider the Master Blackbelt or Lean Master as the Chief Efficiency Counselor; however, these positions have limited scope of authority and are almost never executive level positions.

Principle 4: Discipline

The word discipline has three if not more meanings:

1. The spirit of discipline where the institution is greater than the individual, for example, railroad schedules.
2. The discipline of the rich man who makes his servants wait until his convenience despite a definite program arranged by himself ...
3. The discipline of life which leads us, almost compels us, from intimate contact with the existing order. In the narrowest sense, we use the word to denote the act of punishment inflicted on a bad boy with the object of encouraging observance of prescribed conduct or rules ...

"Discipline as an efficiency principle includes all meanings, from lessons of life to man inflicted punishments."

"The greatest regulator of conduct is the spirit of the organization:

■ If the spirit of the company does not drive an undesirable associate away
■ If standard organization and standard practice, both of which affect conduct, do not drive an undesirable associate away
■ If reliable, immediate, and adequate records, do not drive an undesirable associate away
■ If absence of efficiency rewards does not automatically, effectually, and peaceably eliminate the undesirable (person),

then it is time for the strong hand to descend..."

Emerson goes on to say... "No man enters West Point without passing severe elementary examinations. It is a tremendous privilege to be admitted, a disaster to be excluded. There ought to be a high membership ideal for every plant, no newcomer admitted who is not fit in every way, no man cut off except for cause."

Note: How would this affect your approach to hiring?

- "Discipline begins before the applicant is taken on. Nine-tenths of all the harder discipline ought to be applied to exclude undesirables, men who by reason of bad character, bad and offensive habits, destructive tendencies, laziness, or other faults are unfit to become working members of a high-class organization. It is before he is admitted the applicant should hear of the ideals of the business, of its organization, and of its methods... There can be organization without discipline, as in all plant life; there can be discipline without organization, as in most animal life..."
- "Supernal discipline is inspired by a greater emotion than fear..."
- "The principles of efficiency are not vague platitudes; they are intensely practical, tested, tried out, and successful. The strong leader who employs them prevents waste...
- If the owners and managers of a company of any kind are orderly, enthusiastic, loyal to the work, punctual, courteous, decent, competent; if they feel their obligations toward those they direct; if they are honest, economical, diligent, and sound in health, they can well demand similar qualities in all employees...
- No man ought to be allowed to enlist (in a company) who cannot start in with order, enthusiasm, loyalty, and reliability, who is not courteous and decent; competent, a good brain worker, honest, economical, and diligent. If he has good health so much the better..."

Note: Emerson ties discipline to an expectation of the leadership which must role model the behaviors they expect in others and only hire people who can meet these expectations. Too often we find companies hire warm bodies to fill slots but don't scrutinize their hires or hire with the expectation of developing future leaders in the organization. The goal is to hire the right person, in which the behaviors and discipline desired are already established in alignment with the spirit of the organization or what we might call culture today.

Principle 5: The Fair Deal

"In practice it is difficult to put up a fair deal unless there are three qualities, and these are rarely found in the same person. The qualities are as follows:

1. Sympathy
2. Imagination
3. Above all a sense of Justice"

Note: Wages are a small part of the fair deal but are critical.

The worker wants as high pay as he can enforce; the employer wants his output to be as cheap as that of his competitors, for if it is not, he will be driven out of business. The worker cannot be expected to work for an employer for less pay than is paid under similar conditions for the same class of work by another employer. The wage payer cannot be asked to pay higher wages than the current rate... The worker is selling time, but the purchaser is not buying time, he is buying output. Happily, both can be scientifically determined. Like the other efficiency principles, it should be standardized...

Figure 1.15 Maslow's hierarchy of needs.

Note: In 1959, Frederick Herzberg developed a list of factors based on Maslow's Hierarchy of Needs (see Figure 1.15). Herzberg theorized that hygiene factors were conditions which one would notice if they were not present but would not necessarily notice if they were already present. He postulated that these factors had to be present before additional motivators and could be used to encourage the workers:

Hygiene or dissatisfiers[18]

- Working conditions
- Policies and administrative practices
- Salary and benefits
- Supervision
- Status
- Job security
- Fellow workers
- Personal life

Motivators or satisfiers

- Recognition
- Achievement
- Advancement
- Growth
- Responsibility
- Job challenge

The fair deal to which Emerson speaks satisfies the hygiene factors which support the theory wage rate, while important, is not necessarily a primary motivator for most people.

Principle 6: Reliable, Immediate, and Adequate Records

"The object of records is to increase the scope and number of warnings, to give us more information than is usually received immediately through our senses... Records are anything which provides information.

Men have always felt the need for records, but they have not always known what they wanted, nor how to secure them. In the great industrial plants, one knows not whether to marvel most at the absence of reliable, immediate, and accurate records, or at the super-abundance of permanent records, collected with painstaking and at great expense, but neither reliable, immediate, or adequate. Even if the latter have all these qualities, there is often great duplication, and consequently we find an immense amount of accumulation of very little value, which has cost far more than it needs..."

Note: We find the earlier paragraph to be true at almost every company. The goal of records, as he states, is to have visual controls making the abnormal visible; however, most companies either keep very little data or they have large quantities of data (like hospitals) that is seldom utilized, often inaccurate, and none of which is visual (outside of a computer) or real time in that it can be acted upon to correct a problem.

We violently resist a demand for 10% increase in wages, but we tolerate 50% inefficiency in the worker. One task of the efficiency expert is to convert efficiency records into cost records, since the language of costs is understood by all, but the language of efficiency only by a few. It is of course generally true costs will decline as efficiency increases but this is not always so... We have again and again found machines not in operation over half the time of a 9-hour day. When in operation, they were inefficient. The machine end-efficiency in some plants is not over 4% of the guaranteed capacity... It is a law that it usually pays to increase quality of labor and quality of equipment and materials, provided they are efficiently used. Equipment has hours about half those of labor when it ought to work if materials are available, and be constantly on the job...

This relation of rate per hour to time is generally lost sight of. It is because it has been lost sight of that over-equipment is the rule in America. Materials, service, and equipment are worked up to the general cost formula:

$$\text{Total cost} = \text{materials} + \text{service} + \text{investment charges}$$

$$\text{Total cost} = (\text{quantity} \times \text{price per unit}) + (\text{time in hours} \times \text{wages per hour})$$

$$+ (\text{time in hours} \times \text{cost per hour for capital charges})$$

Note: The over equipment issues still exist today. Sometimes it seems like it is easier to write an ROI to justify the purchase of new equipment and use that capital up before we lose it, than to work to take the waste out of the process to eliminate the need for the new equipment. It is unfathomable for there are so many times we find ourselves fighting to stop the purchase of a new piece of equipment and generally losing! Usually only the greatest of industrial managers realizes:

■ Quantity of units is more important than price
■ Time in hours is more important than wages per hour
■ Cost per hour for capital is more important than time in hours
■ Minimum total cost is realized when all the aforementioned are at their minimum

Note: This book was written in 1911. How much of what is stated here in terms of records and records keeping, even with all the computing power available, could apply to your company today?

Principle 7: Despatching

The name despatching was adopted from train despatching, and the train operation organization was adapted. The foreman corresponded to the train engineer. A new official was created corresponding to the despatcher. A messenger and telephone service kept the despatcher's office in touch with the work… Despatching records, however, were adapted from bank practice… Despatching like other principles, is a subdivision of the science of management. It is a part of planning; but while visible as a distinct pattern, it ought, like inlaid work, to be in tactile.

Note: Despatching (now we say dispatching) is equivalent to execution of the work plan or production schedule as well as the logistics encountered within and outside the company… Despatching today is equivalent to what we would call executing a customer order from order entry to receipt of cash. How efficient is your order entry to collect process today?

Principle 8: Standards and Schedules

There are two kinds, physical and chemical… We use instruments to measure, and physics, chemistry, and mathematics to establish standards and schedules for material things. But when we wish to schedule work for sentimental beings, then our mathematics fails, and we fall back on experiments inspired by faith?…

All around us, nature has been showing us that increased results come from lessened effort not greater effort… To establish rational work standards for men requires motion and time studies of all operations, and in addition, all the skill of the planning manager, physician, psychologist; it requires infinite knowledge, directed, guided, and restrained by hope, faith, and compassion. The promise already partly fulfilled and clearly held out as to the future is greater and greater results shall follow constantly diminishing effort.

Note: Schedules are vital tools to help companies match customer demand, which also ties to the concept of takt time. Takt derived from the German word Taktzeit translates to beat or rhythm and sets the pace for manufacturing lines, such as in car manufacturing. Like a heartbeat, it should be constant. The line must have a couple of known paces, but if level loaded, these paces should not change every day.

Principle 9: Standardized Conditions

There are two distinct methods of standardizing conditions:

1. To standardize ourselves to command the unalterable extraneous facts, earth, water, gravity, and wave vibrations
2. To standardize the outside facts so our personality becomes the pivot on which all else turns

The easiest way for any individual to live his own life in fullest measure is either to standardize himself to suit the environment or to standardize the environment to suit him… In our individual lives, in our shops, in our nation, what are we trying to accomplish? Are we taking too much time, is it costing too much, are we squandering our strength? Are we standardizing conditions so time will not be wasted, so that money will not be thrown away, so that effort will not be in vain?

Principle 10: Standardized Operations

Determines the operational method of standardization, to improve work efficiency. There are two elements to consider:

1. Standardizing the work itself
2. Individual skill: one man may have laid 8,000 bricks and the other only 800 a day

From schedules, dispatching, standardized conditions, and standardized operations, in some shops the methods of efficiency are spreading. Planning pays: the application of all the principles of efficiency pays; but standardized operation is the principle most appeals to the individuality of man, and of the worker.

Note: Part of any hiring process, in addition to what was stated earlier, that is, discipline starts with the hiring process, should be a dexterity test. Is the person physically capable of performing the work within the required cycle time?

Principle 11: Written Standard-Practice Instructions

Makes the written manual the standard course of action. The best results are obtained using the "ratchet" process, by holding onto every gain and by never allowing any slip back; these results being secured by a voluminous book of instructions and suggestions.

Note: Written processes are vital to establishing standard work and form the basis for many ISO9000 Quality management Systems. Toyota has large volumes of untranslated standard work for all their processes.[19]

Emerson goes on to say.

In this book, best ways as ascertained to date, are specifically prescribed, by written, permanent standard-practice instructions, but these instructions are subject to a bombardment of suggestions and all these suggestions, however foolish, are tabulated, printed, and confidentially published.

Only when best practice is carefully and systematically reduced to writing, progress is made and held and built upon in an industrial plant or any other undertaking. Every shop, every institution, has its great body of common law variously understood and interpreted by those most affected.

Note: This is the secret behind Toyota's ability to sustain. They use the ratchet principle combined with the systematic updating of standards, leveraging suggestions, and feedback to drive standards and efficiency as well as sharing best practices within the entire organization.

Often the traditions of the past are treasured up in the brain of some old employee. We have known foremen to refuse deliberately to tell a new official how certain work was done. The defiant stand assumed was this was a personal secret.

Note: We find this often today. Many times, the routings or the work instructions are in one person's head. At Company X, while I was working there, I had an employee who tragically died in a car crash. The next day, no one at the plant could finish the order the employee was working on. They ended up discontinuing the product because literally no one knew how to make it.

Each one of the ten preceding efficiency principles can and should reduce to written, permanent standard-practice instructions so that each may understand the whole and also his own relation to it.

Principle 12: Efficiency-Reward

The worker sells two different possessions: his time and his skill. He should be robbed of neither. Profit sharing and piece rate are inadequate ways of rewarding the worker. Time payments which make no allowance for skill are wrong; skill payments which make no provision for time are also wrong. It is easy to measure time. The ideals are the following:

1. A guaranteed hourly rate.
2. A lower limit of efficiency, which, if not attained, indicates the worker is a misfit and requires either special training or change of occupation.
3. A progressive efficiency reward, beginning at a requirement so low it is inexcusable not to average it.
4. An efficiency standard established after careful and reliable investigations of many kinds, including time and motion studies.
5. For work to be performed, a time standard that is joyful and exhilarating, therefore intermediate between depressing slowness and exhausting effort.
6. A variation in standards for the same work for different machines, conditions, and individuals, the schedules therefore being individual.
7. The determination for each worker of an average efficiency for all jobs over a long period.
8. A continuous correction of time standards and wage rate to suit new conditions. This is essential and inevitable. Time standards have nothing to do with wages. The time standard (i.e., amount of time) to walk a mile on foot is longer than the time it takes to bicycle a mile, which is longer than the time it takes a motorcycle to cover a mile.
9. The worker must have the personal option of working not to a standard time but between limits on either side of standard time.

Efficiency constitutes 9 out of the 18 elements of cost[20]—efficiency of quality and quantity and overhead for materials, for labor, and for fixed charges. It has been found exceedingly satisfactory and convenient to base efficiency rewards/bonus on the cost of efficiencies, the method being so flexible as to be applicable to an individual operation of a few minutes' duration to all the work of a man for a long period, or to all the work of department or plant. Efficiency reward is not a money payment; this is only one of its myriad forms. Men have been willing to die for a smile. Profit sharing does not stimulate as the worker only controls a small percent of the outcome, while management controls the rest.

Emerson goes on to state:

"In most operating plants both discipline and fair deals are defective. Records are neither reliable, immediate, nor adequate, despatching is so elementary as scarcely to be beyond the stage of putting into the shop an order for work, there are few, if any scientifically made work schedules, there are not standard practice instructions, no standardized conditions, no standardized operations, and efficiency rewards are defective.

The self-executing discipline worthy to be an efficiency principle is the allegiance to and observance of all the other eleven principles, so the twelve principles do not become twelve rules unrelated to each other. The twelve principles of efficiency are the strands of a net, each interwoven with the other. No efficiency principle stands alone. Each supports and strengthens the others." It is amazing to see the foundation of what we call Lean today, including the unwavering commitment to eliminate waste and continuously improve based on books dating back to 1911!

Lean and Productivity, Efficiency, and Effectiveness

1. What is productivity?
2. What does it mean to be more efficient?
3. What does it mean to increase your effectiveness?

Our Lean principles strive for the best utilization of man, machine, methods, and materials (the four M's):

1. Productivity
   Productivity is the number of products produced in a certain amount of time with a certain amount of labor. The products could be physical products or transactional such as processing an invoice or internet blogs. Productive means getting things done, outcomes reached, or goals achieved and are measured as output per unit of input (i.e., labor, equipment, and capital).
2. Efficiency
   Efficiency is based on the energy one spends to complete the product or service as well as timing. For example, we all know of the learning curve. The more one performs a new task the better they become each time the task is practiced. As one becomes more efficient, they reduce stress and gain accuracy. A person has achieved efficiency when they are getting more done with the same or better accuracy in a shorter period, with less energy and better results.
3. Effectiveness
   Effectiveness is the ability to achieve stated goals or objectives, judged in terms of both output and impact.

It is (a) the degree to which an activity or initiative is successful in achieving a specified goal; and (b) the degree to which activities of a unit achieve the unit's mission or goal.

Example: The air conditioner on with the windows open is more productive than with no air conditioning. You will still be cooler, but you are losing a lot of energy (efficiency). Closing the windows allows it to get cooler quicker and allows it to remain cooler longer and thus it cools more efficiently. But if it doesn't get cool enough or is too cool then it is not effective.[21]

In manufacturing, one could view a cellular line. The line is more productive than the batch line it replaced, as it is getting more units per hour of labor. It is not as efficient however because we have some new people on the line or more people than are required. It is effective in that we are meeting our planned units for the day at 100% quality.

Another example is the gasoline engine. It is productive in that it gets us there on less fuel, it is effective as it gets us to the right place at the right time, but it is only 30% efficient in its use of fuel.

Making Defects Very Quickly with JIT

On a line where we implemented Lean at Company X back in 1995, we ended up more than doubling production with less than half the people. But the line had a major defect issue which was never solved, so we ended up doubling the defects as well. Ironically, we could also make bad parts fast with less labor! We ended up setting up a full-fledged non-Lean, yet one-piece flow rework line (using some of the people we freed up) and located it next to the production line to rework all the units that failed the final test. This is part of what we call trading labor efficiency for production output. Remember our earlier definitions of productivity versus efficiency versus effective.

Our production line was very efficient and productive but not effective due to the defects it produced. Our defect line was effective but technically not efficient or productive since it was all rework. If we had just taken the time to fix the root cause, we would not have had the rework line. Once the rework line was created, there was no longer a compelling need to change and find the root cause of the problem. We see this phenomenon in many factories still to this day.

> Efficiency is doing things right; effectiveness is doing the right things…
>
> **Peter Drucker**[22]

Apparent versus True Efficiency

By reducing the steps and complexity in the process, we also reduce the opportunity for defects in the process. This is extremely important. Behind this are the wastes of overproduction and overprocessing, and while this sounds simple, it is violated all the time. Toyota differentiates this by highlighting the difference between apparent versus true efficiency. True efficiency occurs only when we increase efficiency without overproducing or overprocessing.

Look at the example in Table 4.3 and decide which kaizen or improvement you believe is true efficiency. Which one did you pick? Why did you pick it?

The answer is kaizen 2. Why is this? While both have the same apparent efficiency (i.e., 15 hours/unit), note kaizen 1 is overproducing which is the number one waste in the system. So, kaizen 2 is an example of true efficiency.[23]

Utility Factor and Efficiency[24]

For a machine, the utility factor is the percentage of the energy supplied to the machine relative to the machine's actual capabilities (never more than 100%). For people, the utility factor is the amount of labor expended for producing a given product in relation to the labor required for making a given product. Efficiency is used when one wishes to compare output. That is, within a given time frame, how many people have produced how many pieces? To compare, one needs to first set a standard.

When we discuss attaining a 20% improvement in efficiency, there are two ways to accomplish improvement:

1. Increase the number of machines per person.
2. Reduce the number of workers.

In some industries, it is said that a 10% decrease in costs can equal a 100% increase in sales. Thus, businesses need to continuously drive costs down, while sustaining or improving quality, this is a key to business growth and competitive advantage.

Trading Labor Efficiency for Output

Under certain circumstances, we all knowingly trade labor efficiency for output. This situation occurs when we cannot utilize a full-time additional person, which implies adding a person will create idle time on the line. This normally is because of a layout issue, for example, a robot feeds a worker, but she is idle half the time, or where an operator must wait on a machine or a line balancing issue where the work cannot be split between both operators. However, to make the output for the day, we may add the extra worker, which is knowingly incurring idle time in exchange for the additional output (yet not the output we should theoretically attain with the additional person). For example, one person in the cell can produce 80 pieces a day, but due to a long machine time in the cell, two persons can only produce 130 pieces per day. This means 30 pieces of idle time are traded for 50 additional pieces of output. It is not efficient but sometimes may be necessary.

Shingo P Course

Another exercise that was used by Dr. Shingo is depicted in Figure 1.16.[25] The question he would ask the class is:

If one man and one machine in 1 hour can make 100 parts, how can they make more parts. The normal answers were of course to:

1. Add people
2. Add machines
3. Add more time

Shingo/ Ohno Training Example

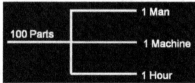

If one man and one machine in one hour can make 100 parts how can we make more parts?

100 Parts

1 Man

1 Machine

1 Hour

"The first step toward improvement is standardization. Where there is no standard. there can be no improvement. " Taiichi Ohno

Source: Kanban / JIT at Toyota/ Management Begins at the Workplace, Japan Management Association

Figure 1.16 Shingo P course example.

These were all unsatisfactory answers because they all add cost to the system. A fourth answer was often given such as "work harder," which was also unsatisfactory since it could not be sustained. When the class was stumped, he would inform them that the right way was to improve the overall method by which the elements work together and produce more efficiently. Either the same combination would be used to make 120 parts per hour or if demand was not needed then instead it should strive to produce 100 parts in 8 hours.

One part of the class would then look in detail at the four categories and draw out symbols corresponding to the workflow. This is called a product flow analysis today. He taught the engineers the basics of time study and how to identify and measure the length of time for the individual elements of each task. Additionally, they had to learn the details of motion analysis and to map out the 17 symbols invented by Frank and Lillian Gilbreth for motion analysis. He taught them the basic discipline of systematic process analysis for which he became so famous, and he showed them manufacturing logically consisted of four primary elements:

- Actual processing work
- Conveyance work
- Inspection work
- Delays

Only the process added value. He would subdivide each of these items further. He taught other methods of looking at how the work was transformed step by step as well as basis operational availability analysis. Once the methods were clear in their head, everyone returned to the shop floor and began to restudy the process in detail. What once seemed highly efficient now seemed utterly wasteful in comparison with their new sets of eye and quantitative analytic techniques.

Where eight machines and four operators previously seemed efficient, now there was suddenly a truer recognition of waste. With proper machine availability, only six machines might be needed instead of eight. Where four operators were needed before, now only two were required. Every aspect of the layout, tooling, motion, walk pattern, operation, and process were fit for more detailed study. During the workshop, some of the items were fixed and improved on the fly and others were left as homework items to be resolved by the time Dr. Shingo returned in a couple of months.

Dr. Shingo and Toyota

Art Smalley asked Kato Isao (Ike) to write about the real relationship between Dr. Shingo and Toyota, which is given here[26]:

As you can see... in Mr. Shingo's courses, there is nothing directly related to the more famous elements of the TPS. In other words, he did not teach or self-develop anything that relates to JIT, jidoka, Kanban, standardized work, or other TPS items. He mainly taught different ways to look at the production process in detail from an industrial engineering point of view, which is his specialty. These were important skills Mr. Ohno and other managers in the company possessed but our engineers and supervisors did not in 1955. Most people don't realize that Mr. Shingo was largely working in a classroom training role at Toyota for most of his visits. Each course visited the shop floor for a few observations and exercises to practice different analysis methods and improvement techniques outlined above. The participants were then expected to use these skills and techniques upon returning to their respective areas after the course.

To put things in proper context Mr. Ohno's primary management direction during this time was to drive production improvements to eliminate waste to reduce cost and improve productivity in manufacturing. The efforts of Mr. Ohno and his chief group of managers alone however were not sufficient to meet all the aggressive goals of the company. Consequently, it was important for Toyota as an organization to develop greater numbers of engineers and supervisors who could actively participate in improvement efforts as well. The P-course contributed to this type of skills development for people in the manufacturing organization. It replaced an earlier training course called Job Methods (JM) from the training within industry (TWI) training programs we previously used in the company. The P-course content was more detailed and varied than the JM course, so we adopted it instead as a part of our training curriculum for supervisors and engineers.

Students of TPS are probably aware Mr. Ohno always maintained a top management philosophy that emphasized the overall production system. He stressed profitability and cost reduction from different viewpoints such as total quality, efficiency, lead-time, and overall system productivity. If you read Dr. Shingo's books published by Nikkan Kogyo in Japan on kaizen techniques, you will see he originally was a much narrower specialist who looked at production mainly from the viewpoint of an operation or a process. His views evolved over time as he studied Toyota which I will comment on later. Unfortunately, since neither his initial books nor the P-course materials were fully translated into English, this reality is lost on non-Japanese speakers. Regardless however this emphasis is a primary difference in how Mr. Ohno viewed Toyota's production system versus how Mr. Shingo typically viewed process improvement.

Over the years, because of Mr. Shingo's instructional efforts, the P-course did indeed produce success in contributing to the development of manufacturing engineers and supervisors in Toyota. In turn, these people improved processes in Toyota in line with Mr. Ohno's priorities and goals. Thus, it is accurate to state that the P-course both helped to improve work as well as to achieve one of the aims related to human resource development Mr. Ohno and top management had set out for my department.

Unfortunately, the success Mr. Shingo experienced in instructing the P-course at Toyota also apparently led him and later others outside the company to believe that he created parts of the TPS. While he is indeed a contributor to the success of Toyota in skills development, it does not make him an inventor of the system in any way. For example, the establishment of the principles of jidoka and JIT predate Mr. Shingo's involvement in the company by several decades. These concepts were put forth by Sakichi Toyoda and Kiichiro Toyoda, respectively, and were well implemented by Mr. Ohno and other key personnel long before Mr. Shingo visited Toyota in late 1955 for the first time.

Please note not even Mr. Ohno claims to have invented these foundational concepts. Most of Mr. Ohno's experiments with process flow, JIT, Kanban, supermarkets, multi-process handling, stop the line, etc. were conducted in his engine machine shops in the period between 1948 and 1955. To state that Mr. Shingo co-invented or taught him all this somehow is simply erroneous and lacks any factual perspective regarding the actual sequence of events from the period. Mr. Shingo's visits began in late 1955 after much of TPS was in fact well developed inside the company. In Mr. Ohno's writing he states between 1945 and 1955 he was merely applying the concepts of Sakichi and Kiichiro Toyoda and other practices he observed at the spinning and weaving part of the company from which he originally came that also built automatic looms. He properly gave credit to the Toyoda family and other many members of his internal group such as Mr. Suzumura and Mr. Mamiya helped develop the system.

For the record, I think it is important to point out that Mr. Shingo taught the exact same versions of his P-course at Matsushita Electric Corporation and many other Japanese companies far more often than he taught at Toyota. Interestingly however these efforts did not result in the establishment of an overall production system at any other location. Nor did he later write entire books about those other companies at which he taught. It was mainly engineering training and skills development and not overall system implementation type of work. Toyota's production system development is truly unique in that it was adapted and created internally by trial and error over many years.

You might be surprised to learn regarding actual TPS implementation Mr. Shingo was initially quite critical of our production methods and ideas for improvement as they differed from his own thoughts on process improvement. His attitude shifted in 1973 however when the first draft of a TPS manual entitled The Toyota Production System for Cost Reduction was written by several managers including recent president of the company Mr. Fujio Cho and a now retired manager named Mr. Sugimori. You might recall during this period there was an oil shock to the economy of Japan due to an embargo placed upon the world by the Organization of the Petroleum Exporting Countries (OPEC) nations. During this period of rising factor costs, Toyota was the only major company in Japan to make a profit including all of Mr. Shingo's other clients. Until this time Mr. Shingo had shown little interest in learning about our overall concept of a production system or the two pillars of JIT and jidoka or even Standardized Work for that matter.

It is also not fair or accurate in my opinion to misconstrue the proper legacy of Mr. Shingo and the type of credit he does honestly deserve. He was a great instructor and contributor to the body of general TPS knowledge as an author especially in the West. No one has ever disputed this point. Furthermore, he deserves credit and recognition as an author, consultant, and instructor regarding development of specific shop floor improvement kaizen techniques as well as helping to develop human resources in Toyota. His instructional efforts and lectures on the Scientific Thinking Mechanism he outlined contributed heavily to the kaizen training course in Toyota for engineers and supervisors even after the P-course was discontinued. Any claims he somehow invented the TPS, especially concepts like process flow, JIT, jidoka, or standardized work, etc. however are deeply flawed and simply misconstrued by uninformed parties.

In this summary, I have attempted to clarify the role of Mr. Shingo, his P-course for industrial engineering, and his actual involvement with Toyota for interested parties. The P-course contributed significantly to the development of engineers and supervisors with regards to their ability to see and think about shop floor kaizen at the process level in Toyota. Anyone who ever took his course in Toyota would agree to this statement and we all thank him for his contribution in this area. However, that is quite different from stating Mr. Shingo personally developed or created the primary elements of the TPS created by the Toyoda family, Mr. Ohno and so many other members of his managerial group. There is simply no person in Toyota Motor Corporation that thinks Mr. Shingo invented TPS even those who value and respect his courses and teachings as much as I do. I would like these facts made clear for the record.

Whatever Happened to the Stopwatch Person?

In the past, almost every company had a work-study or time-study officer. This person was highly trained with the responsibility to observe the work first-hand of several operators doing the same job and then determine, generally using methods-time measurement (MTM)[27] standards, what the output for each operator should be. Sometimes they used video but most often direct observation. The data were transcribed to a work-study form which was used to scientifically determine the capacity of the output of the process. This job turned into more of an industrial engineering job with the person becoming the standards person. However, this person seems to have all but disappeared at most companies.

Lesson Learned: Work-study methods and industrial engineering have critical foundational elements of Lean, and contributions by Frederick Taylor, Frank Gilbreth, Dr. Shigeo Shingo, Taiichi Ohno, Charles Sorenson, and Ralph Barnes were very important to Lean journeys.

"Demonstrated Output Capacity"

The time-study person has all but disappeared today; so how do we figure out our factory or department's capacity? We find the capacity is no longer based on any formal type of calculation but is normally based on the supervisor's experience. Even when we see machine shops scheduled based on equipment hours, the premise for those hours is based on actuals not what it could be. For instance, what if setup hours were reduced or the method for loading and unloading was improved? From what we have seen, most factories are scheduled on nothing but a gut feeling of what can be done versus what could be done or what it should be based on the machine speeds and feeds. Surprisingly many companies don't even run to the recommended machine speeds and feeds. Sometimes operators will slow down the equipment due to problems with running the machine or to get overtime pay. Even in shops that use MRP tools such as rough-cut capacity planning, we find many flaws in the logic used to determine capacity.

We developed a term for this phenomenon, which we call "demonstrated output capacity." "Demonstrated capacity" is when companies or departments use their actual daily or weekly demonstrated output totals as a measure of what they feel they can produce versus scientific methods like time and motion study, or published speeds and feeds, which would tell them what they should really be producing. Ninety percent of companies we work with including government and healthcare initially have metrics based on "demonstrated capacity." A sure sign of this phenomenon is when you ask the supervisor how he knows what can be produced each day and they tell you, "I know from my experience." Many machine shops have shop hours or machine hours of capacity. But seldom is it based on the actual machine cycle time. We find most standards have not been updated for years and when they have it was normally based on the prior year's performance. This wouldn't necessarily be bad if continuous improvements were the mantra and done daily but we have never found this to be the case. Instead, the opposite is true. If you are not constantly improving the system, the waste grows and slowly grows, continually reducing the output of the area over time. When standards are utilized but not updated, there is no way to install checks and balances on the system. The symptom of "demonstrated capacity" is found in the ongoing whining the department does not have enough people and needs to hire more.

Many companies use standard costs and earned hours to set and monitor their capacity and efficiency. The fallacy with this is the standards are seldom updated. We have found standards not updated for over 5 years or more. There are companies which sell their standards expertise. They will provide standards for you based on other companies in industries like yours. They often pitch the Chief Financial Officer (CFO) and convince them how much money they will save using their software systems.

The problem is no two companies are exactly alike. Therefore, if their standards contain waste, yours will as well. Many times, the standards are set against measures which don't even make sense for the business. In Lean, we use our tools like process and operator workflow analysis to determine what the standard should be and then we audit to ensure the processes are continually improved. We work to constantly improve total hours per unit and units per person per day.

Hospital X was using benchmark cost accounting standards data to calculate earned hours and capacity. After we implemented Lean, our hours per unit were significantly below the benchmark data and our capacity increased significantly allowing us to see many more patients. The director of the department insisted we did not have enough people since the software report showed we should have three more people in the area. The manager of the area refused to hire three more people and was chastised by his director because he was not doing a good job of managing his department based on the "report variances."

What's wrong with this picture? First, it is obvious the director never left their office to go to the Gemba and was managing by reading reports. Second, shouldn't the director have been happy they had three less people than the benchmark standards software reported?

Lesson Learned: Measuring your output based on experience and "demonstrated capacity" is a very dangerous way to run your business. Unfortunately, when we tell supervisors we want to collect them before metrics to compare to us after Lean metric, we find that supervisors and managers tend to remember their best days and many times parts of the product have already been subassembled. Therefore, their totals of what they think they produce are very inflated. It becomes almost impossible to convince them Lean is working better when they don't really have a clue of what they were producing before.

How Are You Measured?

During a Lean assessment, we went into the company and interviewed some of the employees and all the supervisors. Each one told us how they were measured to these very tight standards. We asked each one how the standard was calculated. No one could tell us exactly. Next, we asked their performance to standard for the last month. They pulled out a report and showed us their standard versus actual and the variance. They all complained the standard was wrong, could never possibly be met, and how they must spend a lot of time preparing to explain their variance each month, but the bottom line is they fight with accounting each month over the standard.

We then met with the "standards" guy who thought he was going to be in for a big fight and reviewed the calculations with him. He became somewhat animated when we agreed his calculations were correct and there was no reason, we shouldn't be able to meet them. We were the first to ever agree his standards were correct. Every month he had fought with production over the argument his standards were wrong and could not be met and now he was finally vindicated.

Interestingly, over time, to pacify operations management, the standards guy had been forced to revise the standard downward, believe it or not, to 30% of the original. This means if the original standard to put together a subassembly was 1 hour (7 per day based on available time), they were setting the production schedule based on 200 minutes (or 2 per day). So, the company was now scheduling 70% waste into their schedule and increased their quoted lead times by 70% to their customers. When you extrapolate this to the overall business, the effect was huge as this company had five plants. If you think about it, 70% of their plants existed due to this reduction in standards based on demonstrated performance each day. As a footnote to this story, the supervisors were correct when they stated they could not meet the standard. Their work process was so hosed-up that there is no way they could have come close to the standard at which they should have been producing.

Results: At Company X, when we set up their Lean line, we met the original standard in our first week and surpassed it in the weeks to follow. While this company was still doing well from a financial standpoint, can you even begin to imagine how much more money and market share they could have obtained over the years of working to the original standard! Today, after implementing Lean, they have just two plants! The standards guy retired and was not replaced.

Chapter Questions

1. The elimination of what main waste drives the conversion from batch to flow production.
2. What are the six levels of waste?
3. What is the Ohno circle?
4. What is the best way to find waste?
5. It is easiest to find wastes in the area you work in. Is this statement true or false? Why?
6. What was the P course?
7. What is the difference between apparent and true efficiency?
8. What are the eight wastes? Give an example of each.
9. What are some root causes of the eight wastes? Can you think of anymore?
10. How should we eliminate the need to feel defensive when ideas/suggestions are challenged/changed? Describe your approach.
11. What are the principles of efficiency? Are they in any way related to Lean principles? How do they relate to companies today? What lessons can we learn from these principles?
12. What is the concept of strenuousness versus efficiency?
13. Which are the differences between the destructively offensive or constructively defensive company? How are they like plants versus mammals? Which type of company is better? Why?
14. What did you learn from this chapter?

Notes

1. Shingo, *A Study of the Toyota Production System from an Industrial Engineering Viewpoint*, Productivity Press, ©1989, p. 76.
2. C. Protzman III Visit to Japan in 1996.
3. C. Protzman III Visit to Japan in 1996.
4. C. Protzman III Visit to Japan in 1996.
5. Yoshio Kondo, translated by J.H. Loftus, *Company Wide Quality Control (Zenshateki Hinshitsu Kanri)*, JUSE Press, Professor Yoshio Kondo, http://www.hk5sa.com/tqm/tqmex/kondo.htm
6. Acing the Quality Quiz, Joseph M. Juran, *Quality Management Magazine*, 1992. At the time, Joseph M. Juran was the chairman emeritus of the Juran Institute. This article is adapted from a speech he gave at The Conference Boards of quality conference.
7. Partially based on a discussion with ITT Control Technology Team Members: Stephen Deas, Lean Six Sigma Black Belt, Crystal Hamilton, Assembler & Machinist, HazMat Coordinator, Boyd Mashewske—CNC Machinist & Setup, Lloyd Smyly—CNC Machinist and Setup/R&D.
8. Protzman, Kerpchar, *Leveraging Lean in Healthcare*, Mayzell, ©2011.
9. Submitted by James Bond, James Bond, College Professor, Toyota Retiree, and Current International Lean Consultant, Personal Correspondence—Editing Review, January 2, 2013.
10. R. Dave Nelson, Patricia Moody, and Rick B. Mayo, *Powered by Honda*, Hoboken, NJ, John Wiley & Sons, 1998, p. 101.
11. *The Toyota Leaders*, pp. 33–35.
12. R. Dave Nelson, Patricia Moody, and Rick B. Mayo, *Powered by Honda*, Hoboken, NJ, John Wiley & Sons, 1998, p. 25.
13. Jeffery Liker, Toyota Way, New York, McGraw-Hill, 2004, p. 223.
14. Yoshio Kondo, translated by J.H. Loftus, *Company Wide Quality Control (Zenshateki Hinshitsu Kanri)*, JUSE Press, Professor Yoshio Kondo, http://www.hk5sa.com/tqm/tqmex/kondo.htm.
15. Charles Protzman Sr. and Homer Sarasohn, *CCS Training Manual*, an e-book transcription of the version presented at the 1949 Tokyo seminar has been prepared by Nick Fisher and Suzanne Lavery of ValueMetrics, Australia, and is widely available on the Internet. The documents that formed a

final English version that was translated by Bunzaemon Inoue and others and published in 1952 in Japanese by Diamond Press are in the Hopper, Hackettstown, NJ, Civil Communications Section archive, 1949–1950.

16. After a successful tenure as a general manager of a small Pennsylvania glass factory in 1900, Emerson resolved to take up efficiency engineering as a profession. Through meetings of the American Society of Mechanical Engineers, he became personally acquainted with the pioneering work of Frederick W. Taylor, the founder of scientific management, and assimilated much of the methodology for standardizing work and remunerating workers in accordance with productivity. Emerson's most notable consulting assignment was the reorganization of the machine and locomotive repair shops of the sprawling Atchison, Topeka, and Santa Fe Railroad. Three years in duration (1904–1907), this work involved the first successful application of scientific management to a large railroad system. Engineering and railroad periodicals gave much attention to the system of shop betterment which he installed. Emerson also developed and implemented a bonus pay system that was widely accepted in several industries. As a result of his successful work for the Atchison, Topeka, Emerson began to attract an industrial clientele. During his tenure as a Standard Practice Engineer for the American Locomotive Company, Emerson also founded the Emerson Company. This company hired out associate consulting engineers to other firms on a contract basis. Emerson associates were entrusted with the tasks of standardizing work procedures and applying the Emerson bonus plan for client companies. Between 1907 and 1910, the Emerson Company achieved modest success. The company consulted over 200 corporations, submitting reports for which they were paid 25 million dollars. Emerson efficiency methods were applied to department stores, hospitals, colleges, and municipal governments. Between 1911 and 1920 Emerson's firm averaged annual earnings of over $100,000.00. http://vectorstudy.com/management_theories/twelve_principles_of_efficiency.htm Public Domain VectorStudy.com is a free management and marketing portal for management researchers and businesspeople. It provides information about popular management theories, management gurus, management schools, and management topics. All services are totally free.

17. *The Twelve Principles of Efficiency by Harrington Emerson (Sixth I'.nmoif)*, New York, The Engineering Magazine Co., 1924.

18. http://www.nwlink.com/~donclark/hrd/history/herzberg.html

19. From the Art of Lean Website: there are levels of standards and documents inside of Toyota just like in any company. There are governing bodies of standards and regulations inside the company known as Toyota Motor Regulations (TMR) and Toyota Manufacturing Standards (TMS). Both sets together are about the size of 20 encyclopedia volumes and considered highly confidential and proprietary. When I started with the company in the 1980s, they were still costly in Japanese and not very often changed (think application of bearings, etc., where the laws of physics are constant or electrical power coming into the plant), also Inside the Mind of Toyota, Hino, Productivity Press, 2006.

20. Efficiency of quality and quantity and overhead for materials, for labor and for fixed charges (these are nine of the costs). It has been found exceedingly satisfactory and convenient to base efficiency rewards on the cost of efficiencies, the method being so flexible as to be applicable to an individual operation of a few minutes.

21. http://www.google.com/search?hl=en&rls=com.microsoft:*:IE-www.fammed.ouhsc.edu/robhamm/UsersGuide/define.htm, www.balancedscorecard.org/LinkClick.aspxSearchBox&rlz=1I7SNCA&defl=en&q=define:Effectiveness&sa=X&oi=glossary_definition&ct=hensitle, http://www.investorwords.com/3876/productivity.html http://virtuallydistinguished.com/productivity-vs-efficiency-bring-efficiency-to-your-business

22. http://www.brainyquote.com/quotes/quotes/p/peterdruck134881.html#0yceIgbQtZZWrwvE.99

23. Toyota Training Manual.

24. Source: Kanban Just-in-Time at Toyota–Ohno, Japan Management Association.

25. Used with permission—Legacy of Dr. Shingo and TPS, Art Smalley, ©2006, http://www.artoflean.com

26. Email correspondence with Art Smalley, 8/22/2012—Dr. Shigeo Shingo's P-Course and Contribution to TPS, by Art Smalley |1 July 2006| 0 Comments 1997–2010 Factory Strategies Group LLC and the original author. All rights reserved. Isao "Ike" Kato spent 35 years with Toyota Motor Corporation

in a variety of management positions in manufacturing, HR, training and development, and supplier development. Early in his career Ike was responsible for guiding external consultant Dr. Shigeo Shingo around Toyota facilities. Ike also worked extensively developing training material for TPS. This is a reprint of an article that was in a series over at superfactory.com several years ago. This one was written by Mr. Kato, and I edited it, translated it, and submitted to Kevin at the super factory. Earlier he had asked to run a piece I had on my website which I agreed to. I asked Mr. Kato so just lay out the facts of Dr. Shingo's involvement at Toyota. Mr. Kato conducted Dr. Shingo's visits for over two decades. They were good friends even after the Toyota–Shingo breakup.

27. http://www.mtm.org/, The MTM Association for Standards and Research has pioneered in the development of computerized and manual work measurement systems that recognize, classify, describe, and objectively measure the performance of individuals working at various levels within an organization. The Association, a member of the International MTM Directorate, is a nonprofit organization sponsored and supported by member companies throughout the world. With sister organizations located throughout Europe and Asia, membership includes major corporations, governmental agencies, management consulting firms, universities, and individuals. Since 1951, the MTM Association for Standards and Research has provided business and industry with innovative methodologies designed to help them improve profitability, productivity, and quality. Serving a wide cross section of industry, the MTM Association has enabled organizations to not only understand and analyze current operational performance, but also to improve and enhance the work environment as well.

Additional Readings

All these books written in the early 1900s laid the groundwork for the learning organization, standardized work, and what we call Lean today.

Allen, C. 1919. My Life & My Work Henry Ford. New York: Lippincott.

Allen, C.R. 1919. The Instructor the Man and the Job. New York: Lippincott Company.

Barnes, J. 1937. Time and Motion Study. New York: Wiley & Sons.

Barnes, R.M. 1937. Motion and Time Study. New York: John Wiley & Sons.

Folts, F. 1949. Introduction to Industrial Management. New York: McGraw-Hill.

Ford, H. 1926. Today & Tomorrow. New York: Doubleday.

Gilbreth, F.B. 1911. Motion, Study. Easton, PA: Hive Publishing.

Gilbreth, L. 1916. Fatigue Study. New York: Sturgis & Walton.

Given, W.B. 1949. Bottom-Up Management. New York: Harper & Brothers.

Harrington, E. 1911. The Twelve Principles of Efficiency. New York: Engineering Magazine, Co.

Harvard Archives. 1952. Translated by Bunzaemon Inoue et al., in Japanese by Diamond Press. CCS Archive, Hackettstown, NJ, and the Drucker Institute.

Holden, D.P. 1926. Top Management Organization and Control. Stanford, CA: Stanford University Press.

Kimball, D.S. 1939. Principles of Industrial Organizations. New York: McGraw-Hill.

Protzman, C. and Sarasohn, H. 1949. The CCS Industrial Management Manual. Unpublished.

Taylor, F. 1923. Authorized Biography Copley. New York: Harper & Brothers.

Taylor, F.W. 1911. Scientific, Management. New York: Harper.

Chapter 2

BASICS®: Assess—PFA Product Flow Analysis (TIPS)

Time waste differs from material waste in that there can be no salvage. The easiest of all wastes and the hardest to correct is the waste of time because wasted time does not litter the floor like wasted material.

Henry Ford, 1926

This chapter begins the Assessment phase of the BASICS® model. There are three aspects we assess when reviewing an assembly or machining cell. These same tools apply for transactional processes (Figure 2.1). The assessment phase reviews the following:

1. The product—process flow analysis (PFA)
2. The operator—workflow analysis (WFA)
3. Setups—review changeovers and anything that has loading or unloading characteristics

We typically perform our assessment in this order.

Lean Analysis Tools

These tools are used to dissect a process into its finest parts down to the second. (Note: Gilbreth broke motions into a *wink* or 1/1,200th of a second.)[1] First, let's define a process (see Figure 2.2). A process has an input and an output with some transformation occurring in between where the material, or information for an administrative process, is somehow physically changed.

Dr. Shingo states in his book:

When we look at a process, we see a flow from material to semi-processed components to finished product. When we look at operations, on the other hand, we see the work performed to accomplish this transformation—the interaction and flow of equipment

DOI: 10.4324/9781003185789-2

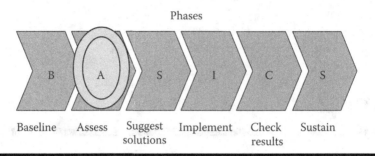

Figure 2.1 BASICS model—Assess and analyze.

and operators in time and space. Process analysis examines the flow of material or product, operator, and machine.

Consider a typical product, a shaft cut and finally finished. This series of changes in the shaft is a process. The lathe (operator) drills holes; rough cuts the outer surface, and finishes cutting the surface. This series of actions is an operation. To make fundamental improvements in the product process, we must distinguish product flow (process) from workflow (operator) and analyze them separately. Although the process is accomplished through a series of operations, it is misleading to visualize it as a single line because it reinforces the mistaken assumption improving individual operations will improve the overall efficiency of the process flow of which they are a part. … Operation improvements made without consideration of their impact on process may reduce overall efficiency…All production, whether carried out in the factory or the office must be understood as a functional network of process and operations… to make effective improvements in production.[2]

Lesson Learned: We have found some of the biggest opportunities occur in improving how the product flows. By looking at the product flow, first, we find that if we eliminate a product step, we have also eliminated the operator step(s) and changeover that goes with it. While simple in understanding, Shingo's discovery is truly remarkable, and when we teach people this, they find it extremely difficult to comprehend at first because we are always so focused on the person doing the job.

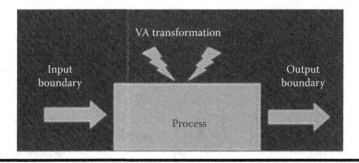

Figure 2.2 Process definition.

Dr. Shingo's Network of Operations—Overview

Dr. Shigeo Shingo described manufacturing as a network of operations[3] (see Figure 2.3). Dr. Shingo credits Frank Gilbreth as the first to discover that operations were different from processes. But Gilbreth defined them as being on the same axis, that is, a process was a large unit, and the operation was a small unit. However, it was Dr. Shigeo Shingo who first realized that they were *not* on the same axis; they were on two separate axes composing a network of operations. This network is composed of two pieces:

1. Process (product) flow
2. Workflow of the operator or those functions carried out by the person(s) doing the job
3. In this book, we are proposing yet another (or third) dimension (axis) to this network, which are setups/changeovers of information processes or products (including loading and unloading parts in machines)

Setups are very important for assembly or machining lines particularly when working in a mixed model environment. A single model line also uses setups when the line is *dried up* (this means all standard work in process [WIP] is consumed) at the end of each shift. We encounter setups on a machining line whenever there is manual or automated loading and unloading of parts in addition to the changeovers we associate with dies, jigs, fixtures, or tooling. We also encounter setups whenever we start a new cycle of the standard work. Sometimes the setup is only composed of the walking distance, and other times it may be using different machines or different fixtures or tooling on machines.

For instance, if I must load and unload a manual machine (like a drill press) or load a part into some type of tooling and then use a machine to press it or weld it and then I remove the tooling, that

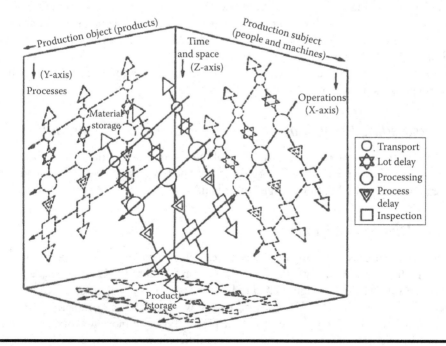

Figure 2.3   Shingo's 3D network of operations.

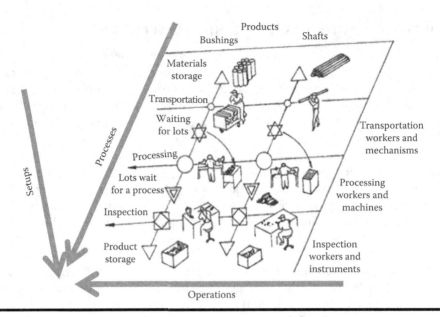

Figure 2.4   Shingo's network of operations.

is a setup! Think about it. Loading a part in or on a fixture for a drill press may require alignment, a trial run with ongoing visual inspection, and periodic adjustments, which are all parts of a setup. Electronic testing may have elements of a setup during each cycle, that is, alignment, calibration, programing adjustments, interaction with software, tweaking, and tuning, again all parts of a setup.

We don't know if anyone has ever reviewed setups in this exact way. We have learned over the last several years working with many mixed model lines; setup is one of our main drivers of inefficiency. It is hidden in the batch world but very exposed in the Lean world as part of or the entire line is generally shut down during the changeover. It should have its rightful place as the third axis in Dr. Shingo's network of operations (see Figure 2.4).

All three elements must be considered when analyzing processes (product or information), and each contributes separately to improved productivity.

Misunderstanding the Relations between Process and Operation[4]

Dr. Shigeo Shingo wrote the following in his book Non-Stock Production: "The phenomena of process and operation have not always been distinguished clearly because they blend together when operations are carried out by a single individual."

Impact of Division of Labor

"Division of labor" means in cutting materials, for example, a worker works successively on different objects, perhaps first on pins P1, P2, P3, etc.; then on bushings Q1,Q2, Q3, etc.; and then on the next part R1, R2, R3, etc. (Figure 2.5, Products).

When a lot of 100 pins (P1, P2, P3, etc.) cut by worker A has accumulated, the items are transferred to worker B who tapers the tips of the pins. Next, they move to worker C who grinds the pin tips. In this way, items flow in succession to different workers (A, B, C, D, etc.), each of whom processes them as required.

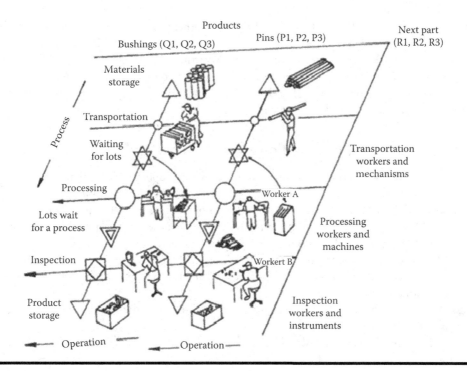

Figure 2.5 Shingo's network of operations—Detail.

Clearly, there is a distinction here:

Process refers to the flow of products from one worker to another, the stage through which raw materials (RMs) gradually move to become finished products.

Operation refers to the discrete stage at which a team member may work on different products, that is, a human temporal and spatial flow consistently centers on the worker.

As these concepts evolved, however, people inevitably became captivated by directly observable human motion—operational movements. Some concluded production consisted exclusively of operations; others who were aware of the process as a separate concept disdained its role in production. In 1921, however, Frank Gilbreth reported in the Journal of the American Society of Mechanical Engineering that production phenomena include the flow leading from RMs to finished product—the phenomenon of process—and that processes are themselves composed of four phenomena: processing (or machining), inspection, transport, and delay. The relationship between process and operation is typically defined as follows:

Processes are large units used in analyzing production.

Operations are small units used in analyzing production.

The West, therefore, ended up imagining that processes and operations are nothing more than overlapping phenomena lying on a single axis. As a result, even in Japan, certain books on production management explained process and operation as classifications dependent merely on the size of units of analysis. We can see where this led. Some people thought that production would improve once you improved operations, the smallest units of analysis. Others developed the obscure notion that if operations were improved, processes—as groups of operations—also would improve.

Lesson Learned: We have learned not just the West thinks this way today. Every country we visit whether the United States, Europe, or Asia still have the old type of thinking, and they constantly mix up process flow (product) and workflow (operator). Even premier universities worldwide teaching Lean courses still mix these up in their training material.

Process/Material and Information Flow[5]

The process flow, defined as the *product piece* of the network of operations, is obtained by configuring machines and materials in the exact order required to produce the product (or in some cases, information, i.e., in a transactional/administrative process, i.e., capital request, quotation, and requisition). Ordering the process flow correctly helps to expose and eliminate bottlenecks and improves overall production flow resulting in increased productivity.

Note: For the purposes of this book, productivity is defined as doing the same amount of work with fewer resources (i.e., people) or gaining more output with the same amount of people (assuming no overproduction).

Lesson Learned: The machines, parts, and tools must be configured in the exact sequence the product is assembled or machined.

Lesson Learned: The product should never go backward. In a transaction area, the service should always continue to move forward.

Our goal should be to always work toward one-piece, balanced, synchronized flow! We should continue to strive for this goal, even if we think or are convinced that it may not be possible. Too many Lean practitioners give up and take the easy way out versus the ongoing pursuit of this goal and settle for sitting operations, WIP caps or batching, and excess inventory in the process. As Lean practitioners, we must eliminate the word *CAN'T* from our dictionary and replace it with "How am I going to do it?" Sometimes you must take some time to figure it out.

The Importance of Lean Implementation Experience

I was working with a certified Lean master, who had his Lean training in a university but had never implemented Lean. He still believed, based on his industrial engineering training, batching was more efficient than one-piece flow. As such, he designed efficient *batch* workstations for the Lean line and even welded the two bin shelves that he fabricated to the workstations. He wanted to put a wall between the two lines that produced the same product.

We asked him why he felt the need to batch, put up a wall, and weld the shelves to the tables. He said batching was better; the wall would separate the two areas, so people could not confuse them; and the welds on the shelves were flexible. You just have to grind them off to remove them.

Have you ever run into Lean masters like this? How would you respond?

I continued to ask him open-ended questions designed to make him think but to no avail. We explained the eight reasons for batching and how we needed to overcome these reasons before we could implement one-piece flow. I did several training exercises with him and the team leaders to show that one-piece flow was more efficient than batching and he still fought me every step of the way. I kept trying to figure out what we were doing wrong.

He would constantly look for reasons to tell the operators it was OK to batch even after we had converted their workstations to Lean. As it turned out, the major cause was his deeply ingrained emotional need to be liked by the workforce. Instead of coaching and training the workforce on one-piece flow, his answer was to make everything a "study to show batching was more efficient." Eventually, I had to work around him and train the workforce directly, and with input and cooperation from the entire workforce, we implemented the lines. Their Lean master just never got it and eventually decided this company was not a good fit for him.

Lesson Learned: Many in Lean are book smart, can talk the talk, but have never implemented and don't know where or how to start implementing on the shop floor. They want everything perfect and are deathly afraid they might make a mistake to the point of not acting.

We generally find that we can achieve a 20%–40% improvement in any area just by getting the product to flow in one direction. Government regulations for biotech industries mandate the product never go backward. In many cases, we may have to duplicate equipment, tooling, or parts within the line to achieve a smooth process flow. Many who are new to Lean will initially object to duplicating parts bins in a cell suggesting that it requires too much work to replenish materials; however, we have found that it is a great way to start mistake-proofing operations. When parts bins are duplicated in the proper order, the assembler does have to go backward and therefore does not forget to go back to the central bin for parts, which helps to reduce errors in the process. World-class goals for the product should be 75%–80% value added (VA), which in most cases is impossible to meet yet still sought. Most products start out around 1%–3% VA and many times less than 1%.

Workflow of the Operator

The next step is to review what the operator does to the part as it flows down the line or information as it flows through an administrative process. It is acceptable for the person to go backward or from side to side if the product continues to move forward; however, we want to minimize and optimize the operator's travel distance. *The goal is for the operator to never have to move more than one step in any direction at one time.*

The operator must be viewed independently from the product and changeover axis.[6] Videos are a very useful tool to fully capture the flow and processes. We video the operator, the person doing the work, and analyze operations down to the second. During the review of the video, we review process, ergonomic concerns, safety risks, and any excess motions of the operator which are then highlighted for corrective actions(s).

We have found that we yield an additional 20%–40% or more improvement in productivity by focusing on the operators; however, *only after we have focused on the product piece.* Think about it this way: one cannot begin to have standard work until such time as all the tools and materials are presented to the operator in the proper order, even if equipment, tooling, or parts bins must be duplicated to do the job. This applies to the office setting as well. In general terms, we can reduce overhead labor by up to 30% or more once we implement efficient flow in the transactional areas.

Therefore, not only is there a network of operations but also a definite priority/order to implementing the Lean tools:

1. Value stream map (VSM) (if applicable)
2. Process flow—product piece
3. Workflow—operator piece
4. Setup improvements

Many company executives want to start where they perceive the bottleneck to be; only to discover, after analysis, the bottleneck is not where they thought it was. Often companies want to start in a subassembly area. Lean should always be started closest to the customer, i.e., with the final assembly area unless it is a service or government business in which case we would start on the transactional/administrative process closest to the customer.

Rule: We always try to incorporate subassembly areas directly into the final assembly lines. Preassembly is batching!

This approach creates the true need for the *pull* from the final assembly to the subassembly area and eventually to the administrative areas including accounting, quality, planning, scheduling, purchasing, engineering, legal, human resource (HR), marketing, and R&D. World class for the operator workflow is 75%–80% VA for assembly with 20% or less required work and zero idle time. For machining lines, the goal is to be as close to 100% required work with zero idle time. Operators should never have to *babysit* a machine.

Setup/Changeovers

The next tool we use is setup reduction that is done by videoing the changeover(s). The goal is to minimize setups by moving as many internal tasks as possible to external tasks with a target of zero setup. World-class changeover for a mixed model assembly operation should be zero, with world class for a machining operation being less than 10 minutes or what is defined as a single-minute exchange of dies (SMED).

Many companies are working on setups that are 3 minutes or less, again with a goal of achieving zero setup or one-touch exchange of dies (OTED) or one-shot (cycle) exchange of dies for assembly operations. We will explore each of these analysis tools in more detail in the following chapters.

History

It is interesting to note in the CCS manual, in 1949, that it differentiated product from operations. "A factory, with all its equipment and services can be thought of as being itself one large machine. The design and organization of this machine, the number of people required to operate it, the number of times materials must be moved from one part of the big machine to another, and the distances involved, and the amount of time required by this production machine to convert the raw materials taken in at one end to the finished products which emerge from the other end—all these factors have a direct influence on operations. Here, too, then, is a relation between factory layout and manufacturing cost."

The US taught the Japanese there were two types of layouts: "The type of factory layout that is becoming most widely used in industry is the so-called straight-line production. In this system materials always move in one direction. There is no backtracking, but rather a continuous flow from the point of entrance of materials to the point of shipment of the product. The machines and equipment are arranged along the line of travel of the product. Mass production organizations are the typical users of this arrangement because

1. There is a minimum amount of material handling.
2. This type of production is easier to supervise.
3. Production costs are usually lower.

In a second type of layout, called the Jobbing layout, all similar types of machines are grouped together in one place and the materials are moved from one group to another during the fabrication of the product."

Analyzing Process (Product), Operation (Operator, Workflow), and Setup (Changeover)[7]

Some of the biggest opportunities lay in improving the process flow. We have studied this separation of process and operation in detail and will explore it through the following chapters. The reader should realize, and we cannot emphasize it enough; each of these pieces, the product, the operator, and setup contribute separately to the overall operational improvement.

For example, just improving the process flow and doing nothing to improve the workflow will reduce inventory and throughput time. Improving the operation will reduce labor time regardless of the process flow. This concept, though rather simple in theory today, holds the secret for process improvement everywhere. It bears repeating here that by just improving product flow, one should realize up to a 20%–40% improvement or more in productivity when converting from a pure *batch production* environment. Likewise, improving the operator piece on its own should realize a similar improvement. However, by combining and optimizing both the product flow and operator pieces, we can achieve improvements not possible looking at each piece individually.

For years, by just looking at the operation, we have been missing all the opportunities found by incorporating the process piece. The goal of the process piece is always striving toward one-piece flow. To improve any process, one must analyze and study each of the analysis components separately and then solve them together as a network of operations.

The third variable in this equation is setup times. Improving setup times can but doesn't necessarily improve productivity but does immediately increase capacity or the ability to perform more setups and deliver mixed models quicker and more efficiently.

It is interesting to note that Productivity Press has two books dating back to 1984 that differentiate process from operation. The first is called *Productivity through Process Analysis*[8] that deals with the product piece. The second is called *Productivity through Motion Study*[9] that deals with the operator piece and explains Gilbreth's therbligs in detail. Both books are part of the IE for the shop floor series. The book does not discriminate between types of delays other than a planned delay, which is storage, and an unplanned delay, which is just called a delay.

Analyzing and Improving the Process (Product) Flow Yields Increased Product Velocity (PFA)

See the Product… Be the Product!—Joe Shipley[10] To conduct a PFA correctly, one must become the *thing* going through the process whether it is a product in manufacturing, a patient in healthcare, a person in a government agency, or information (paper or electronic). This may sound easy but in practice, it is very difficult to do, just ask anyone we test on this exercise in our training classes.

For some reason, maybe human nature, most of us just want to focus on what the operator is doing. To analyze the process or product flow correctly, we utilize what we call a TIPS analysis (see Figure 2.6). TIPS represents the 4 things a product can do i.e. Transport, Inspect, Process, Store. It is important when analyzing to question everything. Don't skip over something because

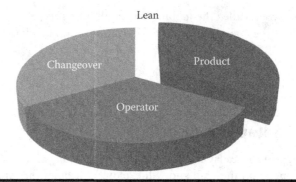

Figure 2.6 The three pieces we analyze—Product piece.

you *already know* why it is being done no matter how trivial. Therefore, we analyze steps down to the second. Act on fact, not on what you are told. This is the reason why the videos of the process are so useful for analysis.

Implementing the TIPS Methodology

These are the steps we utilize to analyze the product flow of the product or information-based process (transactional) we are following:

- Video.
- Analyze and code the product steps.
- Conduct the omits process with the operator and supervisor.
- Create a block diagram of the *to-be* process.
- Reorder the PFA steps to match the *to-be* process.
- Add the times to the block diagram.
- Determine the layout and workstation design and add to the block diagram.
- Determine the new throughput time and WIP calculations.

TIPS Analysis[11,12]

If you want to improve the material or information flow in any process, you must continually perform a TIPS analysis. The PFA is broken down into four basic steps we call TIPS. The acronym TIPS stands for the following:

1. Transport
2. Inspect
3. Process
4. Store (to signify a delay)

Transport (T)

Transport occurs whenever the product is physically moved from one place to another. Transportation is non-VA and we should work to eliminate each transport step or reduce it as much as possible.

Transport is recorded in time and distance. This is just one reason why we try to eliminate forklifts, cranes, conveyors, and even simple movement from one part of the plant or office to another.

Be Aware of Hidden Wastes in Transportation

I toured a plastics assembly company which was a well-known, profitable, and established leader in the marketplace. At first glance, it was very clean, with conveyors and robots everywhere. It looked world class to the non-Lean eye. 5S was the favorite program of the operations VP, yet when we looked closely at the lines, we saw trash on the floor, no visual management, and there was a ton of ongoing human inspection.

The company just installed new robots (see Figure 2.7). The lines prior to the robots had three or four operators (isolated islands) each feeding a conveyor to a manual welder that batched the products, which were then sent via a conveyor to final assembly where they were packed, stickered, tags were applied, and then boxed up and put on an overhead conveyor, which went to shipping. The total labor in the cell varied from six to seven people.

The new cell had two lines with three operators feeding the two robots. The new lines were limited to two products each versus the old lines that could assemble three or even four products. The robots welded and then supplied the parts to two separate final assembly and pack lines, each of which had two operators. The total before and after the robots was still seven operators but we were told they were now faster which saved on their labor reports.

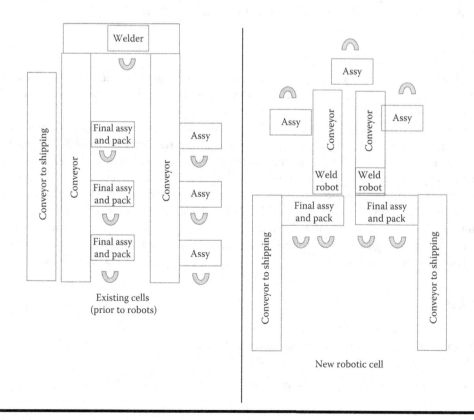

Figure 2.7   Major motorcycle sprocket robotic cell.

When we watched the lines run, we found that the three operators in the front of the line were constantly idle. This is because the final assembly operators were batching off the conveyor line. The line would stop until the product was pulled from the conveyor and tripped the limit switch to start the conveyor again. In addition, if the front-end operators had a delay, they could stop the line. This held up the final operators. I asked the accountant with me if they had a metric that kept track of all this idle time and whether they were really meeting the ROI on these robotic lines. The answer was a resounding NO. These were all hidden wastes!

We looked at the workstation design for the final assembly and noticed that step 1, which was a machine for the product, was located on the opposite side from where the product was pulled from the conveyor, which was the furthest travel distance possible and backward for the product. Stickers were applied and it was put in a queue for the next operator. The next operator had to install a tag and box up the units. WIP was everywhere on the workstations, which were all located off the conveyor. The conveyor provided the illusion of a paced line when it was paced by the operators. I told the accountant that I would bet if we set up manual cells with the old manual welders, we could beat the output of the robot line. He asked me what else I would do. I said I would remove all the conveyors. I asked how he thought that would go over. He said probably not too well since they just purchased and installed them. The accountant has since left the company.

Lesson Learned: What should conveyors do? If you must have them, they should transport (i.e., convey), not store. Most conveyors end up storing product (WIP) and are removed when Lean is implemented. Many companies are very profitable and do a great job until the market turns. The time to implement Lean is when things are going well; however, this is when complacency is at its highest and the compelling need to change at its lowest.

Inspection (I)

Inspection occurs whenever the product or information (paperwork or electronic) is reviewed for any reason. Many times, operators (which can also be a senior executive reading over a report they are ready to submit) don't even realize they are inspecting.

From a Lean purist viewpoint, we have often wondered why Gilbreth found inspection worthy of breaking out as a separate step when in essence it is a process step, which is non-VA. Calling attention to the inspection step allowed Gilbreth, later Dr. Shingo, and now us, to highlight where we fundamentally don't trust the process, or it is out of control and needs attention. If the process was in control, it wouldn't need inspection. As Dr. Shingo argued, the control process belongs as part of the planning, the "p" in plan–do–check–act (PDCA), which immediately requires us to improve or begin to think about mistake proofing the process to eliminate the need for inspection. In addition, one could make the argument that inspection is not a process. This is supported by the fact there is no physical change to the product in which case it should be broken out as a separate step.[13]

Process (P)

Processes are broken down into two categories: VA and non-VA.

A process must meet three criteria to be considered VA:

Value Added Definition[14] (Figure 2.8)

1. The customer must care about the step. If the customer doesn't care about the step, you are not adding anything.

2. The step must physically change the thing going through the process whether a product or paper: form, fit, shape, size, or function. In the healthcare world, we say it must change the patient physically or emotionally for the better.[15]

3. The step must be done right the first time. If the step is not done correctly, it must be reworked. Rework is not VA. So, the step can only add value when it is done correctly the first time and any prior or subsequent rework is to be considered non-VA.

Note: The step must pass all three criteria to be considered VA!

Non Value Added but Necessary: Required Work

Some steps may meet one or two of the three criteria but not all three. We call these steps necessary but not VA. For example, there may be a regulatory requirement one has to meet that doesn't physically change the product, or a part may have to be reworked by design (i.e., tweaking), which physically changes the product but obviously is not done right the first time, or it may physically change the thing and is done right the first time, but the customer doesn't care about it. Many times, this results in the waste of overprocessing.

What about payroll or where employees are paid at a designated frequency? Payroll within the big picture of processes is non-VA because the customer doesn't care if or how you get paid. However, when you are looking just at the payroll process, the definitions may change. For example, within the confines of the payroll process, only the check being cut, or the direct deposit being made, would be considered VA. The timecard being filled in, inspected, or corrected is non-VA. What other examples can you think of in your organization?

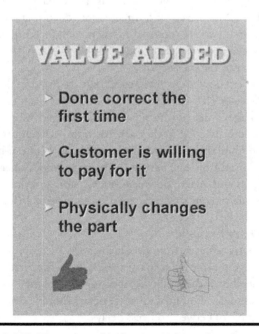

Figure 2.8   Value added definition. (Graphic from Smith's Industries—Barry Rogers.)

Storage (S); Delay

Storage is broken down into three parts: RM, WIP, and finished goods (FG).

1. RM is considered any part that has not had any direct labor added to it. For instance, it may be sitting in the stockroom. It may have had indirect labor added to it to receive it, i.e., receiving inspection labor, but no direct labor has been added to it. While this is a clean definition for products, it can be confusing for office processes. In the office, we technically don't have direct labor. So WIP in the office is whenever indirect labor touches it whether it is paper, or electronic (information). These definitions are based on traditional accounting techniques. In Lean, we don't really differentiate direct from indirect labor. Labor is labor. The goal is to turn as many staff jobs to value stream jobs (line jobs) as possible.

   Sometimes we stretch this definition depending on the process being studied. For example, in the purchasing process, we may be starting from the quote stage. Therefore, any paperwork, which represents quotes received back from suppliers, could be considered RM. In manufacturing, we may start at the cell. So even though labor has been consumed moving the product to the cell warehouse or the beginning of the process or if it was a product made in another cell, we may choose to call it RM even though it may not meet the strict accounting definition. The other option would be to call it WIP; either is acceptable.

   The key is to make sure that whatever it is called in the *before* analysis is called the same in the *after* analysis and make sure the definition is clear and stated somewhere in the project documentation.

   Lesson Learned: It is sometimes not worth splitting hairs over definitions during the TIPS analysis. We have witnessed some very contested and bitter discussions over what something should be called or considered. It is better to move forward with the analysis and just agree to use the same definitions in the before and the after analyses.

2. WIP is defined as any RM received with direct labor added to it. We differentiate WIP into three categories. The first two are standard industrial engineering categories[16] and the third (within process[17]) is a category we created due to the discovery that some products did not fit the criteria for either of the other two.

   WIP storage is broken down into three parts that are listed in the following:

Between-Process Storage (B)

Between-process storage is defined by products sitting and waiting individually or as an entire lot for the next process, that is, they are stored in-between two sequential processes. It is not unusual to find more than one and sometimes many between-process storage locations as the products are moved from one part of the plant or work center staging area to another and then moved again and again. Between-process storage would be like a one-way road with a stop sign. You are moving down the road and must stop before proceeding to the next stretch of road (i.e., the next process).

Between-Process Delay Example

A basket of parts was transported from the shear to the turret punch machine. Now it is in between-process storage *waiting* (all its parts together) for the turret punch process. Another example is on an assembly line—while the operator reaches for a part or a tool, the product is in a between-process delay. Our goal for these delays should be no more than 1–3 seconds. Kanbans are an example of between process delays.

Lot Delays (L)

Lot delays are where we are waiting for the rest of the batch or what we call *our buddies* to be processed. We refer to them affectionately as *buddies* (when we are pretending to "be the part" during the PFA) because we find it is easier for people to remember that we are the product in this way.

Lot Delay Example

Let's say we are analyzing a press operation. The part is moved to the press. What step is this? If you answered transport, that is correct, and we would capture the transport time and distance. Then we get pressed by the machine. What step is that? It is a process. If it is done right the first time and the customer cares about it, it is considered a VA process. We are then moved to a basket or bin. Transport again! Now we are waiting for our *buddies* or the rest of the lot to be processed. This is a *lot* delay. To further clarify, no matter what position we are in the lot, that is, 1 of 5 and 2 of 5, we are still in a lot delay once the first piece is started, and we are waiting to be processed.

Note: As soon as our last buddy has passed through the press operation and has been transported to our bin or basket, we immediately transition from a lot delay to a between-process delay because now we (us and our buddies) are all waiting for the next process.

Generally, lot delays are followed by between-processes delays. However, we occasionally find that we have two or more lot delays in a row. An example would be where I put parts into a bin (transport), and we wait in the bin for six or eight of our buddies (lot delay) and then we are dumped into a basket (transport) and again are still waiting for the rest of our buddies to get completed.

Why do we care about breaking a process step into this detail? The answer is simple; the more you can break the process down, the easier it is to find improvement. We only find lot delays when batching is occurring. Lot Delays are Over Production, our number one waste!

Within-Process Storage[18] (W)

Within-process storage (delay) is a new type of delay that occurs after a process is started on a part or a lot where the part, person, or lot is delayed because the process is interrupted for some reason. It could be a machining operation interrupted for lunch break or a machine that breaks down or a tool bit that breaks, and the piece must wait while it is repaired or reworked. We call this "drive thru parking." It could be someone stuck in an elevator, or a requisition being placed but having to stop the process to check the status of that or another part in a different screen or window.

3. FG storage is defined as when a product is complete except for taking it off the shelf and shipping it. Since storage is waste and again each step is an opportunity for a defect, our goal is to eliminate as many storage steps as possible. Sometimes we may plan to build in WIP or FG storage Kanban, but our goal should be to still minimize the quantity wherever possible.

Note: Many get confused on how to handle time in a PFA, that is, what number of hours to use when a product sits for a "day." We generally use the working hours as the measurement of what a day equals. Keep in mind a person's idle time and product's storage times (which result in excess inventory) are always signs of a problem. Even Kanbans are symptoms of a problem where we have two processes not able to be connected for some reason.

Why Separate Out These Delays (Figure 2.9)

Why separate out these delays? To truly obtain the fastest velocity possible for material or information flow and to understand the nature of the operation and where the waste exists, it becomes imperative to break down each step the product goes through on its journey from RM to the shipping dock. Think about what your products would say to you if they could talk. You would probably hear things like "why have I been sitting on this shelf for three months? Why have I been in this inbox for hours?" However, if you are the product in a hospital, that is, a patient, wouldn't you want to count every step that you go through in the process and see how long it takes? If you are sitting for hours in a waiting room, how many times do you go to the front desk to ask when you will be seen by the doctor? Unlike hospitals, for most of us, our products can't talk, but think about what yours would say if they could!

Many times, there are so many moves of the product from operation to operation that going through the pain of literally walking every single step of the process and writing down each move helps give us the incentive or big C in our change equation (see Figure 2.10) which is our compelling need to change. It is not unusual to find products or paper literally traveling miles (kilometers) from their RM stage to FG stage. Imagine doing a PFA from the iron ore to the soda can recycling.

What We Normally Find (Figure 2.11)

We seldom find cases where the product has more than 1%–3% VA activity happening to it throughout the process. Ninety-seven percent or more of the time, it is normally sitting … waiting for the next thing to happen to it. The batch size and waiting time seem to be correlated; the larger the batch size, the more waiting occurs, and the more delays are inherent in the process.

Laundry Example of PFA

To illustrate that a PFA can be applied to any product, let's analyze it with an example of doing a load of laundry:

Step 1: The first thing we need to decide is what we are going to follow.

So, let's pick a shirt in the load of laundry and assume we are the dirty shirt sitting in the laundry pile in the closet.

Step 2: We need to follow the process in detail. Walk every step of the process.

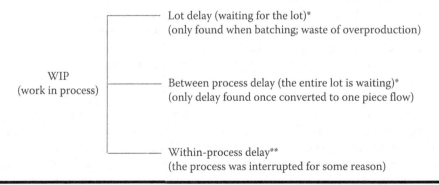

Figure 2.9   WIP delays.

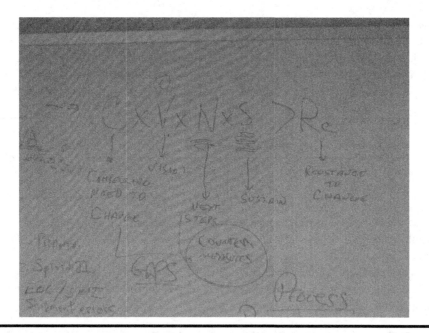

Figure 2.10 Change equation.

Since we are sitting in a pile waiting to be cleaned, what PFA stage are we in?

Notice that we (the group doing the PFA) refer to ourselves as *we*—the shirt. Otherwise, it is easy to get trapped into following what the operator is doing.

Answer: Since we are sitting in a pile, we are obviously in storage. But which type of storage?

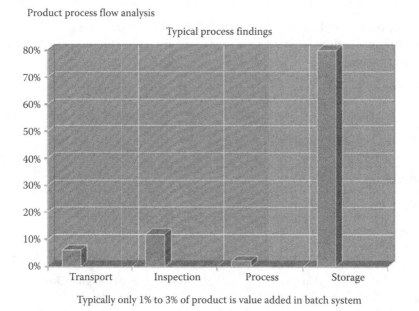

Figure 2.11 Steps of the product and typical percentages found.

Answer: We would call waiting in the closet for the laundry process as *RM* storage.

We ask the following question: "How long have we (the shirt) been waiting there?"

If you do your laundry about once a week (excluding weekends), let's say we have been waiting for 5 days. We would enter 5 days × 24 hours/day × 60 minutes/hour × 60 seconds/minute on our sheet of paper. This would give us 432,000 seconds. We always do the analysis in seconds.

Step	Description	Type	Time	Distance	Total Time	Cumulative Distance
1	Waiting in pile for washing machine	RM	432,000	0	432,000	0

The next step would be to pick us up and move us to the laundry basket. Since we are picked up, we would code it as NV for non-VA process and put in 1 second for the time. We are then transported (2 seconds, 2 ft).

Note: Wherever there is a transport, there must be a distance traveled. It is also possible to be transported during other steps, so sometimes there may be a process where a part is transported, and the distance should be captured as well.

Step	Description	Type	Time	Distance	Total Time	Cumulative Distance
1	Waiting in pile for washing machine	RM	432,000	0	432,000	0
2	Pick us up	NV	1	0	432,001	0
3	Move to laundry basket	T	2	2	432,003	2

We wait for the rest of the laundry to be loaded into the basket. What step is this?

Answer: This is a lot delay since we are waiting for our buddies (the other shirts) to be loaded. Let's call it 10 seconds.

Step	Description	Type	Time	Distance	Total Time	Cumulative Distance
1	Waiting in pile for washing machine	RM	432,000	0	432,000	0
2	Pick us up	NV	1	0	432,001	0
3	Move to laundry basket	T	2	2	432,003	2
4	Wait for rest of laundry to be loaded	L	10	0	432,013	2

We would then assume that we are moved right away to the washing machine, but this is not always the case. When we asked what happened next, we were told by the operator that we (the basket of laundry) had to wait to be moved while the operator prepared another pile of laundry for the next wash. So how do we code this step?

Answer: As soon as the last shirt is put in the basket, we immediately transition from the lot delay to a *between-processes* delay for 60 seconds.

Note: It is important to ask the operator at each step if we ever sit and wait for something else to happen or if they do it right away. Many times, the operators forget that they did not move something right away. In this case, let's assume that we move the basket as soon as the next load is completed.

Step	Description	Type	Time	Distance	Total Time	Cumulative Distance
5	Wait while next load is prepped	B	60	0	432,073	2

Then we (the basket of laundry) are moved to the washing machine, picked up (1 second), and then transported (30 seconds, to the 1st floor, 150 ft).

Step	Description	Type	Time	Distance	Total Time	Cumulative Distance
6	Pick up basket	NV	1	0	432,074	2
7	Move basket to laundry machine on 1st floor	T	30	150	432,104	152

Then we wait for the washing machine to finish the load already in it. This is a between-processes storage step—20 minutes.

Step	Description	Type	Time	Distance	Total Time	Cumulative Distance
8	Wait for washing machine to finish previous load	B	1,200	0	433,304	152

Once the washing machine finishes, the operator moves the previous load to the dryer. What step is this? I know many of you immediately thought of transport. If you were one of them, I am sorry to tell you that you are wrong! Why is that? Well let's go back to what we are following. We are following the first shirt in the basket. What is the first shirt doing while we moved the previous load of clothes from the washer to the dryer? Sitting of course. So, we are still between-processes storage—2 minutes.

Step	Description	Type	Time	Distance	Total Time	Cumulative Distance
9	Wait while washer's previous batch is unloaded	B	120	0	433,424	152

Then we wait while the other shirts are loaded into the washer—this again is a lot delay because we lost FIFO and we are waiting for the armload where we are picked up—5 seconds.

| 10 | Wait in the pile while first shirts (our buddies) are loaded | L | 5 | 0 | 433,429 | 152 |

Then we are loaded into the washer.

| 11 | Pick us up (with other shirts) | NV | 1 | 0 | 433,430 | 152 |
| 12 | Move to washer | T | 1 | 2 | 433,431 | 154 |

Then we wait for the rest of the basket to be loaded. (Lot delay—10 seconds.)

| 13 | Wait for rest of shirts to be loaded | L | 10 | 0 | 433,441 | 154 |

Next, the operator reaches for the detergent and takes off the cap. What step is this?

How many think it is a process step?
If so, is it VA or non-VA?
Answer: Actually, it is neither because we are following the shirt. So, we are in storage in the washing machine. But what kind of storage?
Answer: It is between processes because me and my buddies are all waiting for the detergent.

| 14 | Wait while detergent is grabbed | B | 2 | 0 | 433,443 | 154 |

As you can see, it is not as easy as you might think to become the product and do this analysis. Next, the detergent is poured over us. We would consider this to be a NV step—2 seconds.

| 15 | Detergent added to machine | NV | 2 | 0 | 433,445 | 154 |

Then we close the door and spin the dial on the machine to the wash position. What step is this? Hopefully you answered between-processes storage—5 seconds.

| 16 | Wait while door is closed and setup machine cycle | B | 5 | 0 | 433,450 | 154 |

Now the washing machine runs—30 minutes. This is our first VA step.

| 17 | Cycle machine | VA | 1,800 | 0 | 435,250 | 154 |

Note: Here, we captured the entire wash as one process, but we could break down each individual step of the machine. Many times, we do this analysis on machines. For example, while the machine is filling with water, we are waiting in between processes until such time the washer starts to rotate. Once it starts to rotate, then we are being washed, which is the true VA. Then we wait while the machine changes over to the rinse cycle, and then we get rinsed. Rinsing would not be considered VA since it is removing the soap, which while necessary is not VA because technically it is a rework. This is because the VA was in removing the dirt and/or stains from the shirt, which was done in the wash cycle. Then we wait while the machine changes over to the spin cycle. The spin cycle again would be a no-VA (NVA) process because it is not physically changing the shirt. It is just removing the water necessary to activate the soap. The temptation would be to argue that adding soap, washing, rinsing, and spinning are all VA. But this is misleading because the only real VA is removing the dirt (of course, you could always argue we shouldn't have gotten the shirt dirty in the first place and the entire process is rework). Regardless of the outcome, it is the discussion which is most important. Just getting people to THINK and ask questions about the process is the VA portion of Lean thinking. At this stage, our 30 minutes of VA is somewhat misleading and is probably only actually 5 or 10 minutes of the cycle.

Once we are washed, we wait to be unloaded (between process—10 minutes to half a day).

Note: The dryer runs longer than the washing machine, so we end up waiting for the dryer to finish and then we wait some more while the operator is busy doing something else.

| 18 | Wait to be unloaded | B | 600 | 0 | 435,850 | 154 |

Next, the operator unloads the dryer. What step is this? It is the between process (5 minutes).

| 19 | Wait while the dryer is unloaded | B | 300 | 0 | 436,150 | 154 |

Then we get moved from the washer to the dryer—2 seconds, 5 ft.

| 20 | Pick us up | NV | 1 | 0 | 436,151 | 154 |
| 21 | Move us to the dryer with a bunch of other shirts | T | 2 | 2 | 436,153 | 156 |

Then we wait for our buddies to get moved, which is a lot delay—10 seconds.

| 22 | Wait for our buddies to be moved | L | 10 | 0 | 436,163 | 156 |

Then we wait in the dryer while the washer is loaded (between process—3 minutes).

| 23 | Wait in dryer while washer is loaded | B | 180 | 0 | 436,343 | 156 |

Note: For those of you who are more advanced, we are in a changeover at this point as loading and unloading are changeovers and we are on internal time. We really should have started the dryer first and then loaded the washer since the dryer has a longer cycle time than the washer.

The next step is to turn the knob on the dryer to the desired cycle. What step is this? If you said VA or non-VA, you are wrong! Remember that we don't care what the operator or person is doing; we are still sitting in the dryer while waiting—10 seconds.

| 24 | Wait while dryer is setup for the cycle | B | 10 | 0 | 436,353 | 156 |

Then we go through the drying cycle—40 minutes.

| 25 | Go through dry cycle | NV | 2,400 | 0 | 438,753 | 156 |

Note: Technically the drying is non-VA because it has nothing to do with cleaning the shirt. We are still dealing with the water needed to activate the soap. What if we could clean it without water? Assuming we consider dry as VA, at what point do we become *dry*? Until that point, we could call it a VA process, but after that we are not really being dried anymore. At the exact point where we become *dry*, we turn into either between-process storage assuming the entire load is dry or a lot delay until all our *buddies* are dry. In either way, we are technically being overprocessed if we are in the dryer longer than it takes to dry just us (the shirt).

At this point the dryer is done. But do we get unloaded right away? No! The operator is busy watching TV. So, we wait for 10 minutes. We are normally unloaded before the washer so there is room to move the washed clothes over directly into the dryer. Unload is transport—2 seconds, 5 ft.

26	Wait to be unloaded	B	600	0	439,353	156
27	Pick us up	NV	1	0	439,354	156
28	Unload—move to basket	T	2	2	439,356	158

Then we are in a lot delay, while the rest are unloaded—20 seconds.

29	Wait for rest of buddies	L	20	0	439,376	158

The next step is that the operator cleans out the lint trap. What step is this? You should have said between-processes storage—1 minute.

30	Wait in basket while lint trap cleaned	B	60	0	439,436	158

Then we wait in the basket while the dryer is loaded, the washer is loaded, and both machines are started—5 minutes.

31	Wait—washer and dryer are loaded	B	300	0	439,766	158

The next step is to move us back to the second floor and lay us on the bed—30 seconds, 150 ft.

32	Move us back to 2nd floor	T	30	150	439,766	308

Go get the hangers—60 seconds.

33	Wait while hangers are retrieved	B	60	0	439,826	308

Put us on a hanger—5 seconds.

34	Pick us up	NV	1	0	439,827	308
35	Put us on a hanger	NV	5	0	439,832	308

Move us to the closet—10 seconds.

| 36 | Hang us up in the closet | T | 10 | 10 | 439,842 | 318 |

At this point, we have a choice. Technically we could take us out of the closet to wear us, so one could argue that the next step is between-processes storage. However, normally in manufacturing or administrative processes, we must wait for the batch to be completed. So, the next step would be a lot delay, while the rest of the shirts are hung up and put in the closet—10 minutes.

| 37 | Wait for rest of buddies to be hung | L | 600 | 0 | 440,442 | 318 |

The last step is waiting to be pulled from the closet to be worn.

| 38 | Wait to be worn | B or FG | 600 | 0 | 441,042 | 318 |

We will assign our output boundary here; but it is easy to see how we could have followed the shirt all the way back to the laundry pile waiting again to be washed. Notice our time of 441,042 seconds is our throughput time, which is equal to 5.1 days. If we remove the RM storage and just look at the laundry cycle, it would be equal to 150.7 minutes from start to finish. We capture things when we follow the product that we will never see following the operator. For instance, while the machines are washing or drying, the operator is gone. So, if you were just following the operator, you would miss these times in the analysis. That is why we must look at both the product and the operator separately.

Omits Process and Improvement Questions ERSC[19]

Think about how this process could be improved. What ideas do you have? We always walk our team through four questions that we call the OMITS process. Look at and question each step and ask if it can be somehow:

1. Eliminated
2. Rearranged
3. Simplified
4. Combined

Eliminate the Step

If we can eliminate the step, we do not have to do an operator analysis on that step, and we immediately speed up the process without adding any additional work. This is what we were referring to earlier in this chapter when we said we could improve productivity without even looking at the operator! Eliminating a step does not mean moving the step to another department; although if this happens, we haven't really eliminated the step but shifted it to another area. Eliminating it means the need for the step no longer exists. When we are conducting the PFA, we keep track of two sets of times. These are *as-is* or current state times for each step and future state or *to-be* times for each step. Sometimes we may have to estimate how long the step will take in the new Lean environment, but if we can eliminate it, the *to-be* time goes to zero! It is important to make sure that all stakeholders, who may be affected by the step, agree that it can be eliminated. This ties in with the systems thinking discussion earlier in the book.

What steps could we possibly eliminate in the following? If we can eliminate it, we call this omitting the step and we mark an X on the step or cross it out (see Figure 2.12) if we are doing it by hand. For instance, we could eliminate grabbing the detergent if we have it set up to dump into the washer (we did this at home).

Lesson Learned: It seems like almost every team falls into the trap of getting excited about making an improvement and they make the change thinking (or in some cases not thinking) no one else could possibly object. Yet, the mere fact of not communicating the change, even if everyone agrees with it, will upset people. It is important to remember that change tends to create unintended consequences. Communication to all stakeholders affected by the change must be part of every Lean activity.

Rearrange

If we can't eliminate it, we look to see if the step is in the proper order, makes sense, and allows the product to flow smoothly. Many times, the engineers that create the router or process have no idea what happens on the floor. Sometimes we find parts, within the same product line or family, with totally different manufacturing paths or routers. This is normally because different engineers designed the parts or routings for the parts. Instead of starting from the existing part drawings, the engineer started the process completely over from scratch. This is not Lean! Sometimes reordering the steps can allow us to accomplish the steps quicker, with the same product flow for the entire product family, which then lends itself to setting up Lean workflow cells.

Example: The Morgan Motor Company, famous for their *hand-built* cars, used to put their engines in their cars at the beginning of the process. In their old batched-up processes, the cars used to spend 3 months in the production process. This meant that in addition to creating difficulties moving the car from building to building, the cost of the engine was absorbed for over 3 months. Their engineer Morris Owen suggested building the car differently. He said, "…they should build the car in different units, build the bodies separately, build the chassis separately and put the engines in at the end… because there are (British) pounds laying all around the factory in cars there for 12 or 14 weeks."[20]

Lesson Learned: By looking at the product separately from the operator, it exposes this waste of inventory that lays around our factories for weeks, months, or even years at a time. We have seen parts in factories that have been physically inventoried for years. They should have birthday celebrations for them each year! These are all costs that negatively impact your bottom line; but you don't see them if you just look at what the operators are doing. As Sir John Harvey Jones said, "A company that is not progressing is regressing."[21]

Simplify

If we can't eliminate it, or rearrange it, our next option is to try to simplify the step or reduce part of a step-in order to reduce the time. By removing the complexity in the operation, we expose the waste and simplify the process. We may be able to simplify setting the washer cycle by eliminating some of the options or by using a pre-measured detergent cup.

Step	Description	Type	Time	Distance	Total Time	Cumulative Distance
1	Waiting in pile for the washing machine	RM	432,000	0	432,000	0
2	Picking us up	NV	1	0	432,001	0
3	Moving to the laundry basket	T	2	2	432,003	2
4	Waiting for the rest of the laundry to be loaded	L	10	0	432,013	2
5	~~Waiting while the next load is prepped~~	~~B~~	~~60~~	~~0~~	~~432,073~~	~~2~~
6	Picking up basket	NV	1	0	432,074	2
7	Moving the basket to the laundry machine	T	30	150	432,104	152
8	Waiting for the machine to finish	B	1,200	0	433,304	152
9	Waiting while the washer is unloaded	B	120	0	433,424	152
10	Waiting while the first shirts are loaded	L	5	0	433,429	152
11	Picking us up	NV	1	0	433,430	152
12	Moving to the washer	T	1	2	433,431	154
13	Waiting for the rest of the shirts to be loaded	L	10	0	433,441	154
14	~~Waiting while the detergent is grabbed~~	~~T~~	~~2~~	~~0~~	~~433,443~~	~~154~~
15	Detergent added to the machine	NV	2	0	433,445	154
16	Waiting while the door is closed and the machine cycle is set up and started	B	5	0	433,450	154
17	Machine is washing	VA	1,800	0	435,250	154
18	Waiting to be unloaded	B	600	0	435,850	154
19	Waiting while we unload the dryer	B	300	0	436,150	154
20	Picking us up	NV	1	0	436,151	154
21	Moving us to the dryer with a bunch of other shirts	T		0	436,153	154
22	Waiting for our buddies to be moved	L	10	0	436,163	154
23	Waiting in the dryer while the washer is loaded	B	180	0	436,343	154
24	Waiting while the dryer is set up for the cycle	B	10	0	436,353	154
25	Going through dry cycle	VA	1,200	0	437,553	154
26	Waiting to be unloaded	B	600	0	438,153	154
27	Picking us up	NV	1	0	438,153	154
28	Unloading—moving to the basket	T	2	2	438,155	156
29	Waiting for the rest of the buddies	L	20	0	438,175	156
30	Waiting in the basket while the lint trap is cleaned	B	60	0	438,235	156
31	Waiting—the washer and the dryer are loaded	B	300	0	438,535	156
32	Moving us back to the second floor	T	30	0	438,565	156
33	Waiting while the hangers are retrieved	B	60	60	438,625	216
34	Picking us up	NV	1	0	438,625	216
35	Putting us on a hanger	NV	5	0	438,630	216
36	Hanging us up in the closet	T	10	10	438,640	226
37	Waiting for the rest of the buddies to be hung	L	600	0	439,240	226
38	Waiting to be worn	B	600	0	439,840	226

Figure 2.12   Process flow steps eliminated.

Combine

The next option is to combine it with another step assuming we can reduce the time or improve the flow by finding a better method. For instance, if we could stagger the times on the washer and the dryer, we could probably unload the dryer while the washer is still running; the goal here is to try to combine steps to create as simple a method as possible. At this stage, the subprocess operators now feel quality is the responsibility of the person doing the final inspection versus themselves. To this end, try to separate the work and then combine it. An example of separation would be like the following: assume a visual inspection is conducted at the final assembly stage in the line. It takes about 60 seconds. This inspection process could be broken down and distributed among each of the four prior subprocesses on the line by the person doing the work or prior to starting the operation by the next person in the line. Let's say it takes 5 seconds for the subassembly operator to inspect their work and another 5 seconds for the next operator to check the assembly prior to starting. Overall, we reduce the time to 40 seconds but even better we catch the mistake sooner versus at the end. Also, the chances of catching a problem while looking at the end of each subprocess where there are fewer things to check are better than trying to inspect the whole assembly at the end. Doing the centralized inspection at the end can now be eliminated, save time, and possibly improve quality. It also puts the responsibility for quality back on each operator.

When ERSC May Not Even Be Enough

The last resort, but sometimes necessary, is to take no action at all. It may be that the step just must be there. In this case, we need to determine where we have reached entitlement (entitlement is the best you can get with the current process) for the process, in which case we may need to brainstorm a completely new way to perform the work (we call this benchmark developing a new process), that is, progressing from a vinyl, record player to CD player to IPHONE® or wood glue to hot-melt glue to UV cure.

The other objective of the OMITS process is to really question why we do each step and understand the true need as to why it exists. It could be that we have always done it that way or at one time we had a failure, and a root cause corrective action (RCCA) process was put in place, but the corrective action step implemented previously is no longer required. Technology may have changed, or we may have created a new more process-capable production approach. There could have been a step required due to an old supplier's process, but the new supplier has included the step in their process. The list goes on and on. The important thing is to question every step in the process.

Homework: Go back through each step of the laundry process above and jot down some ideas on how we might improve. For example, could we move the washing machine to the second floor? Or install a laundry chute to the washer? But keep in mind that we would still have to get the clothes back upstairs. Could the washing machine itself be improved? Could it be one-piece flow? Would it be faster if it was manual? Think about it for our shirt. We wait to be washed, and then we are transported to the sink, washed by hand in the sink, and wrung out and hung on a clothesline. The whole process would probably take less than 30–60 seconds to get to the clothesline. What if we could design a machine that worked like this and did one at a time? If we introduced a dryer, we would go back to batching because we wouldn't want to run the dryer for just one shirt. So again, we would have to design a one-piece flow dryer. Could we have saved time by getting things ready while the machines were running? We will discuss this concept later in the setup section.

Conducting a PFA

There are at least three different ways to map products:

1. Manually record the process by walking it through.
2. Record the process by video.
3. Create a process wall map.

Walking the Process

To walk the process, you first need to involve the operations director of manufacturing and department managers to let them know you are going to be in the area, and you will be interrupting their operators. (You can never communicate enough!) We then need to decide what part of the product we are going to become (Figure 2.13). We generally try to find a component part that must travel through the entire process starting with unloading from the truck in receiving. If you choose to start somewhere else in the process, we must scope the flow from start (input boundary) to finish (output boundary). For the first one you conduct, we suggest starting at the receiving dock.

PFA Worksheet

We use a worksheet to capture the PFA steps (Figure 2.14 and Table 2.1). We capture each step and note where it fits into our TIPS definition. We break down each process step as to whether it is VA, non-VA, and if it is a storage step, we identify which type of storage the step fits. We accumulate

Figure 2.13   Walking the product process flow.

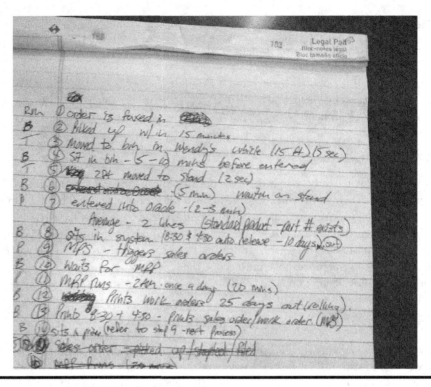

Figure 2.14   Example of PFA on notebook paper.

Table 2.1   PFA Excel Spreadsheet Version

No. of Steps	OMIT	Flow Code	Description	Baseline Time (Second)	Baseline Time (Minute)	Post Lean Estimate Time	Distance (in ft)
1		rm	Order is faxed in and waiting on machine	900	15	3,600	
2		t	Moved to bin into CSR cubicle	5	0	5	15
3		b	Sit in CSR bin	450	8	450	
4		t	Moved to CSR stand	2	0	2	2
5		b	Wait on CSR stand	300	5	300	
6		nv	Entered into Oracle	150	3	150	
7	x	b	Sits in system until 4:30	25,200	420	0	

Source: BIG Archives.

the times the product spends in each step and the distance traveled. Every step is questioned as we capture it as to why we do what we do and if we need to do it. We then look for opportunities to eliminate (omit), rearrange, simplify, or combine each step. We are left with a before and after analysis that gives us an *as-is* versus a *to-be* number of process steps and times within each part of TIPS. The process analysis should yield a 20%–40% productivity improvement to the overall process versus a batch environment.

The other choice is to start with the component part that you are following sitting on the shelf. Wherever you start, we normally consider the first step as RM. If you are starting on the WIP shelf, you could also consider it to be between-process storage. We then follow the part through the process capturing each step as we go.

Assign Jobs to Each Person

When we walk the process, we assign jobs to each person: first, we assign a team leader, who communicates with management, safety, provides proper PPE for the team, etc., and leads the team through the process and is responsible for the outcome of the PFA tool. The team leader then assigns the following:

- The first person keeps track of each step on a pad of paper.
- The second person makes a point-to-point diagram of how the product flows through the shop with pencil and paper.
- The third person counts off the steps or feet/meters between each step (sometimes a surveyor's wheel is helpful for this).
- The fourth person keeps track of the machines utilized.
- The fifth person keeps track of any ideas people come up with during the walk through.
- The sixth person keeps track of how long it takes to walk between steps and can time processes where necessary.
- The seventh person keeps track of WIP inventory located throughout the process and checks dates to determine the oldest stock.
- Anyone else on the team can write down observations, ask operators for ideas, determine operator morale, etc.

These jobs can be rotated and/or combined.

Video The Process Flow

Videoing versus Walking the Process

If a picture is worth a thousand words, what is a video worth?[22]

—Sam Mitchell

We have found over and over that wherever one can video the process (obviously we would not video long periods of storage), we find steps we don't find when we walk through a process with a supervisor or even the employees that do it every day. They simply forget the steps they do. When we video and review it with the operators and compare it to what they told us, they are surprised that they left the step out. Sometimes you will hear "that doesn't normally happen." But our experience shows that if you capture it on video, it probably happens much more than anyone thinks or cares to believe.

Lesson Learned: Using Lean tools enables you to understand and optimize what happens to the product as it moves through the process. Just analyzing and fixing the product axis piece of the network can yield as much as a 20%–40% productivity improvement.

Exercise: Pick a product and do a point-to-point diagram.

Did you remember to do the following?

- Physically walk every step of the process. You fail if you try to just do it on a whiteboard.
- Select the *thing* you are going to follow. Do *not* follow the operator!
- Number each step.
- Calculate the travel distance.
- Count the WIP at each station.
- Identify all the machines correctly.
- Get cycle times for each machine.

The Importance of Video

For any of you that have played or know anything about football, you know the importance of watching tape! The pros use it to better understand their opponents and to improve their game from both a team perspective and an individual perspective. The same should go for manufacturing and office processes. The video camera, which was invented by William Lincoln in 1867 followed by the Lumiere brothers and Edison, was used by Gilbreth back in the early 1900s. In our opinion, it was the greatest industrial engineering tool ever invented. There is no way one can observe everything that goes on in a football play (see Figure 2.15) from the football sidelines or from the stands. If so, we wouldn't need *instant replay*. How many times do we all see and observe

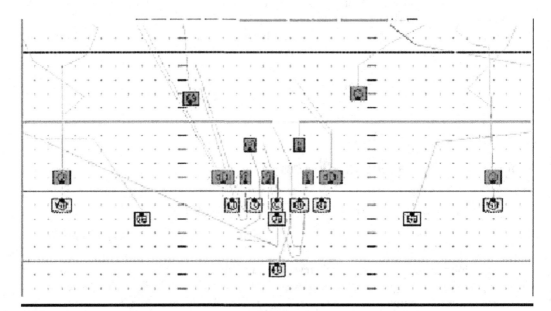

Figure 2.15 Football play example.

the same play only to find out that during the instant replay, we were indeed so wrong! Of course, admitting to it is another story. The same is true for manufacturing. If you are filling in a typical point kaizen key observation sheet, you cannot possibly capture everything the operator does down to a second or in some cases fraction of a second.

There is no substitute for video. Despite objections, you may hear from some consultants that you just need to go observe and then do, that is, make rapid *fire, aim, ready* (vs. ready, aim, fire) changes. One cannot possibly see all the waste in the process by just observing or truly understanding the process without videoing and reviewing it with the operators you filmed. Videoing is a great way to get the operators and supervisor involved. When you just observe, the operator can say, "I didn't do that" but they can't argue with the video. We utilize video for both office and shop floor processes. In union facilities, it pays to let the union know ahead of time and get someone from their leadership on the team with you. We have never had a problem implementing in union or nonunion facilities. It is best to put a communication plan together and get HR and the union involved from the start. Again, get all the stakeholders involved before starting any initiative (in this case videoing).

Seeing the Light

At one union plant in upstate New York, the local union president told me he enjoyed working with us during a system Lean implementation, but he was very frustrated with the management. I asked him why? He said he was working very closely with the plant manager to grow the business, so they could not only protect their jobs but add jobs. Twelve months prior, the parent company had threatened to close them down because they were doing so poorly. They had come a long way in improving their plant, but the president told me he was frustrated because he had identified two or three employees that in his opinion were deadwood and not pulling their weight. They were also dragging down the people they were working with. He was upset because the management would not deal with the individuals when he had indicated he would go through the motions but not block their exit. I had never heard of anything like this before. He told me if I told anyone, of course he would deny it. I asked why he was helping the management. He said simply because he wanted a place he could retire from. He said they had not laid anyone off since they started Lean (it was all handled through attrition). Management never lied to the employees, and they were successful in turning the plant around. He said people now took pride in their jobs and the workplace and management listened to them and respected them.

Lesson Learned: Sometimes when you get rid of the deadwood, you become much more productive, and people see you as serious about waste and efficiency. Trust me, there are great workers on your plant floors that don't want to participate in soldiering and are just waiting for you to deal with those that don't want to work.

Product and Operator Video Guidelines

1. Communicate to everyone about the videoing ahead of time (see Figure 2.16). Let them know they will be invited back to review the videos and that it is not about the person but the process. If possible, do not make the filming voluntary. Add a clause into your HR forms that people are accepting videoing as one of the expectations and conditions for hiring.
2. Remember to make clear what you are following with the video, i.e., product or operator. Many times, people forget or get confused and stay filming the machine instead of following the operator wherever they go. Never stop the camera. Operators will make a mistake and tell

January 11, 2012

To: All employees
From: HR person
Re: Video taping for lean

Videotaping is essential for us to continue our lean business system efforts. This videotaping will be taking place plantwide. We are videotaping in order to make improvements to our processes, look for ways to make your jobs easier, and to be more competitive in the market place. The core team will initially be doing this filming but in the future anyone may be called upon to help videotape. Many of you will be invited to review the videotapes with the core team. Videotaping used for our lean improvement efforts will not and is not to be used for disciplinary purposes. Any questions regarding this policy should be directed to my attention.

Figure 2.16 Video letter sample.

you to turn off the camera because they must go get something. Don't do it. The only time we stop the camera is when they are headed to the restroom. We need to explain to the operator ahead of time that if we need to take a step out, we can do it when we review the tape, and if they must get something not at their station, it is exactly the point of the video. We need to see the stupid things on the video that we (management) make them do every day.

Unexpected Reaction

At Company X, we videoed a line and called in the operator to review the tape with us. She was literally so thankful that we were finally paying attention to what they were doing. She said in the past that management had improved other lines, but their line was never important enough to try to improve, and they were told they should just keep making parts!

Lesson Learned: It pays to call the supervisor and everyone in the area for a brief meeting prior to filming and let them know ahead of time what to expect. Some key points are that the video will never be used against them or for disciplinary purposes. It is not about them; it is about the process (this is key for all to understand) and finding ways to make their job easier. Let them know we need them to help us with ideas on how we can do things better even if they have suggested them before and no one ever listened.

1. Film as far away as possible but close enough to be able to see exactly what the operator is doing. This is a big advantage of videoing over traditional time study. Instead of standing over top of someone with a stopwatch, you can normally be a good distance away and still see everything the operator's hands are doing. Sometimes they even forget you are there.
2. Have fun but not too much fun. When you video, there are those who love to be filmed and others truly hate it. Be aware of this fact and compassionate to those who don't like to be filmed. Empathize with them but still insist on filming them. Some operators will try to lose you as they travel through the plant trying to find what they need. Others will joke around and tease the operators as being film stars, wanting rights and royalties to the video, etc. Some of this can't be prevented but too much joking around will result eventually in someone getting upset or their feelings hurt.

3. Let people know eventually everyone will be filmed. The first time filmed is the hardest. Once people see everyone getting filmed, it will eventually become second nature and people won't even think about it. In some cases, they come to us now and even request to be filmed to rebalance the line (if it was station balanced) or show a problem in the process or to highlight someone who is not working.

4. Resist the temptation to zoom in and out constantly, and if doing so, do it slowly. There is nothing worse than reviewing someone's first video. Many times, you feel like you are on a boat and feel seasick. Sometimes they forget to follow the operator's hands and you find yourself moving your head trying to see what the operator's hands (which are just out of view) are doing. When you ask the operator what they did most times, they don't remember.

5. Try not to have the operators talk to you while you are filming. This slows the operator down and sometimes they forget the steps because they are talking. It can remove the normalcy from the video and not show what truly happens each day.

6. Don't give operators advance warning. This normally results in them getting ready to be filmed and they go and retrieve all their parts, etc., which defeats the whole purpose of filming. This is especially true in setups.

7. When panning an area, do it very, very slowly like walking down the aisle at a wedding. When we initially start the Lean process on a cell, the first thing we do is document the area with digital photos and video pans of the area. This is so we have a *before* video and pictures to compare once the area has been improved. People tend to forget very quickly what the area used to look like.

8. Always involve the operators from the beginning when viewing the video. Don't analyze the video and then bring them in. This is a trap everyone falls into. Two things lead to this trap. The first is the thought process that the engineers are too busy to be bothered with watching the videos and we should find the problems and then hand them over to them. This almost never works. If you don't involve the engineers during the process, they can't possibly hear directly from the operators or feel their pain. Many times, I will make the engineers go build what they have designed. The operators love this!

The other pitfall is when we are told that we can't afford to free up the operators to review the videos. There is too much pressure on production! My response is, "What do you do when they call in sick?" If you don't take the time to fix the process, you will never get out of the firefight. Whenever I have given in to this argument, it inevitably impacts the overall quality and outcome of the project during and after, and it becomes much more difficult to sustain because the operators weren't involved. If you don't have the operator there, you can't possibly understand what they are doing. You miss steps, tribal knowledge, learning about the tools they developed, and all the other problems in the process like the interruptions from quality or planning or engineering. You don't learn why they do what they do or the way they do it. The output lost by having the operators involved is always quickly made up and then some when the process is Leaned out.

Lesson Learned: The overall discovery process that occurs during video review is too important to miss, and by not getting the operator's involvement, they will fight the solution even if they like it better. Always set up or frame the video analysis session by telling the operators that watching the videos is for continuous improvement purposes only. No one is ever written up for anything witnessed on the video. Remember that it is not about them; it is about the process!

Converting a Skeptic to a Believer

At Company X, an employee was overheard saying Lean wasn't working very well and not much progress had been made. We called the employee in and asked him to sit down and review the before videos of his process. After reviewing, we asked the employee if he would like us to put everything back the way it was before. He apologized for his remark and said he truly forgot how it was before and admitted a lot of improvements had been made. We then encouraged that if he was going to complain about how things are today, that is fine but give us a recommendation to go with the complaint or take a leadership role in making the improvements with his supervisor's support. He eventually became one of our biggest advocates. The advantage to this approach is that through the request for a recommendation it continues to demonstrate to the employee that they provide value to the customer as well as value to the organization.

Lesson Learned: If you can take a skeptic and convert them, they generally will become zealots.

Point-to-Point Diagram

Point-to-point diagrams (see Figure 2.17) are utilized to show the path of the product through the layout of the area. This differs from the spaghetti diagram we use for operators. It is utilized to identify only product flow patterns. Because our layout will come from the PFA, this diagram is used to guarantee the product always moves forward in a point-to-point fashion. If any stations are out of order, they will immediately show up as you draw the point-to-point flow of the product. Stations out of order will force the product to move backward and must be corrected in future revisions to your layout.

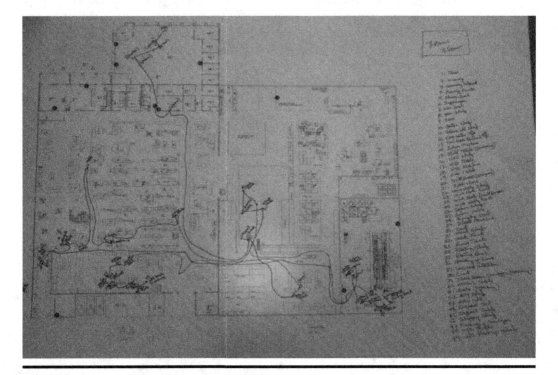

Figure 2.17   Point-to-point diagram example.

Lesson Learned: The product should never move backward. It is OK for the person to move backward but never the product.

From the product's perspective, the point-to-point diagram assists in creating a logical grouping of operations or machines based on the flow of the product. Any time a renovation or new construction is being considered, the layout should be tested utilizing point-to-point diagramming for all products flowing through the process to ensure that whatever is being conceptualized will result in a good flow through the area from the product and operator's perspective. Layouts are one of our biggest drivers of waste.

How to Do a Point-to-Point Diagram

The same teams who have participated in the PFA analysis should be involved in the point-to-point diagramming activity. The product point-to-point diagram is performed independently. A team member is provided with a CAD drawing of the layout or sketches the layout on paper. As the product flows through the area, each movement is noted on the layout. Point-to-point diagrams should be created for both the baseline and revised *to-be* layouts. We have also found that if the sequence is numbered in the point-to-point diagram, it helps in reviewing and utilizing the data to assist in sequencing equipment and supplies within a layout. We also recommend the diagram is time- and date-stamped, as you may find varying product flows at different times, that is, days versus nights and weekdays versus weekends.

After Completing the Point to Point ask the following questions:

1. Is it one smooth continuous flow?
2. Is the product flowing one piece at a time?
3. Does the product go backward at any time?
4. Are there areas where the product crisscrosses as it travels through the layout?
5. Is there excess inventory or idle time on the line?

The answer to the first two questions should be yes and the other no. We will come back and revisit the PFA later once we have completed the operator analysis and have a better idea of the flow.

Total Throughput Time

This is your material flow or velocity by which you can get a product through your system. It can be an enabling constraint if we can continually reduce the time. A primary goal of the PFA (see Figure 2.18) is to determine the total throughput time of the process. The total throughput time is the sum of all the time the product, patient, or information spent in the process. If you divide the total throughput time by the takt time (TT) or factory cycle time, it will tell you how much inventory should be in the system.[23]

Even though we are not looking at operators at this point, throughput time impacts the number of staff or labor required to run the organization. The longer a product stays within a system, the more staff are generally required to manage it. In a Lean initiative, capturing this data should be done at the beginning of the project. Throughput time has a big impact on the inventory in the system and many times the labor required for moving it, storing it, and counting it. Most companies do not have throughput time built into their objectives.

No. of Steps	OMIT	Flow Code	Flow Symbol	Description	Alt. Start Time (sec) (optional)	Cumulative Time (sec)	Baseline Time (sec)	Baseline Time (min)	Post Lean Estimate Time	Distance (in feet)	Distance Post (with omits)	Machine	Department
							This totals of these columns become our baseline and post Lean throughput time						
1		rm	□	Received as an e-mail				0	0		0		Customer service
2		b	□	Waiting to be opened			21600	360	21600		0		
3		b	□	Open e-mail			1	0	1		0		
4		nv	○	I am opened as an attachment			2	0.0	2		0		
5		nv	○	I am printed on the printer			10	0.2	10		0		
6		l	■	Waiting on the printer while other POs are printed			270	5	270		0		
7		b	□	Waiting while Kathy walks to the printer			10	0	10		0		
8		t	◉	I am picked up			1	0.0	1	2	2		
9		nv	○	Sort through the papers to make sure others are not with us			3	0.1	3		0		
10		t	◉	We are walked back to the desk			10	0.2	10	30	30		
11		nv	○	I am stapled			2	0.0	2		0		
12		l	■	Wait while others are stapled			13	0	13		0		
13		b	□	Wait while oracle opens			5	0	5		0		
14		b	□	Checking if i am available in inventory and status checked			120	2	120		0		
15		b	□	Waiting while looking up the "opportunity #" is looked up and files saved to the smart team file			1800	30	1800		0		
16		b	□	Waiting while an EAR is created and attachments downloaded onto EAR			2100	35	2100		0		
17		b	□	Waiting while EAR is e-mailed to engineering			30	1	30		0		Engineering
18		b	□	Waiting while EAR sits in engineering e-mail box			28800	480	28800		0		
19		b	□	Waiting while EAR's application data is reviewed			300	5	300		0		
20		b	□	Waiting while application sizing program is being performed			600	10	600		0		
21		b	□	Waiting while p/n is being assigned from book			300	5	300		0		
22		b	□	Waiting for the simulation program to be performed and orifice designed			900	15	900		0		
23		b	□	Waiting for counter-drill calculations			300	5	300		0		
24		b	□	Waiting for drawings and solid works models to be created			900	15	900		0		
25		b	□	Waiting for design folder to be created in smart team			300	5	300		0		
26		b	□	Waiting while drawing folder is linked to the EAR			600	10	600		0		
27		b	□	Waiting while the drawing folder is linked to the EAR			480	8	480		0		
28		b	□	Waiting while the part number is added to the			180	3	180		0		
29		b	□	Waiting while the EAR is updated with "hours worked" and e-mail sent to Kathy with p/n			60	1	60		0		

Figure 2.18 PFA Example—Goal is to get total throughput time by adding up the times for all the steps.

Process Wall Map

To create a process wall map (see Figure 2.19), we first layout either flip chart paper or a roll of paper on the wall. We then decide what we are going to follow or become since we are now the product! We begin in a conference room with each of the participants that do the jobs on the team and ask them to write down on yellow stickies step-by-step what they do in the process. The wall map:

- Shows what is happening to the product
- Shows all the details of every step the product goes through, including transport, storage, and inspection, no matter how small (TIPS)
- Shows the number of activities and the time required for each activity
- Shows who touches the product and does each step
- Shows overall length of the process (throughput time) by having each yellow sticky represent a standard amount of time

Have the team start by putting yellow stickies on the left-hand side with who or what position does the job. We then start by having each person write each individual step in the order that they perform on a different sticky with a magic marker. As soon as they write the first step, for example, *match up the paperwork*, we have them break the step down (a big bucket) into finer detail (granularity of big bucket) of what is really involved in the step. For instance, broken down "match up the paperwork" is:

1. Move the receiving and invoice folders to the desk (transport).
2. Get the incoming mail and move to the desk (transport).
3. Open all the mail (process—NVA).
4. Wait while the rest of the mail is opened (lot delay).
5. Sort out the invoices received by the vendor (process—NVA).
6. Wait while the rest of the mail is sorted (lot delay).
7. Search through the receiver folder until you find the receiver to match the invoice (process—NVA).
8. Staple the invoice and receiver together (process—NVA).
9. Wait while the rest of the invoices are matched (lot delay).
10. Wait while invoices that can't be matched are put back into the invoice folders (lot delay).

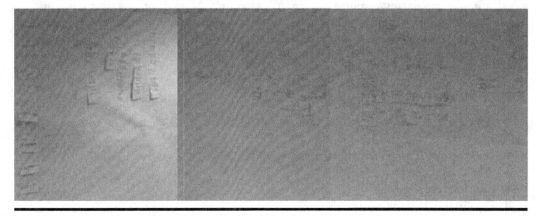

Figure 2.19 Process wall map.

Figure 2.20 Accounts payable example.

Note: It is important to follow up the PFA wall map exercise, if performed in a conference room with becoming the product and going to the floor or office to experience each step with operators participating (see Figure 2.20). No matter how good the person is at doing the job, there will be steps missed when just listing them out in a conference room. In addition, you will find things to improve by walking and videoing the process you can't possibly come up with in the conference room.

For example, one step might be retrieving the receiver from the printer. However, the printer was located over the operator's head so he or she couldn't even see if it was printed without reaching up to see if it was there. This requires constant inspection and rework steps to see if the paper is there and then reprinting it if it is not. The other thing we noticed was the response time of the computer, which we found out had to be rebooted several times a day.

Lesson Learned: You can see Lean tools work just as well for the office. People will do the best job they can with the tools and systems you provide them to do the job! Ensure they have the right tools at the right time to perform the required task.

PFA Process Wall Map versus Swim Lanes

These tools are similar in that they show the steps by function; however, the PFA process flow wall map is not a flowchart per se and is more detailed in that it shows the classification of person doing the job, that is, staff accountant, accounts payable (AP) supervisor, AP clerk, or controller versus just AP department. It also includes the type of step (i.e., TIPS), who does it, how far it travels, and the length of time that one does not normally find in a swim lane process flow (see Figure 2.21). The process wall map does show rework loops and all different paths an item can take as it morphs through the process.

Yellow Sticky Legend (See Figure 2.22)

Each of these steps is now recorded on a yellow sticky. We then label each sticky with:

- The type of TIPS step noted previously.
- Who does the step?
- How long the step takes (cycle time)
- The distance the product travels

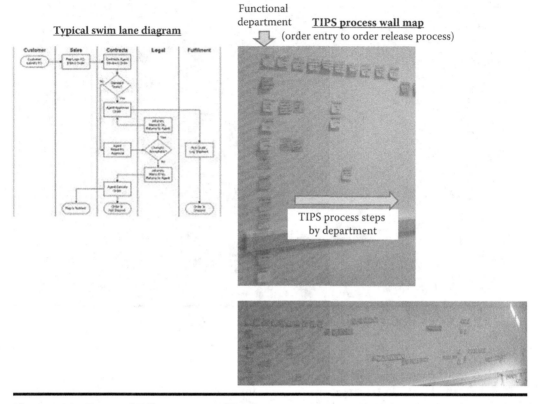

Figure 2.21 Process Wall map versus flowchart.

Analysis of a Wall Map: ERSC

So, when completed the team reviews (see Figure 2.23) the following:

- Which activities can be eliminated, rearranged, simplified, or combined (ERSC)?
- Which events can be done in parallel?
- What is the critical path?

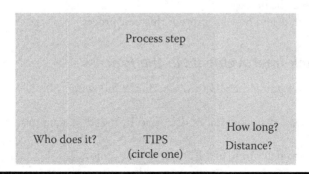

Figure 2.22 Example of process wall map sticky format.

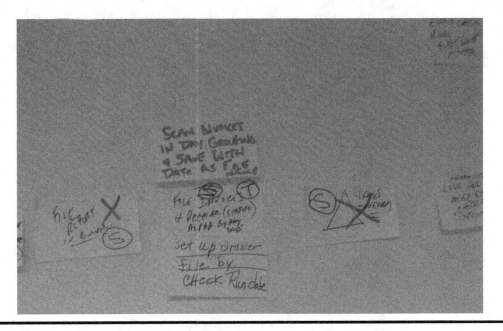

Figure 2.23 X's are steps eliminated in the process using ERSC.

- How many people touch it?
- Where are the handoffs between participants (mistakes, waits)?
- Where are the duplicated activities by the same or another person or department?

Map the Ideal Process

Next map the process with no barriers.

- What could it look like?
- How would you set this process up if it were your business or if you were a small business?
- What happens when you must get something through this process right away?
- List the major problems preventing you from realizing your ideal process.
- Identify the real purpose for the process you are improving.
- Do we even need the process?
- What would it take and how long to put this new process in place?

Identify and Rank Improvements to the Process

After reviewing and designing the *to-be* process, do the following:

1. List all the ideas and opportunities discussed in the ideal state to improve process speed/velocity.
2. Filter each idea to determine first if it is a task or project. If it is a task, it should be able to be assigned to one person with a due date. This ensures accountability and point of contact. Record these as action items from the project.

3. What will be left are the projects that generally require a cross-functional team to work on it.
   a. Next, consider the amount of resources available and the strategic planning goals, and identify each project with the time horizon. That is, can it be completed within a year? Is it 2–3 years out? Is it 5 years out?
4. Then list all the projects that can be completed in a year with the expected results and anticipated project cost.
5. Now categorize each of these projects using an impact/difficulty chart and prioritize them according to your strategic plan goals. Which one should we work on first? The answer is low cost, high benefit.
6. Make sure to consider the risk and impact to the other departments for each project.

Then create an implementation plan and action item list (see Table 2.2) for improvements and expected results phased in by month.

The Quality Paradox

Every step in the PFA we can remove or simplify eliminates the step and thus the opportunity for a defect to occur that can and almost always will improve quality. This enables the paradox often scoffed at which is why it is possible to do a job quicker and have better quality. We cannot express how important it is to separate the product flow from the operator when analyzing or assessing a process in any area. It is this principle that allows process improvement in any situation, and in any environment at home or at work.

While simple in understanding, Shingo's discovery is truly remarkable, and when we teach people this, they find it extremely difficult to conceive that it has such implications for improvement. We find that people also have much difficulty when first trying to apply the product tools since looking at the operator and applying the operator tools are so ingrained in all of us. In addition, while Dr. Shingo doesn't necessarily indicate this, there is a definite priority to implementing the tools inherent in this network of operations. The priority must start with looking at the product flow first; the operator(s) second, whether they are on the shop floor or in an executive office; and then applying the setup reduction tools third or in conjunction with the operator step if there is unloading and loading involved.

Off-Line Operations/Pre-Assembly

One common mistake people make in implementing Lean is that people want to keep certain operations off-line. We are not sure why this is, but it is commonplace and widespread. Generally, keeping off-line operations in a separate area results in much waste. For instance, one must figure out how to link the area up to the line that it is feeding. This means that there needs to be an inventory buffer between the lines or, if not, the final line cannot start until all the subassemblies are available. For some reason as human beings, we are literally compelled to want to keep subassemblies off-line as if this gives them some type of leg up on the process. However, they still require labor; the labor is sporadic and inefficient and normally ends up holding up the line. We constantly fight companies that think there is something to be gained by keeping subassemblies manufactured off-line. This also impacts the quality because if a mistake is made, we have lost the opportunity to find the root cause, and the entire batch of parts is now impacted which stops the final line.

Table 2.2 Action List Filtered for Task versus Project and Prioritized

Item	Product Cell / Team Leader / Action	Task or Project	Impact on Problem (A)	Mistake Proofing Potential (B)	Ease of Implementation (C)	Priority Number (A×B×C)	Resp.	Due	Status
			Impact from 1 to 10 (1, Low; 5, Medium; 10, High)						
1	Dedicate person to prestage setups	Task	10	10	10	1,000	Joe	8/15/2012	In process, person identified, TBA on 08/09
2	Develop format for Gauge list that will be used for each order. Add to or similar to tools sheets. This will be the *recipe* for the job	Task	10	10	1	100	Mike	8/30/2012	On schedule
3	Develop Kanban bins for all good candidates that run through the shop	Task	5	1	10	50	Jim	8/25/2012	On schedule
4	Determine inspection sampling plan to be used by shop. Decide whether last piece inspection is still needed and if so, can it be done after the machine is already running the next job to move it to external time	Project				0	Joe	Ongoing	First batch of parts handed to QC to develop IPs (on 08/03)

Source: BIG Archives.

In the material requirement planning (MRP) world, subassemblies are synonymous with a lower-level bill of material (BOM). Think of the waste this creates. A separate work order must be created, with a unique part number, ordered, released to the floor, produced, and then normally stocked only to be pulled again out of the stockroom for the final assembly or in many cases another subassembly. This creates all types of barriers with Lean as we run into resistance from engineering, not to flatten the BOM, but in the engineering man-hours required to change all the bills and routings. The other waste this creates is overproduction (i.e., making parts before we need them) and then the storage space for those parts. How often are the parts then redesigned and become obsolete or stored in the wrong location and must be made again because we can't find them?

So, make sure you capture all the subassemblies in your analysis with a goal to put all the sub-assemblies in line to the extent it makes sense, that is, we have enough equipment to dedicate to the line. If you can't get them in line right away, then keep it as a goal for the future.

Lesson Learned: Doing operations off-line results in waste. This waste is manifested in BOM levels, additional part numbers and drawings that must be created and maintained, fractional labor necessary to produce the parts, somewhere to store the parts, transactions in and out of the stockroom, specialization of the operator doing the job, inventory buffers, schedule inefficiencies, and space. *We should never release work orders for Lean lines until we have all the parts.*

Why Look at the Product First?

Let's back up to the VSM before we answer this question. We were careful to include the VSM as more of a baselining tool for a process, and it is a great way to track your progress on improvements. While it could be considered an analysis tool, we feel it is better utilized to look at the big picture and force one to view the entire system. If one can eliminate a step at the VSM level, one does not have to conduct a PFA or WFA as the step is removed (see Figure 2.24). This was a big issue with total quality management (TQM) and point kaizen events where we would launch team after team to improve steps in the process only to discover later, they could be eliminated by looking at the overall system. While the VSM tool is based on following the product, it mixes up the product and operator steps in the process boxes. It also ignores the impact of transportation and inspection.

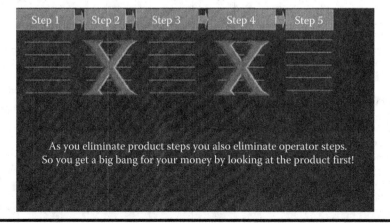

Figure 2.24   Steps removed at PFA level don't need FWA or setup analysis. There is a hierarchy to using the BASICS tools.

Value Engineering and Manufacturing Methods

Dr. Shingo then breaks process improvement into two pieces[24]:

1. Value engineering
2. Manufacturing methods

Today value engineering is known as design for assembly (DFA) or design for manufacturing and assembly (DFMA)[25] and Toyota's 3P (process, product, preparation) process.[26] Manufacturing methods question how a product can be improved by looking at the basic manufacturing processes including speeds and feeds, tool selection, curing or melting temperatures, high-speed plating, and instantaneous drying.

Levels of PFA Analysis

Where the current state process is strictly at the batching level, then we find there is so much waste in the process analysis that we generally do the PFA at a higher level. For instance, we may call a step clamping a unit together with three clamps and assign it 76 seconds and call it a NVA process.

Step	Description	Type	Time	Distance	Total Time	Cumulative Distance
	Start time		76		76	0
1	Wait—while the clamp is picked up	B	5		81	0
2	The 1st clamp is attached	NV	2		83	0
3	Wait—while the screwdriver is picked up	B	3		86	0
4	*Wait while the operator looks for the right screwdriver*	W	25		111	0
4	The 1st clamp is tightened	NV	5		116	0
5	Wait while the screwdriver is put down	B	2		118	0
5	Wait while the second clamp is picked up	B	5		123	0
6	The second clamp is attached to me	NV	2		125	0
7	Wait while the screwdriver is picked up	B	3		128	0
8	The second clamp is tightened	NV	5		133	0

(Continued)

Step	Description	Type	Time	Distance	Total Time	Cumulative Distance
9	Wait while the screwdriver is put down	B	2		135	0
10	The 3rd clamp is picked up	B	5		140	0
11	The 3rd clamp is attached to me	NV	2		142	0
12	Wait while the screwdriver is picked up	B	3		145	0
13	The 3rd clamp is tightened	NV	5		150	0
14	Wait while the screwdriver is put down	B	2		152	0

There are many more steps (see the previous text). Had we not done the detail, we would have missed the in-process delay where the wrong screwdriver was at the station. This created a within-process delay while he had to search and find the correct screwdriver. Someone had taken the correct screwdriver and not returned it with the clamps. In the batch environment, there is so much waste we may not care at that point about the within-process delay. But as you continue to refine and improve the process, these delays become more important. That delay was over 33% of the total process time.

You Decide?

What else could be improved? Why do we have to pick up and put down the screwdriver each time? Could it be hanging over the workstation on a tool balancer? Is there a better clamping system we could utilize? Could the product be redesigned to fit together without clamping it all?

Learning to See

Recently at Company X looking at work content and tools in a cell, we discovered that one tool was being shared by four operators and it was also the wrong tool. The correct tool went missing and one of the operators in their haste grabbed a tool that accomplished the task but took 20% longer. The more granularity you have, the easier it is to identify non-VA, as well as things delaying the work and output.[27]

Coding PFA Steps

Sometimes it is not always clear how to code a particular step. Take the example in the following:

Some time ago I was stuck in an elevator between floors. What step would you call it? Technically I was stuck within the process of being transported. So would it be transport 2 seconds, within-process delay 10 minutes, transport 5 seconds, or would it be transport 10 minutes 7 seconds since technically NVA process was started. There are a lot of gray areas when coding steps. Just make sure whatever you code is consistent between the before and the after.

Flowcharts versus PFA

Flowcharting (see Figure 2.25) is not the same as PFA analysis. Flowcharting doesn't give you times, what type of step it is, what the VA content is in the process when you are done, or all the delays a product will encounter. Flowcharts simply don't capture all the steps and times within a process. They do give us a high-level view of the process and decision points but do not nearly get into enough detail to expose all the steps or waste in the process. For instance, the flowchart in Figure 2.25 shows at most 26 steps. The PFA we conducted for the same process within the same boundaries was 147 steps (see Figure 2.26). The flowchart has no data. So, as we discussed previously, it is more qualitative than quantitative. The PFA process produces both qualitative and quantitative views. From the PFA, we now know there are 147 steps with an opportunity to reduce it to 76 steps. The current VA percentage is only 0.2% with 99.8% of the time being storage and it travels 435 ft with 10 people touching it. Try getting that kind of data from a flowchart! The same

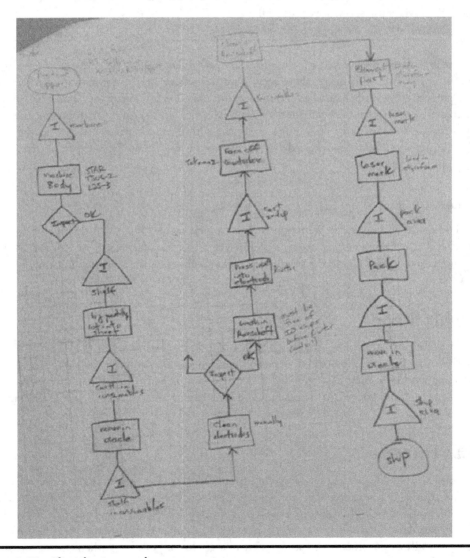

Figure 2.25 Flowchart example.

TAPE name	
Description	Electrodes
Input boundary	Receipt
Output boundary	Ship
Available time/day (hours)	8
Number of people touch it	10
Notes:	

Summary	Baseline	Post-Lean projected	Reduction	Reduction %
Total steps	147.0	76.0	71.00	48%
Orig sec:	996,644	901,502	95,142	10%
Min:	16,610.7	15,025.0	1,585.70	10%
Hours:	276.8	250.4	26.43	10%
Days	34.6	31.3	3.30	10%
Weeks	6.9	6.3	0.7	
Distance	424.9	265.8	159.10	37%
# of people	10.0	10.0	—	0%
Check:	996,644	901,502	95,142	10%
Va %	0.0226%	0.02%	0.00%	−11%
NVA %	0.11%	0.12%	−0.01%	−10%
Storage	99.80%	99.81%	0.00%	0%
Inspect	0.01%	0.01%	0.01%	45%
Transport	0.05%	0.04%	0.01%	19%

Enter PPF drawing here

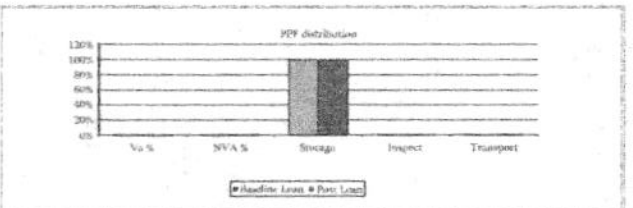

No. of steps	OMIT	Flow code	Flow symbol	Description	Alt. start time (Optional)	Cumulative time	Baseline time	Post-Lean estimate time	Distance (in feet)	Distance post	Machine	Person who touches it (job)	Notes
1		rm	□	Copper bars stored in cart at TSUGII	000000		194400	194400		0	TSUGII	Machinist	18 hours per day for 3 days
2		t	⊙	Bar transported to machine-3 at a time			30	30	12	12			
3		t	⊙	Fill magazine with bars			12	12		0	TSUGII		
4		b	□	Bars sits in feeder			28800	28800		0			5 or 6 bars loaded
5		t	⊙	Bar feeds in to head stock collet			120	120	6	6			
6		va	○	Part machined			124	124		0	TSUGII or Star or L25-3		

	Baseline Lean: Storage Time: Raw material (RM)	Between process delay (B)	Lot delay (L)	Within process delay (W)	Finished goods (FG)	Transportation: Time (T)	Distance (in feet)	Inspection: Time (I)	Processing time: non-value added (NV)	Value added (VA)	Check numbers	Post Lean: Storage Time: Raw material (RM)	Between process delay (B)	Lot delay (L)	Within process delay (W)	Finished goods (FG)	Transportation: Time (T)	Distance (in feet)	Inspection: Time (I)	Processing time: non-value added (NV)	Value added (VA)
Numer of steps	3	21	27	0	1	70	424.9	5	14	8		1	21	27	6	1	70	265.8	5	11	3
Baseline time (secs)	194400	189617	34673	0	576000	460	425	138	1131	225		194400	121329	7520	0	576000	336	266	69	1123	225
Percent	19.51%	19.03%	3.48%	0.00%	57.79%	0.05%		0.01%	0.11%	0.02%		21.56%	13.51%	0.83%	0.00%	63.89%	0.04%	0.03%	0.01%	0.12%	0.02%
1	194400						0					194400									
2						30	12										30	12			
3						12	0										12				
4		28800					0						28800								
5						120	6										120	6			
6							0			124											124

Summary	Baseline	Post-Lean projected	Reduction	Reduction %
Total steps	147.0	76.0	71.00	48%
Orig sec:	996,644	901,502	95,142	10%
Min:	16,610.7	15,025.0	1,585.70	10%
Hours:	276.8	250.4	26.43	10%
Days	34.6	31.3	3.30	10%
Weeks	6.9	6.3	0.7	
Distance	424.9	265.8	159.10	37%
# of people	10.0	10.0	—	0%
check:	996,644	901,502	95,142	10%
Va %	0.0226%	0.02%	0.00%	−11%
NVA %	0.11%	0.12%	−0.01%	−10%
Storage	99.80%	99.81%	0.00%	0%
Inspect	0.01%	0.01%	0.01%	45%
Transport	0.05%	0.04%	0.01%	19%

Figure 2.26 PFA has more detail and meaning than a simple flowchart.

can be said for a VSM. The VSM only gives you high-level steps with the resulting process time versus storage time. Within the process time, VA and non-VA get mixed up.

Conducting PFAs on Machines

One can conduct a PFA on a machine just like a product. Pick the first piece and note each step. Where there is external loading and batching on or around machines, one will find many in-between processes and a lot of delays. In the past, we have been able to significantly increase the speed of machines by eliminating unnecessary steps and optimizing the computer numerical control (CNC) programing (see Figure 2.27a and b). For example, making sure it selects the tools in order versus going from one end to the other to retrieve tools for each step.

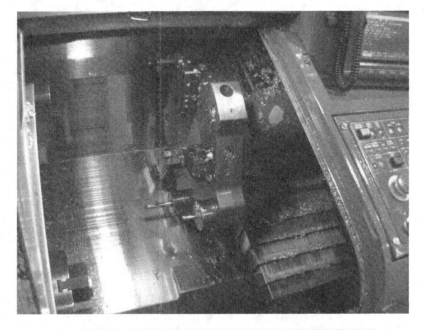

Step	Description	Code	Time (s)
1	Load bar	T	2
2	Wait for turret	B	2
3	Grind part	VA	1
4	Wait for turret	B	4
5	Drill part	VA	2
6	Wait for turret	B	3

(a)

Figure 2.27 (a and b) PFA for CNC machine. *(Continued)*

Step	Description	Code	Time (s)
1	Load four-sided pallet	T	2
2	Wait for turret	B	2
3	Grind 1st Part	VA	1
4	Wait for rest of parts	L	15
5	Rotate pallet	VA	2
6	Wait for turret	B	3

(b)

Figure 2.27 *(Continued)*

PFA on a Machine Cell

The cell was making parts for a well-known motorcycle company. Prior to starting to work on improving the cell, they were frequently late on supplying parts to their customer and in jeopardy of losing the business. They were supposed to always have a 2-week Kanban in place (see Figure 2.28). When we were done with our first round of improvements, they not only filled the Kanban but also had a week of extra time to work on other products within the same cell. Within the cell were two robots used to load machines. We conducted a PFA and WFA on the two robots working in the cell. When we completed the analysis, we determined that we could free up one of the robots because much of the cycle time was tied up with programed-in delays so the robots would not hit each other!

Figure 2.28 Week visual Kanban—Couldn't keep it full prior to Lean—After Lean it was always caught up.

High-Level Process Map

The high-level process map (see Figure 2.29) identifies steps at the highest level and is normally used as a starting point to grasp the process. Under each of these boxes will be several subprocesses that are then broken down into further detail using the PFA tool. Listing the steps at this level is normally a good starting point for teams doing process mapping. The advantage of a high-level process map is it allows the users to see and agree on the big picture first prior to drilling down into the subprocesses.

Then we need to list out who does each step (see Figure 2.30) in the left-hand column with the stickies showing the timeline for each step. It is easy to confuse operator steps with product flow steps. For instance, how would you categorize the step *clerk checks credit history*? How many would agree that it is a VA process? If you agree, you would be wrong. The step is written as an operator step. So, if we are the order, then we are sitting and waiting while the clerk checks the credit history, so from the product's point of view, it is a between-processes storage step for us.

Network of Process versus Operations Defined

We have attempted to expand Dr. Shingo's separation among product, operator, and changeover and take it to the next level. To our knowledge, no one has broken down these processes into the pieces of Lean thinking each one provides. We studied this for literally years before it dawned on

High-level process map

| Take the order | Process the order | Pick the order | Check credit history | Ship the order |

Figure 2.29 High level process map example.

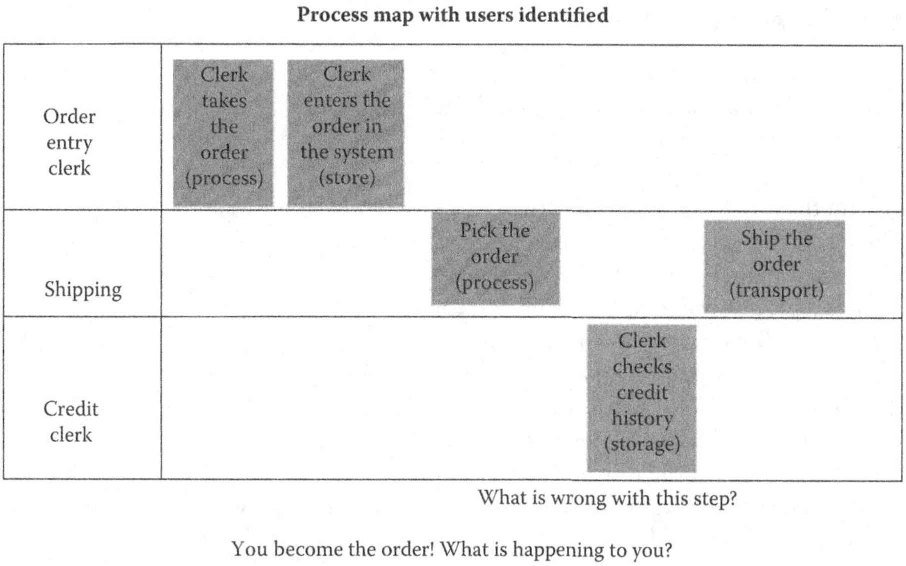

Process map with users identified

Order entry clerk	Clerk takes the order (process)	Clerk enters the order in the system (store)				
Shipping			Pick the order (process)		Ship the order (transport)	
Credit clerk				Clerk checks credit history (storage)		

What is wrong with this step?

You become the order! What is happening to you?

Figure 2.30   High level process map example with who does each step.

us that each analysis tool (product vs. operator's axis plus changeover) provides different answers for Lean improvement. We would like to propose that analyzing the product axis will provide the following pieces of the Lean implementation:

- Total throughput time
- Flow, flow, flow
- Layout and workstations
- In hospitals it shows where rooms should be in relation to the activity that is occurring
- Where the workstations should be located
- The proper sequence for equipment and supplies
- The location of where standard WIP (or number of rooms in hospitals) will be needed
- Machine times (running time of the process within a piece of equipment)
- Routings: which are the paths or sequence of steps the product or patients follow as they progress through the process?
- Percent VA for the product
- Percent of storage for the product
- Percent time inspecting the product
- Capacity analysis when combined with operator and setup analysis
- Travel distance for the product
- Point-to-point diagram: numbered steps the product follows

Lesson Learned: Using Lean tools enables you to understand and optimize what happens to the product or information as it moves through the process. Just analyzing and fixing the product axis piece of the network can yield as much as a 20%–40% productivity improvement.

Chapter Questions

1. What are the four things the product can do?
2. What is the world-class goal for the product?
3. What are the three types of storage?
4. What are the three types of WIP?
5. Explain the difference among a between-process delay, lot delay, and within-process delay?
6. What is the network of operations?
7. What are the three criteria for VA for the product?
8. What is a process wall map? How do you construct it?
9. What is the difference between flowcharts and process flows?
10. What is a point-to-point diagram? Can you draw one?
11. What is the importance of ERSC?
12. What is the importance of following the product?
13. What are the four of the things the product gives us toward a Lean culture?
14. What is the total throughput time of the process, and how do we determine it?
15. PFA and flowchart are the same. Is this statement true or false? Why?
16. What did you learn from this chapter?

Notes

1. *The Handbook of Advanced Time-Motion Study*, Sylvester, Magazines of Industry, ©1950, pp. 32–33.
2. Shigeo Shingo, *The Study of the Toyota Production System from an Engineering Viewpoint*, ©1981, 1989 English version, p. 4.
3. *Non-Stock Production*, Shigeo Shingo, Productivity Press, 1988, p. 6 Dr. Shingo reported during a speech to the *JMA Engineering Conference* 1945.
4. *Non-Stock Production*—Shingo, Productivity Press, ©2006, pp. 4–5.
5. Process and product flow are used synonymously as well as workflow and operator flow.
6. This is the fundamental premise of Dr. Shingo's network of operations theory, and yet mostly every Lean internal and external consultant still misses this piece. They always look at them on one axis. The real secret is to analyze the product and operator and setup separately and then develop the solution by marrying them together. VSM, for instance, is the tool of choice for Toyota Kata and others but VSMs mix up all three pieces. It may separate out the changeover time, but they almost always refer to the process steps as VA. Each process step however can generally be broken down into the three axes—Charlie Protzman.
7. It should be noted that we will use the terms process flow and product flow synonymously as well as operation, workflow and operator piece, and setups and changeovers.
8. *Productivity through Process Analysis*, Ishiwata, Productivity Press, ©1984.
9. *Productivity through Motion Study*, Kato, Productivity Press, ©1983.
10. Quote used with permission from Joe Shipley.
11. These steps came from Dr. Shingo's *A Study of The Toyota Production System from an Engineering Standpoint* but originally from a 1921 article by Frank Gilbreth reported in the *Journal of the American Society of Mechanical Engineering*.
12. These steps are also in the productivity book: *Productivity through Process Analysis*, Ishiwata, Productivity Press, ©1984, p. 36, Transportation, Operation, Inspection, Retention (storage and unplanned delay).
13. Based on conversation on 3-3-15 with Mike Meyers.
14. AMA video, *Time Is the Next Dimension of Quality*, Rath and Strong.
15. *Leveraging Lean in Healthcare*, Protzman, Mayzell, Kerpchar, Productivity Press, 2011.

16. *Non-Stock Production*, Productivity Press, Shingo, pp. 9–12, Figure 1.2.
17. *Leveraging Lean in Healthcare*, Protzman, Mayzell, Kerpchar, CRC Press, ©2011.
18. *Leveraging Lean in Healthcare*, Protzman, Mayzell, Kerpchar, CRC Press, 2011. This concept of within process storage was first published in this book.
19. Ralph M. Barnes, Motion and Time Study Design and Measurement of Work, Wiley, © 1937 London pg. 23 3rd edition
20. Video—*Troubleshooter Series, Episode Six, BBC Training Series* with Sir John Harvey Jones, Chairman of ICI, 1982–1987, ©1990.
21. Video—*Troubleshooter Series, Episode Six, BBC Training Series* with Sir John Harvey Jones, Chairman of ICI 1982–1987, ©1990.
22. Sam Mitchell, Sam Mitchell a Steel Foundry Operations Executive.
23. Hopp, W. Spearman, M. *Factory Physics*, 3rd edn, Waveland Pr Inc. (August 31, 2011).
24. A study of the *Toyota Production System from an Engineering Viewpoint*, Shingo, Productivity Press, ©1989.
25. DFMA is a registered trademarked of Boothroyd and Dewhurst.
26. *Design News*, http://www.designnews.com/document.asp?doc_id=219434, *Spiegel*, March 15, 2004. "The roots of 3P go back to the Toyota production system of the mid-1980s. '3P was developed by Sensei Nakao, who worked for the consulting company Shingijutsu in Japan,' explains Godt. Shingijutsu designed Toyota's groundbreaking production system which became the quality standard in the automotive industry. '3P uses the principles of Lean manufacturing. It can be used when there is design change, a new product launch, or a significant change in the production rate,' says Godt."yes
27. Submitted by Professor James Bond person correspondence February 2013.

Additional Readings

Ishiwata, J. 1997. Productivity through Process Analysis I.E. for the Shop Floor. Productivity Press.
Shingo, S. 1988. Non-Stock Production. Portland Oregon: Productivity Press.

Chapter 3

BASICS Assess:
WFA—Workflow Analysis

> Anyone who has never made a mistake has never tried anything new.
>
> **Albert Einstein[1]**

> Your most unhappy customers are your greatest source of learning.
>
> **Bill Gates[2]**

Now that we have completed our process flow analysis (PFA), we move on to the workflow analysis (WFA), which is the second step in our analysis process (Figure 3.1). We switch from being the product to being the person(s) doing the work. We have seen these tools utilized in home and building construction, landscaping contracts, banks, insurance companies, clinics, veterinarian clinics, executive offices, manufacturing companies, and people's garages. You name it, if you follow the BASICS® model by analyzing the product, operator, and setup separately, the process always works. Remember if we eliminate a step at the PFA level, we don't have to do video analysis or conduct a WFA on the step.

WFA Steps

1. Video.
2. Break down the job—Analyze the operator steps.
3. Follow the Eliminating, Rearranging, Simplifying, and Combining (ERSC) process (sometimes referred to as the Omits process because we Omit steps or update the "to be" or future state estimated times).
4. Reorder the steps.
5. Determine the total labor time (TLT).
6. Create standard work for the operator and the supervisor.

DOI: 10.4324/9781003185789-3

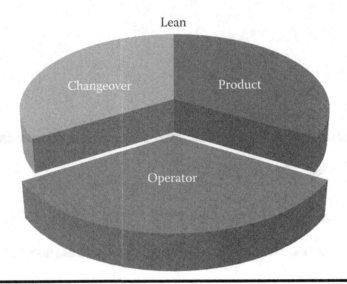

Figure 3.1 Pieces we analyze—Operator piece.

Conducting a WFA

To conduct a WFA properly, we suggest one follow the steps listed above. Prior to filming, it may be necessary to fill out certain company permits and obtain permission from the area supervisor. A meeting should be called with all the people in the area to advise them they are going to be filmed. We are sensitive to the fact some people are *hams* and some people literally hate to be filmed. However, we must remember this is about the process not the person. We need to work together to find ways to make everyone's jobs easier and grow the business. We let everyone filmed know they will be invited back to review their video to explain what they are doing and why. They will be able to describe what problems they run into each day and to give us their ideas on how we can improve the process.

What We Normally Find When Doing a WFA

Initially people are very fearful that the videos will be used against them somehow, so it is important to let everyone know that no one will be chastised or written up based on what is on the video. It is also important to let them know if they have a problem doing their work; it is ok to encourage them to do the operation the same way they always do it. We need to see the problems they run into every day, or we can't begin to work on fixing or improving the process.

Many times, people will get nervous and do things they normally don't do, just because they are being filmed. They will try to do what they think we want to see versus how the job is done every day. For instance, it is not unusual to see them look at the work instructions before each step, which they never do normally. It is important for the team members to perform tasks just like they would if no one was there. We all know that won't exactly happen, and some people slow down a little, and some speed up a little, but we take all that into account when we review the videos.

It is better to film your best person at the job, and sometimes we will film the best, worst, and someone in between. Remember to review the video guidelines presented earlier in the book. With rare exceptions, it is important not to talk to the operators or have them talk to you when filming them.

Step 1

The first step in this process is to video the operator (Figure 3.2). Videoing has many advantages over watching an operator with a stopwatch in hand or filling in a key observation sheet. If one trains their eyes properly, one will see things on the video that would never be noticed while just standing and watching the operator. Also, the operator can't argue with you once they see what they did on the video.

Note: It is really important not to stop the video during the recording until the operation is complete. This means from the very beginning of the job … asking what the next work order is, looking for the first tool or part, etc., until they put all the tools down which in some cases may mean returning the sub assembled part to the stockroom. We do ask the operator to let us know if they are going to the restroom, for a break, lunch, etc., so we can restart the video if necessary. It is best to video a clock with the time you stopped and started because when downloading digital video, we may lose the time and date stamp.

Step 2: Analyze the Video

We hold an analysis session in a conference room or on the floor if there is room and project the video up on the wall. We invite the operator(s), supervisor, engineer, and someone unfamiliar with the process. We also assign each person a task. For instance, one person will map the operator movements (spaghetti chart), another counts the number of steps (feet/meters) the operator travels, and one writes down each part and tool the operator uses. We use this information later when we create the block diagram. We explain the overall improvement process we are about to follow and explain we are looking for their ideas, problems, and to help us understand what they are doing and why at each step.

Don't confuse motion with progress

Figure 3.2 Videoing operators.

Lesson Learned: Lean, safety, and ergonomics all work together—safety and ergonomics are most important, no matter what. We never compromise those items. The goal is to improve their process and make it easier for them. We have never found a situation where we have had to compromise on safety or ergonomics to improve the current state.

The first thing we always look for when reviewing videos is anything unsafe or that results in poor ergonomic positions. We point out these conditions to the operators and supervisor and work to root cause and develop new solutions as we go. Sometimes you have to get outside the box to determine a solution.

We have the operators write down each step by hand (Figure 3.3), how long it takes, and code it with what type of step it is. The codes are value added (VA), required or necessary work, unnecessary work (UW), idle time (IT), reaching for parts or tools, material handling (MH), and others depending on the process. Many times, we will also put the same information into the computer. The purpose of this is twofold. By having the operator write down the steps, it shows them how to analyze the video and that it can be done by hand. This means there is no excuse in the future why this process cannot be continued by anyone virtually on the floor or in the office.

By putting the analysis into the computer (Figure 3.4), we can preserve the information and make it easier to put together the standard work in a more readable form. We can also easily calculate how much time is spent on each step and summarize all the data. When we ask the operators what problems they have, they normally start to unload on us. We write every problem down so when we put in the new Lean system, we can come back and review this list to make sure we fixed all the problems. We explain to the operators, "As long as you have this current-system, you will have this madness every day."

We also discuss freeing up people. Freeing up a person should not be a bad thing. Your goals as operators should be "How can I free myself up? How can we replace two operators with one?" If you want to be competitive, make more money, or put bonus systems in place, you have to be

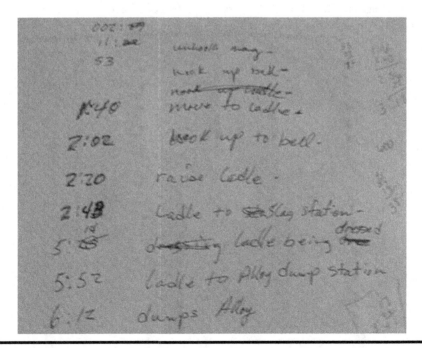

Figure 3.3   We write down each step the operator is doing along with the times.

									Each	Est	VA	NVA	MH Water Spider	Idle time (IT)
		Check No:		236		NVA Total Current	186	79%						
		Idle Time:		2		NVA Total Est	133	81%						
									Current	236	50	183	1	2
PPF step	OP step	Omit	Description	Key quality and safety notes	Running total process time estimate	Analysis code	Start time (optional)	Cumulative time	Estimated	164	31	133	0	0
									% Change	−30.5%	−38.0%	−27.3%	−100.0%	−100.0%
	1	x	Pick up housing	Alysia cycle—operator is sitting—should be standing.	0	nva	3:00:05	3:00:06	1	0		1		
0	2	x	Place on table	Why place on table and not into fixture	0	mh		3:00:07	1	0			1	
0	3		Pick up filter		1	nva		3:00:08	1	1		1		
0	4		Place in fixtue	Must be placed acording to the drawing	3	nva		3:00:10	2	2		2		
0	5		Pick up housing		4	nva		3:00:11	1	1		1		
0	6		Place in fixtue	Make sure housing is facing toward you	4	it		3:00:13	2	0				2
0	7		Reach for arbor press handle	Reach is too far!	5	nva		3:00:14	1	1		1		

Figure 3.4   Workflow analysis spreadsheet—Part of our cell design workbook.

more productive. The goal of every operator should be—"How can I get double the output with zero defects?" This type of thinking becomes job security for you. Free up enough people and space, and you can bring in more business or bring in business you used to have but now contract out locally or to other countries.

We also explain the goal is not to rush (Figure 3.5) however, we find no matter how many times we tell them this, they still think we want them to rush or skip/shortcut steps. We tell them,

Figure 3.5   Quality first the speed will come—Graphics from Smiths industries—Barry Rodgers.

"This is not the goal. Work at a normal pace. It is not about you (the operator)—but the process. No chastising, no blaming."

Note: It is extremely important the operator be present during the analysis. Many times, people will get the idea of reviewing the video first and bringing the operator in later because they feel there is no time and they can't meet the schedule if we bring the operators in to watch the video. But this is a big mistake! When the operator is not involved, they do not get the on-the-spot learning discussed during the video and many times we really don't know what or why the operator is doing what they are doing. Dr. Shingo called this "knowing what" versus "knowing why."

The WFA analyzes the operator steps while the product is flowing through the system down to the second. We break the operator steps into two categories:

1. VA
2. Non-VA (NVA)

We have the same definition for VA we had for the product piece, which is as follows:
VA:

1. Customer cares
2. Physically changes the product (form, fit, shape, size, or function)
3. Done right the first time

We break NVA steps up into three main categories:

1. Required work (RW)
2. UW
3. IT

We break operator steps into the elements listed in the following and sometimes other elements, depending on the process. Eventually one can get to the Therblig elements of motion study.[3]

Required Work[4] (RW)

RW comprises steps that are required but don't necessarily meet all three of the VA criteria. These steps may be taping a shipping box closed, deburring a part, or filling out a requisition form, or some work in transactional areas. Many times, something has to be done in the current state that might not have to be done later; however, this does not make it IT or UW. If the operator has to do the step-in today's world, we must consider it RW. This can also be for things the customer cares but doesn't physically change the product.

Parts (P)

This is any step that involves reaching for, grasping, and picking up a part and moving it to the unit. It must immediately be placed into the unit to be considered a part step. We generally include the time it takes to move the part to the unit, assuming it is within a step or simple reach of the operator. If the operator does not immediately put the part in the assembly and puts it on the table or puts it in another hand, etc., it is considered MH.

Tools or Tooling (T)

This is any step that involves reaching for a tool being used right away or loading a part into a tool or loading a tool onto a part. This includes loading the part onto a fixture or into a machine.

Inspection (I)

This is any step that includes inspection whether it be by a final inspector, in-process inspector, certified operator, or neighbor operator (successive checks), etc. It includes any operator inspection, formal or informal. Whether they just glance at it to check it out when taking it out of a machine or formally put calipers to it, we consider it inspection. In the office, we may look at papers coming off the copier machine to make sure they are printed correctly or in the right order. This is an inspection. It also includes part or product testing, engineering review, first article, and some types of oven cures (burn-in) or life cycle testing that are not physically changing the form, fit, size, shape, or function of the part. Our goal is always to eliminate inspection. However, to do this, we must eliminate the need for the inspection by using mistake proofing or by using 100% inspection by a machine (optical recognition).

Material Handling (MH)

Whenever an operator gets a part but does not put it immediately into the unit or grabs a tool but then sets it down before using it, it is considered MH. It should be equal to 0 seconds in the after condition. Tests for this code are as follows: is this step something we can hand off to a water spider (material handler) to do for the line, or could the operator have put the part directly on the assembly or used the tool immediately after he/she picked it up? This includes an operator reaching for screws and putting them on the worktable or an office worker going to the supply room or copy room for paper or office supplies.

The idea of MH/using a waters spider is not new. In fact, Gilbreth had people dedicated to making sure the concrete was always just the right consistency for the brick layers (Figure 3.6). They would also raise and lower the adjustable scaffolding (Figure 3.7) that Gilbreth invented to eliminate excess motion for the bricklayers. An example of applying the idea of adjustable scaffolding in use today is the scissor lifts used in the construction industry and manufactured by firms such as JLG or Genie. As we engage employees in redesigning their workstations and eliminating excess motions to provide safe and ergonomically designed jobs for our shop floor and administrative team members, we realize increased productivity, morale, and job satisfaction, which usually leads to higher profits.

Unnecessary Work (UW)

These steps do not meet any of the three VA criteria in the current condition (i.e., searching or overprocessing waste)! Sometimes we don't have a clue, nor does the operator why they did what they did, so we consider the step UW. We see this especially in transactional types of settings as well; for example, circling information on an invoice for data entry or putting a payable date on an invoice that is already assigned by the computer system. In the assembly area, primarily in-sit down operations, you will see the team members sit down and just start making wholesale changes to their workstation area, moving this, moving that, etc., for really no reason other than to get settled and ready to start working.

Old way materials presented

Concrete kept mixed to right consistency by a water spider, so bricklayers spent their time laying bricks

Figure 3.6 Example of bricklayers material presentation before and after from Gilbreth's *Motion Study* book.

The test for unnecessary steps is they should be equal to 0 seconds in the after condition (i.e., we should be able to omit the step in the after condition). If it cannot be omitted, it must be considered RW. For instance, if the operator has to change bits on a screw gun or change a fixture over because they only have one screw gun or one arbor press, it is RW because in the current condition it is required.

For example, sometimes operators will take assemblies apart prior to reassembling them. This is because they don't trust the operator before them. This is also a good indicator and there is no certification for the assembly operators and no standard work. It may also suggest they were blamed in the past because of something that someone else did incorrectly. Therefore, they have resigned themselves to this pattern of ongoing rework to make sure they are never blamed again. The wastes of overprocessing, transportation, excess inventory, inspection (defects), excess motion, all are things to look for during the videos that can be categorized as UW. Another thing to look for is to see if the operator is using the correct tooling. Many times, they will use whatever tool is available or that they can find to try to do a job. Many times, they do not have the right tool for the job, which results in overprocessing and sometimes defects or safety concerns.

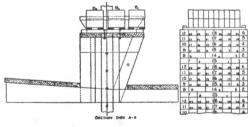

The numbers show the correct sequence of courses and tiers as laid from the nonstooping scaffold for the fewest, shortest, and most economical motions under the "pack-on-the-wall" method.

Figure 3.7 Example of adjustable scaffolding from Gilbreth's *Motion Study* book.

Idle Time (IT)

This step denotes where the operator is doing nothing but sitting or standing idle and waiting. This is not used for an operator searching for parts, etc. That would fall under MH (if we can't get rid of it right away) or UW (if we can get rid of it right away). We also call IT pure waste or the Japanese word muda. Operators should never be idle. Every operator analysis step should get one of these codes; however, please keep in mind, these codes are guidelines and can and should be changed based on your application. Every company is unique. You may decide you just want to capture each step at a high level simply using VA, NVA, and IT or you may want to capture computer time or paperwork time. Do not get locked into a template. Do whatever makes sense for the process on which you are working.

Example

Let's go back to our laundry example from the last chapter, only looking at it through the lens of the person doing the laundry. Our first step in the laundry example is when we grab the shirts and put them into the basket. Now we are focused totally on the operator. We don't care how long the shirts have been sitting there because we are following the operator not the product. So, the first step would look like this:

Step	Description	Type	Time (Seconds)	Distance (ft)	Total Time (Seconds)	Cumulative Distance
1	Pick up shirts from the pile	RW	1		1	0

Notice for this first step when watching the operator, we ended up combining the first and second PFA steps. The next operator steps are as follows:

2	Load us (shirts) in a basket	RW	1	1	2	0
3	Load the rest of the shirts in the basket	RW	10		12	0
4	Prepare (sort) the rest of the clothes for future loads	UW	60		72	0
5	Move the basket to the laundry room	RW	30	150	102	150

Sorting the clothes for the next load is out of sequence here and unnecessary.

6	Wait for the machine to finish the previous load	UW	1,200	0	1,302	150

We are stuck now waiting for the machines to finish. Many times, in the factory we stand there and watch machines just in case they might crash or a tool breaks, etc., so we put that time in here, but chances are we would be working on or doing something else while the clothes are washing. For example, how many of you watch your washing machine or dryer run? Isn't it ironic we pay people to watch machines in the factory? Our next step is to unload the washer.

7	Unload the washer	RW	120	0	1,422	150

Once we have unloaded all the clothes and placed them in the dryer, the next step is to start with picking up the shirts in the basket.

8	Pick shirts up from the basket	RW	1	0	1,423	150
9	Load them into the washer	RW	2	0	1,425	150
10	Load the rest of the shirts	RW	15	0	1,440	150
11	Grab detergent	RW	2	0	1,442	150
12	Remove the cap	RW	2	0	1,444	150
13	Add detergent to the machine	RW	2	0	1,446	150
14	Put detergent down	RW	1	0	1,447	150
15	Close the door	RW	1	0	1,448	150
16	Set dial	RW	4	0	1,452	150

Now we start the washing

17	Cycle the washer machine (press start)	RW	1	0	1,453	150

Notice at this point there is no VA. Why? Because the machine adds the value. We leave and do something else for 2,400 seconds, while the washer is running our load and the dryer is running a prior load. We return 600 seconds after the washer has been stopped because the dryer takes 40 minutes versus the 30 minutes for the washer.

18	Unload the prior load from the dryer	RW	300	0	1,753	150
19	Move our first armload of clothes from the washer into the dryer	RW	1	0	1,754	150
20	Move the rest of the clothes in the dryer	RW	15	0	1,769	150
21	We then put the next load in the washer (before starting the dryer), add the detergent, and cycle the washer	UW	180	0	1,949	150

Note: For those of you more advanced, we are actually in a changeover at this point as loading and unloading are changeovers and we are on internal time. We really should have started the dryer first and then loaded the washer since the dryer has a longer cycle time (2,400 seconds) than the washer (1,800 seconds). The next step is to turn the knob on the dryer to the desired cycle.

22	Turn the knob to the desired dryer cycle	RW	10	0	1,959	150
23	Cycle the dryer	RW	1	0	1,960	150

Then we press the start button or pull out the knob to start it up and wait for 40 minutes. Now we go do something else for 2,400 seconds until the dryer buzzes to let us know it is completed the cycle.

24	Pick up a shirt from the first load in the dryer	RW	2	0	1,962	150
25	Move the clothes to the basket	RW	1	0	1,963	150
26	Remove the rest of the clothe	RW	13	0	1,976	150
27	Clean out the lint trap	RW	5	0	1,981	150
28	Load the washer and the dryer again	RW	120	0	2,101	150

We did not break down this next step because it is all RW. The next step is to move the clothes back to the second floor and lay them on the bed—30 seconds, 150 ft.

| 29 | Move the clothes back to the second floor. | RW | 30 | 150 | 2,131 | 300 |

Go get hangers (60 seconds) and then hang up the rest of the shirts.

30	Get hangers	RW	60	0	2,191	300
31	Pick shirts up	RW	2	0	2,193	300
32	Put them on a hanger	RW	3	0	2,196	300
33	Set them on hook	RW	1	0	2,197	300
34	Put the rest of the shirts on hangers	RW	120	0	2,317	300
35	Pick all shirts up that are on hangers	RW	5	0	2,322	300
36	Move them to the closet	RW	10	0	2,332	300
37	Hang some of them up in the closet	RW	2	0	2,334	300
38	Hang up the rest of the shirts in the closet	RW	30	0	2,364	300

Notice that this analysis generates our TLT. Our TLT is 2,364 seconds or 39.4 minutes. Compare this to the product process flow (PPF) time of 137.8 minutes for just the laundry (not including the 5 days we are waiting). Following the operator gives us TLT and steps we would not get by just following the product. Why is the TLT so much less? Well, it is because we are off doing something else while the machines are running. We call this external time. We will discuss external time in the next chapter.

Analyze to the Second

Do not shortcut the process. If you take steps larger than a second, you can end up combining steps that mix up different codes, which affects true content of the work and eventually impacts the standard work that is derived from this analysis. It will affect the steps when we go to balance the line where splits in the work between operators occur later. If the steps are too big (i.e., too much time per step), we will not know exactly where the split is within that step. Also, when you revise how the work is to be done, the steps within the larger block of time cannot be split out and apportioned properly. This is one reason why videoing is an excellent tool. You will not miss steps.

WFA Lessons Learned

Listed below are a small set of a collection of lessons learned from performing WFA.

1. When talking about one very methodical and diligent worker, her co-worker said, "I believe she assembles in her sleep." The operators are the experts in how the work is performed in the current state processes.
2. Don't just analyze the process videos—make decisions about what should stay in the process and what shouldn't with a goal of one-piece flow with no rework.
3. Have the operator there during as much of the analysis as possible—and have them help in the decision-making. They have to learn to recognize waste and call it waste. They also have the best suggestions and can make the change happen but only if you involve them.
4. Operators need to understand what will happen to their operation once something is defined as waste since they won't be doing it anymore (i.e., sitting down and standing up, etc.).
5. Simulate or pilot a new process whenever possible before putting it in place.
6. Filming—catch the entire operation—not just hands or product. Try not to zoom in and out all the time. Only zoom in when absolutely necessary.
7. Make sure the team agrees on coding definitions ahead of time.
8. Streamline each operation—recognize what is significant and capture all the operations. Many times, operators forget some of the steps they perform.
9. Analysis in teams is better than by one individual—particularly when all members are not comfortable with the process.
10. Follow through on "agreed to" operator suggestions. It's the best thing you can do to secure an operator buy-in and get future suggestions.

Equipment Lessons Learned

1. Most people work at the same height. For example, ask the person next to you to hold their arms out as if they were going to work at the station. In 90% of cases no matter how tall we are, our work height is within a couple of inches unless you are vertically challenged. However, our eyes are all at different heights. So, equipment and instruments used by the eyes must be vertically adjustable. Microscopy work and having machines tied to bench height have special needs in terms of equipment.
2. Have all capital equipment available and in-line or as close to in-line as possible, to integrate into the Lean line at the time of implementation.
3. Maximum flexibility must be built into the equipment to support different flows and volumes for mixed model environments and must meet needs of workers.
4. Once good equipment is found, it should be recorded for development of standards.

5. Equipment budget must be available to address ergonomic issues.
6. Equipment must support one-piece flow and must be easy to manage visually.

Major Process Changes

Pick the hills you want to die on—there isn't always time to change everything. Go for low-hanging fruit—not world hunger—and let everyone know, going in, this is the intention.

Legal WFA Shortcuts

We generally want to capture every step as close to the second as possible. If we know a step is going to be all one unnecessary step or all MH or all IT, or we know we are going to omit it later, it is ok to capture it as a lump sum time amount. We find this often with rework on the line or operators gathering parts or tools prior to starting their work. Otherwise, if it is VA or RW, we must capture it to the second or it will make the line balancing future improvement updating and proper coding during the analysis session more difficult.

Occupational Ergonomic Assessment Tools[5]

Lean and ergonomic principles overlap considerably. People are a critical element of any work system and when work demands exceed the capabilities of the human element, system performance is threatened and output becomes unreliable. This human overburden (muri) is wasteful and manifests itself most obviously in the form of unnecessary motion and rework as well as that excessive workload or anything too difficult to:

- Do
- See
- Hear
- Reach
- Learn
- Train
- Remember
- Teach
- Lift
- Process

For example, wasted human motion may be the result of reaching too far to retrieve tools or bending over to pick up parts from a pallet on the floor. This not only results in wasted motion and therefore time but also subjects the worker to safety risk in the form of awkward postures and excessive force. It is also more fatiguing. Occupational ergonomics is the science of improving employee performance and well-being through the design of job tasks, equipment, and the overall work environment. When coupled with a continuous improvement mindset, it is a relentless effort to design the workplace for what people do well, and design against (mistake proof where possible) what people do not do well. For example, at one plant, we could not get the operators from filling and moving very heavy carts, so we cut the carts to one-third of the size in order to mistake proof safety and ergonomics into the system. This way even if the carts were filled, they were still within the acceptable weight limits. The risk factors ergonomics addresses are conditions in the workplace that increase one's chance of developing a musculoskeletal disorder (MSD). The three categories of MSD risk factors are as follows:

1. *Posture*: Extreme postures stress joints and occlude blood flow.
2. *Force*: Tasks with forceful exertions place higher loads on joints and connective tissues.
3. *Frequency*: Extreme frequencies can contribute to fatigue debt. Also, the longer the period of continuous work, the longer the recovery time needed. These also lead to conditions that may not be discovered until much later in life like tendonitis, carpal tunnel, and arthritis.

When these risk factors surpass known thresholds, the probability of injury increases, and exposure to them should be limited or totally avoided. However, avoidance of injury is not the sole benefit of risk reduction as job tasks with elevated MSD risks are also more likely to take more time and present more opportunities for error, thereby influencing quality, delivery, and safety metrics. For this reason, workplaces should be assessed for MSD risk and the results of these assessments viewed by operational leaders as opportunities to improve the performance of their entire system.

Generally, analyzing jobs for MSD risk takes one of the following three forms: simple checklist, interactive form-based assessment, or a narrative (open-ended) method. No matter which form of analysis one favors, a comprehensive ergonomic assessment requires the following process steps:

Recognize	Collect background job information (preferably via video)
	Break the job into its essential functions
Evaluate	Identify risk factors for each task
	Identify root causes for each risk factor
Control	Generate and implement solutions
	Follow-up after solutions has been implemented

Humantech's Baseline Risk Identification of Ergonomic Factors[6]

Baseline risk identification of ergonomic factors (BRIEF) is an initial screening tool, which uses a structured and formalized rating system to identify ergonomic acceptability on a task-by-task basis. The BRIEF examines nine work-related MSD (WMSDs) such as body areas for WMSD risk factors (posture, force, frequency, and duration for hands/wrists, elbows, shoulders, neck, back, and legs). The BRIEF also takes into consideration physical stressors that tend to accelerate WMSDs: vibration, low temperatures, soft tissue compression, impact stress, and glove issues (Figure 3.8a). Risk prioritization is a proven strategy for ensuring resources that are directed at the jobs and/or tasks that will benefit the most from ergonomic improvements. Without risk prioritization, ergonomics initiatives tend to become bogged down in reactionary activities and progress stalls. By prioritizing ergonomic risks, and therefore jobs for improvement, one is able to manage resources efficiently, maximize the impact, and make steady progress toward the company's goals.

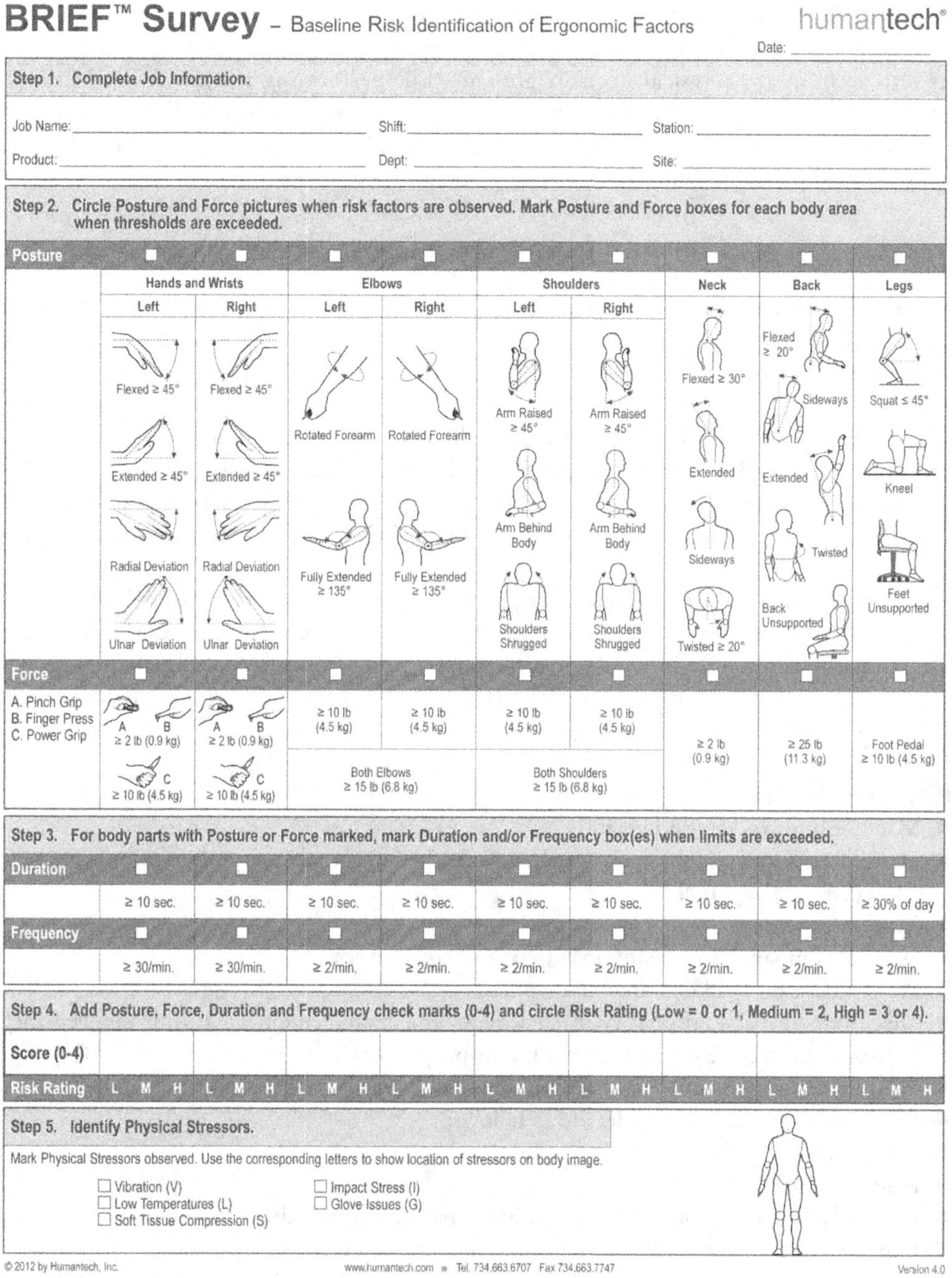

BRIEF™ Survey – Baseline Risk Identification of Ergonomic Factors

humantech®

Date: ______

Step 1. Complete Job Information.

Job Name: ______ Shift: ______ Station: ______

Product: ______ Dept: ______ Site: ______

Step 2. Circle Posture and Force pictures when risk factors are observed. Mark Posture and Force boxes for each body area when thresholds are exceeded.

	Hands and Wrists		Elbows		Shoulders		Neck	Back	Legs
	Left	Right	Left	Right	Left	Right			
Posture	■	■	■	■	■	■	■	■	■
	Flexed ≥ 45° Extended ≥ 45° Radial Deviation Ulnar Deviation	Flexed ≥ 45° Extended ≥ 45° Radial Deviation Ulnar Deviation	Rotated Forearm Fully Extended ≥ 135°	Rotated Forearm Fully Extended ≥ 135°	Arm Raised ≥ 45° Arm Behind Body Shoulders Shrugged	Arm Raised ≥ 45° Arm Behind Body Shoulders Shrugged	Flexed ≥ 30° Extended Sideways Twisted ≥ 20°	Flexed ≥ 20° Sideways Extended Twisted Back Unsupported	Squat ≤ 45° Kneel Feet Unsupported
Force	■	■	■	■	■	■	■	■	■
A. Pinch Grip B. Finger Press C. Power Grip	A B ≥ 2 lb (0.9 kg) C ≥ 10 lb (4.5 kg)	A B ≥ 2 lb (0.9 kg) C ≥ 10 lb (4.5 kg)	≥ 10 lb (4.5 kg) Both Elbows ≥ 15 lb (6.8 kg)	≥ 10 lb (4.5 kg)	≥ 10 lb (4.5 kg) Both Shoulders ≥ 15 lb (6.8 kg)	≥ 10 lb (4.5 kg)	≥ 2 lb (0.9 kg)	≥ 25 lb (11.3 kg)	Foot Pedal ≥ 10 lb (4.5 kg)

Step 3. For body parts with Posture or Force marked, mark Duration and/or Frequency box(es) when limits are exceeded.

Duration	■	■	■	■	■	■	■	■	■
	≥ 10 sec.	≥ 10 sec.	≥ 10 sec.	≥ 10 sec.	≥ 10 sec.	≥ 10 sec.	≥ 10 sec.	≥ 10 sec.	≥ 30% of day
Frequency	■	■	■	■	■	■	■	■	■
	≥ 30/min.	≥ 30/min.	≥ 2/min.	≥ 2/min.	≥ 2/min.	≥ 2/min.	≥ 2/min.	≥ 2/min.	≥ 2/min.

Step 4. Add Posture, Force, Duration and Frequency check marks (0-4) and circle Risk Rating (Low = 0 or 1, Medium = 2, High = 3 or 4).

Score (0-4)									
Risk Rating	L M H	L M H	L M H	L M H	L M H	L M H	L M H	L M H	L M H

Step 5. Identify Physical Stressors.

Mark Physical Stressors observed. Use the corresponding letters to show location of stressors on body image.

- ☐ Vibration (V)
- ☐ Low Temperatures (L)
- ☐ Soft Tissue Compression (S)
- ☐ Impact Stress (I)
- ☐ Glove Issues (G)

 www.humantech.com ■ Tel. 734.663.6707 Fax 734.663.7747 Version 4.0

Figure 3.8a The BRIEF™ exposure scoring technique.

The BRIEF™ Exposure Scoring Technique or BEST™ builds on the BRIEF Survey to determine a job hazard score. It adjusts for different time exposures to ergonomic risk and takes into account any physical stressors present while performing the job. A BRIEF Survey must be completed for a job prior to completing the BEST form. The BEST generates a score from 0 to 125, with a higher score representing a higher priority level. A job hazard score is generated based on the following:

BRIEF Survey Scores

- Physical stressors (vibration, low temperatures, soft tissue compression, impact stress, and glove issues)
- Task exposure times

BEST scores are classified as low, medium, high, or very high priority for ergonomic improvement/intervention (Figure 3.8b). Lean practitioners can use these tools as a quantitative method to understand the *human overburden* risk at an operation. By prioritizing jobs, practitioners can manage resources, time, and costs by focusing on the improvements with the highest impact (Figure 3.8c).

The BRIEF is designed to analyze a job with specific tasks repeated throughout the cycle. The BRIEF Survey works best in environments where operators routinely perform jobs/tasks using repeatable methods or procedures. In addition to looking at the workload of a person, it is also important to look at the overall environment in which the person is working. For instance,

- Workstation design
- Machine and workstation heights
- Flexibility: With everything on wheels, what is the force it takes to push or pull (for example, a full cart load of parts)?
- Machine openings
- General company attitude toward safety and ergonomics
- Weight belts for MH or warehouse workers
- Discipline and accountability of employees and management regarding the wearing of (personal protective equipment) PPE and proper PPE
- Use of mats on concrete
- Other safety factors to consider are as follows:
- Air quality
- Noise levels
- External aids such as breathing or cooling apparatus for certain welding jobs
- Exposure to slick chemicals like oil on the workstation or floor
- Allergic reactions to certain chemicals

Priority			
Low	Medium	High	Very high
0–9	10–29	30–49	>50

Figure 3.8b   Best scores breakdown.

BEST™ – BRIEF™ Exposure Scoring Technique

humantech®

Date: _____

Step 1. Complete Job Information.

Job Name: _____ Shift: _____ Station: _____

Product: _____ Dept: _____ Site: _____

Step 2. Transfer BRIEF Scores.

Transfer scores (0-4) from a completed BRIEF Survey.

Hands and Wrists		Elbows		Shoulders				
Left	Right	Left	Right	Left	Right	Neck	Back	Legs

Step 3. Determine Conversion Factors.

Find each BRIEF Score in the table to the right and determine the Conversion Factor for each body part. Add the Conversion Factors together and enter the total.

BRIEF Score	Conversion Factor
4	10
3	5
2	3
1	1
0	0

▼

Step 4. Summarize Physical Stressors.

Place a 2 in the box for each physical stressor marked on the BRIEF, and a 0 for each physical stressor not marked. Add the Physical Stressors together and enter the total.

Vibration	Low Temperatures	Soft Tissue Compression	Impact Stress	Glove Issues

+

Step 5. Calculate Job Risk Factor Score.

Add Conversion Factors and the Physical Stressor Scores together and enter the total.

=

Step 6. Determine Time Exposure Multiplier.

Use the table to the right to determine the appropriate multiplier.

Time on Task Per Week	Multiplier
> 40 hours	1.25
20 - 40 hours	1.0
4 - 19 hours	0.8
< 4 hours	0.4

X

Step 7. Calculate Job Hazard Score.

Multiply the Job Risk Factor Score by the Time Exposure Multiplier.

Job Hazard Score	Priority
0 - 9	Low
10 - 29	Medium
30 - 49	High
50+	Very High

=

Figure 3.8c   BEST scores highest impact form.

Lean Principle: Separate Man from Machine

One of our main Lean principles is to separate man from machine. When we follow the product, we get the machine time compared to following the operator where we get the time to unload, load, and cycle the machine. It is important to keep these times separate. If an operator is standing there watching the machine, it is considered IT. We utilize Jidoka techniques in order to free up operators from machines.

Total Labor Time (TLT)

One of our major deliverables of WFA is the TLT. TLT is the amount of VA and NVA labor or work performed during the process by the operator(s) to produce one completed piece (or lot as in our laundry example) of an item. Some refer to this as touch time. Machine time is not included in the labor time. This is part of the principle of separating man from machine work.

Step 3: The Omits Process (Eliminating, Rearranging, Simplifying, and Combining [ERSC])

What we call the Omits process is crucial to the analysis process and it should be done with the operator(s) present. If we can omit the step, we reduce the time to zero. If we can't completely omit it, we change the time for the step to a new estimated time. It is critical to have the employees participate in the process so they can help contribute their ideas and understand how we arrived at the new times for the overall work. It not only incorporates their improvement ideas, but the estimated times now come from them. For example, if we can't omit the step but we think we can improve it, we ask the operator, "How long do you think it will take with this new process?" So, when we end up with a 30%–50% reduction in the TLT, they understand why and how it was calculated and agree to and accept it. In this way, they are included in determining their standard work, which will be the resulting process after the steps are reviewed (see Figures 3.9).

If operators are not included as part of the process, you risk the following:

■ They will not understand how you expect them to get the work done twice as fast as they are now!
■ They will think you only want to lower the standard.
■ They will think you want to create more work for them and make them work harder.
■ They will feel they have to rush.
■ They will argue they should be compensated more for the additional output even though they are not working any harder.

The next step is to review and question each step and ask if it can be somehow:

1. Eliminated
   If a step can be eliminated, we mark it with an X, which shows that step will be *omitted* and the estimated time is set to zero (0).
2. Rearranged
   Many times, we can rearrange the steps in an order which makes more sense for the product being assembled or for the operator to utilize their tools and equipment. Rearranging will

SAMPLE CHART USED ON PICK–AND–DIP METHOD, EXTERIOR BRICKWORK,
BEFORE THE DAYS OF THE PACKET

Operation No.	The Wrong Way, Motions per Brick, ¼ ½ ¾ ¼	The Right Way, Motions per Brick, ¼ ½ ¾ ¼	Pick-and-Dip Method. The Exterior 4 inches (Laying to the Line).
1	Step for mortar	Omit	On the scaffold the inside edge of mortar box should be plumb with inside edge of stock platform. On floor the inside edge of mortar box should be 21 in. from wall. Mortar boxes never over 4 ft. apart.
2	Reaching for mortar	¼	Do not bend any more than absolutely necessary to reach mortar with a straight arm.
3	Working up mortar	Omit	Provide mortar of right consistency. Examine sand screen and keep in repair so that no pebbles can get through. Keep tender on scaffold to temper up and keep mortar worked up right.
4	Step for brick	Omit	If tubs are kept 4 ft. apart, no stepping will be necessary on scaffold. On floor keep brick in a pile not nearer than 1 ft. nor more than 4 ft. 6 in. from the wall.
5	Reach for brick	Included in 2	Brick must be reached for at the same time that mortar is reached for and picked up at exactly the same time the mortar is picked up. If it is not picked up at the same time, allowance must be made for operation.
6	Pick up right brick	Omit	Train the leaders of the tenders to vary the kind of brick used as much as possible to suit the conditions; that is, to bring the best brick when the men are working on the line.
7	Mortar box to wall	¼	Carry stock from the staging to the wall in the straightest possible line and with an even speed, without pause or hitch. It is important to move the stock with an even speed and not by quick jerks.
8	Brick pile to wall	Included in 7	Brick must be carried from pile to wall at exactly the same time the mortar is carried to the wall, without pause or jerk.

Figure 3.9 Standard work sheet with omits—ERSC from Gilbreth's *Motion Study* book.

generally but may not always reduce time but can improve ergonomics, safety, employee morale, and flow.

3. Simplified

Our goal is always to simplify steps wherever possible and eliminate any unnecessary steps, searching, waiting, or rework to make the operator's job easier. This almost always results in a reduced estimated time or sometimes in omitting steps.

4. Combined

Combining steps is the process of taking two steps and doing them in parallel, making them one step or moving a step from one operator to another; for example, when cooking instead of adding salt and pepper separately, we get a new shaker and add them at the same time or we combine two motions into one.

The WFA is a time-consuming process, but in the end, it is where all the value of performing the analysis resides. We want to continuously ask these questions whenever possible for each step … Forever! Much can be learned from motion study and questioning every step in the process. Our goal is to always cut at least 50% of the labor in the process. The WFA leads ultimately to our work instructions and standard work process for doing the job (see Figure 3.10a and b).

Omits Process

You Must Involve the Operators!

Repeatedly, especially at the end of the month, we are told there is no time to pull the operators to review the videos. We have gotten to the point where we will not conduct the WFA without them. This is because when they are not included there, it ends up being so much resistance to

PICK-AND-DIP METHOD — WORKING RIGHT TO LEFT (Continued)

Fig. 28. — Throwing mortar on interior face tier.

Fig. 29. — Spreading mortar on interior face tier.

Fig. 30. — Cutting off mortar before brick is laid.

Fig. 31. — Tapping down brick after laying on interior face tier.

Fig. 32. — Cutting off mortar after brick is laid on interior face tier (here working left to right).

Fig. 33. — Handling mortar for two brick at one time on interior face tier.

Figure 3.10 (a and b) Work flow example from Gilbreth's *Motion Study* book. *(Continued)*

STRINGING–MORTAR METHOD

Fig. 34.—Working right to left.—Spreading mortar on exterior face tier.

Fig. 35.—Working left to right.—Buttering end of laid brick on exterior face tier.

Fig. 36.—Working left to right.—Cutting off mortar after brick is laid on exterior face tier.

Fig. 37.—Working right to left.—Spreading mortar on the interior face tier.

Fig. 38.—Working left to right.—Cutting off mortar after brick is laid on exterior face tier.

Fig. 39.—Working left to right.—Spreading mortar on the interior face tier.

Figure 3.10 *(Continued)*

the new process, it takes twice as long as to try to implement, morale is poor, and it is harder to sustain. This gets blamed on the team implementing versus the root cause, which is the manager or supervisor not willing to involve their people. With one exception, we have always been able to make up any time lost because of pulling the operators from the line to work with us on the videos in a day and worst case within a week after the implementation.

Lesson Learned: You can either do it to them or with them!

Some Notes on the Analysis

When we code the analysis steps, we code the steps assuming we are going to be able to make the improvements right away when the new line is set up. If the improvements cannot be made right away, they should not be estimated or set to zero in the after condition, but a note should remain with the improvement idea and who is assigned to it.

Power of the Video: Case Study

Funny Thing Happened when Attempting to Solve a Safety Issue: A True Account of Lean Eyes in a Process[7]

Project Background

Shortly after I began in my current position, I was asked to participate on a team that had been assembled to identify safety improvement opportunities. The process involved the assembling, sanding, cutting, and coating of large components, which included multiple steps where employees were required to team lift (and in some cases flip over) very large and heavy assemblies, thus creating the safety concerns of potential back injury.

General Observations

There are multiple cure stages built into the process that created a delay time of 24 hours per curing cycle (as dictated by the material supplier) used to glue the large assemblies together, which totaled three individual curing cycles in the process (three cycles of 24 hours each). A significant amount of floor space was consumed during these delays.

One of the suspected areas of low-hanging fruit was within the final coating applications. This portion of the process was filmed and analyzed for improvement opportunities. Based on extensive experience with other material systems (of which offered a significantly quicker cure time), we began an R&D project to develop a replacement. With testing completed and now approved, we were set to introduce this as a process improvement that eliminated one of the three handling steps and obviously reduced the required floor space as each cure would now only take 3 hours each (total of 6 hours vs. 72 total hours). In addition to improving our safety concerns, the improvements now improved our agility to market/customer demand.

Two months after we started this portion of the improvement process, we suffered a quality issue that we'd investigated by use of another film event to aid in identifying the root cause of the conditions that allowed bad products to escape our facility. This portion of the process included the actual assembly of the components, gluing and squaring, and alignment of these massive assemblies. It also included hand lifting and moving these large assemblies from the assembly fixture to a gluing station. Immediately after the adhesive was applied, the assembly was hand lifted to a staging area on the floor where employees then pushed and prodded the assembly into some form of squareness, followed by covering it with plastic to prevent the glue from the subsequently added assembly on top from dripping all over it. This created a subsequent processing step to flip the assembly over and scrape the excess glue off the underside of the assembly.

Based on the analysis of the film, we next determined to extract a large sampling of the assembly's joints that were glued together and tested them to failure to determine the bond strength of the assemblies (which was thought to contribute to our quality issue). We'd expected to see a minimum value of 1,000 psi in tensile strength development. We were surprised to see that our average was only achieving 280 psi with only one single value in 30 meeting the 1,000 mark.

Based on how the product was glued together, we typically flood the joint area with a very expensive two-component adhesive and, based on a generous guess, it was calculated that we were about 5% utilized in the way that we were applying it versus the amount of adhesive that actually created the needed bond joint.

Now there's a Lean and a quality opportunity—95% waste and not able to achieve minimum bond strength characteristics!

The adhesive came in drums of approximately 425 pounds. At 5% transfer efficiency, we were using 22 pounds of material (and very ineffectively I might add based on our bond strength test results), and the rest goes in the trash can (of course after it's paid for!). This is another portion of the process that also took another 24 hours and ate up the valuable floor space to cure (along with several floor-mounted electric space heaters that are very expensive to operate)!

This prompted the exploration of a new adhesive system with the intent of pinpoint placement accuracy and improved cure. We identified a single component that provides the 1,000 psi bond strength in 10–15 minutes. This now allows us to apply the adhesive as we are assembling the components in the fixture, which aligns everything squarely to one another then, allowing it to cure sufficiently to achieve the desired bond strength.

These enhancements will eliminate approximately 50% of the total process steps, not to mention the savings in adhesive transfer efficiency/utilization, we no longer have to purchase/apply plastic, tie up scads of floor space for curing the product, and safeguard both the quality (squareness guaranteed off the assembly fixture) and safety of our employees. Several assembly holding fixtures are being removed and a new layout is being performed to accommodate the streamlined process.

This is one of countless examples of identifying and eliminating waste from a process. By filming any process, it is remarkably easy to identify waste streams and opportunities for improvements, providing the user has (a) a camera and (b) an understanding of basic Lean tools and ability to identify the seven great wastes.

Just When You Thought You Were *There*: Motion Study

If you think you have improved all you can, let us provide you with a second thought.

Dr. Shingo has an example in one of his books where he takes a towel and soaks it in water to exemplify waste. One by one, he asks his students to come up and wring out the towel. The first person squeezes out a lot of water, later several students are still able to still squeeze some water but not as much. Even the last student was able to squeeze out some additional drops.[8]

Once you are trained to see the waste for what it is, there is much to see. But sometimes waste is hidden by batching, excess material, and just because that is the way we have always done it (boiled frog syndrome). Once you *Lean out* the area, it becomes easy to see where there is variation and waste. But as you continuously improve the area, the waste becomes harder to find, yet it is there. Excess material always hides problems and represents the level of risk in the process. In some cases, it would be easy to say we have improved enough, and we don't need to improve anymore; however, just like in the towel example, the waste is always there. You just must keep squeezing the towel.

The tool to ultimately expose this waste is Frank Gilbreth's motion study. Motion study involves analyzing what we do in the fraction of a second. As we discussed earlier, Gilbreth did his work with bricklayers. He owned a bricklaying company and was constantly searching for ways to improve the work processes and build buildings faster yet make it easier on those doing the work. Gilbreth filmed and studied the motions of his bricklayers and developed what he called Therbligs, or the 18 fundamental motions of the worker. He found many of his bricklayers were wasting time getting their own cement or having to constantly mix the cement to the right consistency.

He also noticed they were doing a lot of walking, searching, and bending over. He analyzed their work down to the right and wrong way to pick up a brick (Figure 3.11). He totally standardized how the wall should be built, brick by brick (see Figure 3.12) In addition he even figured out where they should plant their feet and how to move (see Figure 3.13). Ironically, Toyota has markings on their line to show workers where to place their feet when working on the cars. He hired people to make sure the cement was always of the right consistency. He invented and patented adjustable scaffolding to adjust the height of the bricklayers to the wall so they did not have to bend over (Figure 3.14). He had a rule his bricklayers should always be laying brick and should never have to take more than one step in any direction. This was all part of the scientific management movement of the Industrial Revolution in the early twentieth century. Gilbreth's Therbligs are listed here (see Figure 3.15) as follows:

Class 1—The essence of an operation (highest value):
- – Assemble
- – Disassemble
- – Use

Figure 3.11 The right and wrong way to pick up a brick—Gilbreth's *Motion Study* book.

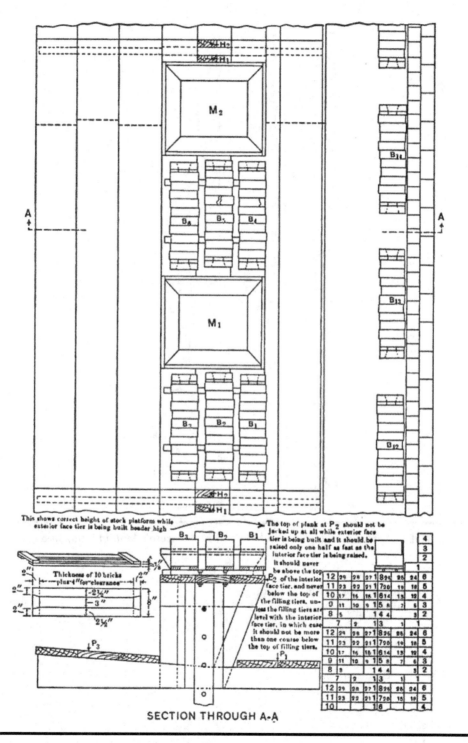

Figure 3.12 How the wall should be built from Gilbreth's *Motion Study* book.

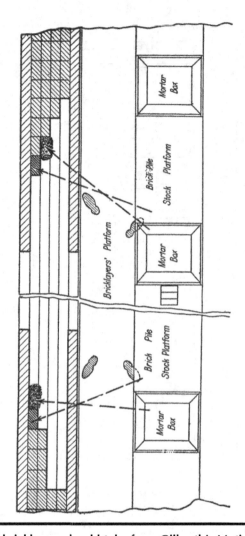

Figure 3.13 Exact steps bricklayers should take from Gilbreth's *Motion Study* book.

Class 2—Preparatory or follow-up motions:
- – Transport empty
- – Grasp
- – Transport loaded
- – Release load

Class 3—Incidental motions:
- – Search
- – Find
- – Select
- – Inspect
- – Pre-position or re-position
- – Hold
- – Prepare

Figure 3.14 **Bricklayers never have to bend over from Gilbreth's *Motion Study* book**

Class 4—These should be eliminated, if possible:
- – Think or plan
- – Rest for overcoming fatigue
- – Unavoidable delay
- – Avoidable delay

Therbligs

Class	No.	Name	Symbol	Description
1	1	Assemble	♯	Shape of combined rods
	2	Disassemble	♯	One rod removed from a combined shape
	3	Deform (use)	U	U for "use", or a cup placed upright
2	4	Transport empty (extending or retracting your hand)	∪	Shape of palm opened up
	5	Grab	∩	Shape of hand grabbing
	6	Transport	◡	Shape of object being transported with hand
	7	Release	⌒	Shape of object with hand facing down
3	8	Search	⊙	Symbol of searching eye
	9	Find	⊙	Symbol of eye having located object after search
	10	Select	→	Symbol of finger pointing at selected object
	11	Inspect	0	Shape of a lens
	12	Regrasp (reposition)	9	Symbol of regrasping object held by finger tips
	13	Hold	⋂	Shape of rod held with hand
	14*	Prepare	♉	Shape of a cuestick standing erect
4	15*	Think	♀	Shape of a thinking person with hand by head
	16*	Rest	♀	Shape of a person sitting on chair
	17	Unavoidable delay	⌒o	Shape of tripped person on ground
	18*	Avoidable delay	↳o	Shape of person lying down

Note: An asterisk indicates a therblig that does not usually arise during normal tasks.

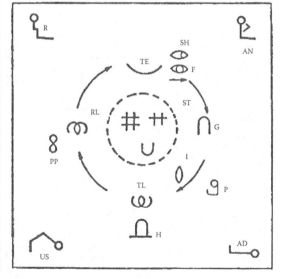

Figure 3.15 **Therbligs from Gilbreth's *Motion Study* book.**

The only VA Therbligs are assemble, used, and sometimes disassembly (i.e., re-manufacturer). Gilbreth's work done with bricklayers is documented in a book called Motion Study, circa 1911. Gilbreth also used the techniques we are describing in a hospital setting. He created an OR in his home, which was depicted in the original film *Cheaper by the Dozen*. Gilbreth videoed the tonsillectomy operations on his children and himself so he could study the motions the doctors were utilizing and work to streamline them. Our approach is to analyze operations to the second and, when we have exhausted improvement opportunities at that level, move to motion study. We have come across operations in manufacturing and healthcare where each person only has a few seconds' worth of work in their process. We have successfully used motion study techniques to reduce these times by more than 50% per operator, effectively doubling their capacity. The concept of eliminating waste in motions and transforming them into work is known as *labor density*. The formula for this is work divided by motion with a goal of 100%.[9] One thing to keep in mind is not all motion is work. Only work that is VA or necessary should be considered true work.

Motion Study Process[10] In his book, *The Handbook of Advanced Time and Motion Study*, Sylvester states:

> The end served by the time and motion study process (see Figure 3.16) is to rationalize human work. Its purposes are specifically to reduce the energy expended per unit of product, to develop skill, pace, and to make improvements. Finding better tools and equipment, adapting work to people and vice versa, development of better and simpler methods, and the modification and control of surrounding physical and organizational conditions are ways of creating or inventing improvements in human work. Thus, it can be seen what is meant by the process of time and motion study is

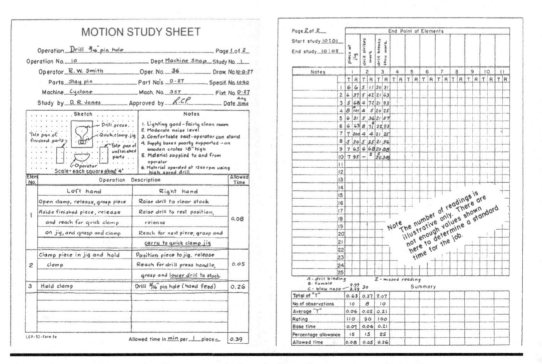

Figure 3.16   Motion study Sheet example from Gilbreth's *Motion Study* book.

a pattern of thought that rationalizes human work. Improvements and knowledge are the practical end results. The technique of preparing a time and motion study record should not be referred to as measurement. It is a technique of estimation of a quantitative value of an observed event.

Motion Study Defined[11]

Sylvester also stated:

In the simplest of terms the time and motion study process is the application of human work of five specific steps:

1. Analysis of work into subdivisions
2. Descriptive classification of each subdivision with or without measurement
3. Experimenting
4. Changing the work by elimination, rearrangement, addition, or reduction
5. Synthesis into a new described or described and measured combination

In other words, the result of the study process can be either qualitative, quantitative, or both, which result from the second step. If the second step is purely descriptive, the result will be purely qualitative, if it includes measurement, the result will be quantitative; to derive exact knowledge it must be both qualitative and quantitative.

One can see the processes are very similar though from two different authors. Inherent in each is the idea that first we analyze and measure the work, conduct experiments that we call pilots today, then question every step, referred today as the 5 Whys or 5W2H (What, When, Where, Why, Who, How, and How much). This questioning is also noted in *Motion and Time Study*, a book dating back to 1937, where Ralph Barnes outlines the following steps[12]:

■ What is done? What is the purpose of the operation? Why should it be done? What would happen if it were not done? Is every part of the activity or detail necessary?
■ Who does the work? Why does this person do it? Who could do it better? Can changes be made to permit a person with less skill and training to do the work?
■ Where is the work done? Why is it done there? Could it be done somewhere else more economically?
■ When is the work done? Why should it be done then? Would it be better to do it at some other time?
■ How is the work done? Why is it done this way?

After all phases of the work have been subjected to the above questions, consider the following possibilities for job improvement:

■ Eliminate all UW
■ Change the sequence of operations
■ Simplify the operations
■ Combine operations or elements

Today we still utilize the same questioning of work in our analysis but we have modified the four possibilities a bit. We call it the Omits process. Whenever we do a PFA, WFA, or setup analysis, we ask:

- Can we eliminate the step (whether it is unnecessary, required, or VA)?
- Can we rearrange the steps?
- Can we simplify the step?
- Can we combine the steps?

You Must Take Away All the Excuses

When doing your analysis from the videos, the team will come up with all types of great ideas on how to improve the process. However, each idea tends to be met with significant resistance from those doing the job. Since they have done this job for quite a while they think, "Who are these people to come in and change things?" It is not unusual to get every excuse in the book as to why something cannot be done. This is symptomatic of the boiled frog syndrome. You must capture, address, fix, and eliminate all the excuses, or gaining acceptance to the final Lean line or office process will be difficult if not impossible. It is best if you can make the idea, the operators', or if you can get the operators to come up with ideas that would counter the excuses. People tend to zero in on every special case problem or situation they have ever had on the line to ease their fears. Normally these special cases represent less than 3% of the time or volume or were incurred 5 or 10 years ago! The best way to address this is to say, "Let's start out by focusing on the 80% which fit the model" or "Let's pick your highest volume part and try that out first." Ask the operator to just try it on a couple pieces and see what happens; but, make sure you give it enough time to work. In many cases, the operator will make it fail, go painfully slow just to prove they were right; but, sometimes the change really is worse! We recommend, wherever possible you learn to do the job yourself. Then you can judge for yourself and explain to the operator how to make the necessary changes. Always video the changes to determine if it is better and faster and so you can also look for more improvements.

Trust but Verify

At Company X, we asked the operator to take a part from the saw and put it into the CNC (computer numerical control) machine without putting it into a large batch washer first. Instead, we asked him to wash the chips off using the hose for the coolant already in place on the saw. This would get the chips off the parts prior to putting them into the CNC machine. The operator told us there was a regulation against this. We asked about the regulation and he told us we should not mix the saw oil (coolant) with the CNC coolant because it would cause a chemical reaction which would make the CNC machine break down. We asked if he could show us the regulation. He looked all around and said no, but there used to be a sign on the machine and that he was told by the CNC guy before him about this. Once we investigated this claim with process engineering, we found the saw actually used the same coolant as the CNC machine. We let the operator know and thanked him for his concerns and asked him what other concerns he had. It's not that the operators are lying to you; they honestly believe most of the time in what they are saying. They just don't know what they don't know.

At a company in Ohio, we were working on a new layout for a welding cell. During the exercise, a welder who had been working there for over 30 years told us we could not set up the welding cell because the welding machines had to point toward magnetic north. We asked why and he looked at us like we were totally incompetent and said "magnetic arc blow of course." We asked what that was and he proceeded to tell us the welds on the parts would suffer magnetic arc blow if we did not have the weld machines facing magnetic north.

We proceeded to look up the information on the Internet and found, to our surprise, there was such a thing as magnetic arc blow, but manufacturers had compensated for it many years ago in the design of the equipment. We went back and thanked him for bringing this to our attention and told him what we discovered. We asked if he had any other concerns we needed to consider.

Lesson Learned: The objections are real. People honestly believe what they are telling you although sometimes they are just making it up. We trust what people tell us but we verify to make sure it is true. The second we hear words like I think, it should, I believe, we know we are not being told facts. If someone says there is a regulation, ask to see it. There is nothing wrong with verifying the information.

100% Efficiency with Humans

1. Looking at it from a very analytical point of view, only an operator who uses both hands and feet (Figure 3.17) at the same time is 100% efficient (a piano player or drummer is a good example). Normally, we look at use of both hands simultaneously as 100% efficient, but technically it is only 50% efficient since we are not using our feet. People who use one hand as a fixture to hold something while the other hand is working on it are only 25% efficient and are also a common reason an operation cannot be split between two persons (see Figure 3.18).

2. Watch the work being performed. Can a fixture be made to hold the part for the person and free up the other hand? Can we use their feet? In some cells in Japan, the operators use their legs as they are walking forward to hit the switch for the machine.

Figure 3.17 Foot pedal used for labeling machine.

The three don'ts of assembly are:
1. Don't choose
2. Don't search
3. Don't turn around

The three don'ts of quality are:
1. Don't accept poor quality
2. Don't make poor quality
3. Don't pass on poor quality

The 12 motion mudas breakdown the 6th muda (hidden) waste, they are specifically aimed at improving light assembly workstations:

1. Waiting with both hands free
Both hands are not used during process

2. Waiting with one hand free
Waiting time while one hand is used for the process the other hand is not used for anything

3. Pausing
Pause between movements (eg., a pause to think before moving to the next process.)

4. Excessive movement
Moving more than is necessary to do the work

5. Switching
Switch parts or tool from one hand to the other before the process begins

6. Walking
Additional walking due to distance between process area and parts/tools

7. Turning angle
Additional walking or turning due to parts location.

8. Wasted process by single operation
Nonsimultaneous operation even though it is possible to combine and operate more than two processes together

9. Rework due to wrong operation
Rework due to process problem

10. Stretching
Stretching due to higher location of parts or process

11. Bending
Bending due to low location of parts or process

12. Useless movement
Movement with no added value such as confirmation movement, repeated movement, preparation movement, etc.

Figure 3.18　Wastes to look for in operator analysis.

3. You must have the right tool for the job. Don't use general-purpose tools for jobs that require specific tools. People will do the best job with the tools you give them. Sometimes general-purpose tools are convenient but they are not the best tool for the job. Use power tools versus hand tools wherever possible.

4. When the same operator is using two separate tools consecutively, see if you can combine them.

5. Design tools that fit people's hands. Tom Peters refers to this in the video *Speed is Life*[13] where the Ingersoll Rand design team went to visit customers to see how they used their grinders. Here the workers had wrapped the tools with tape so their cold, aching, hands wouldn't slide into the grinding end of the tool. This was an example of how handles can be wrapped with cloth or tape to make them easier to grip. It should be noted with Lean Design principles, Ingersoll Rand designed their new tools with grips that replaced the tape and cloth. It all starts with not only listening to your customer by going to their workplace to see them use your tools and then take their place and use them yourself.

6. Always look for ways to make the job easier and safer.

7. Keep in mind light assembly jobs are less fatiguing. The 10-minute breaks built into most shifts were developed by Frederick Taylor. Therefore, there is no reason to build in a fatigue allowance to the job. However, medium-to-heavy assembly jobs may require more rest during the shift to increase output.

8. Use assists to hold tools, reducing the ergo burden on the operator and position the tool for easiest use to meet requirements.

Motion Study Observations for Operators[14]

Some findings from *Time and Motion Handbooks* by Gilbreth (Figure 3.19), Ralph Barnes, Gilbreth's disciple, as well as conclusions noted in a master's thesis by Ranveer Singh Rathore are listed here:

1. "Motions of the hands should be made in opposite and symmetrical directions and should be made simultaneously:
   a. When work is done with two hands simultaneously, it can be done quickest and with the least mental effort, particularly if the work is done by both hands in a similar manner, that is to say when one hand makes the same motions to the right as the other does to the left.
   b. Symmetrical movements of the arms tend to balance each other, reducing the shock and jar on the body and thus enabling the worker to perform the task with less mental and physical effort. The aforementioned principle was demonstrated by the task of bolts and washers assembly.
   c. Make two-handed motions as small as possible.
   d. Make small motions with short duration. Make sure tools and parts are as close to the operator or machine as possible including setup tools.
   e. When both hands are involved in simultaneous motions, the performance of one hand is affected by the performance of the other.
   f. The angle of best response for each hand, when involved in simultaneous motions, is not the same angle of best response when the same hand is making independent motions.

First photograph of wire models showing one man's progress of learning paths of least waste. These wires represent the paths of the left hand of a manager on a drill press—a machine which he had not touched for 25 years.

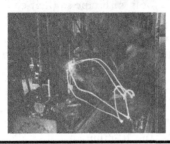

Chronocyclegraph showing two cycles of a foreman's left hand on the same machine—showing habits of *positioning* before *transporting loaded.*

Figure 3.19 Example of operator movement from Gilbreth's *Motion Study* book.

g. In single-hand motions, a hand can move much faster than when it is involved in simultaneous motions.

h. Simultaneous and symmetrical motions of hands are faster and more accurate than the simultaneous and asymmetrical motions in the horizontal plane.

i. For light assembly it is better to move hands and forearms versus upper arms and shoulders.

2. Avoid abrupt changes in the direction of motion:

a. As the distance of movement increases, the number of errors also increases.

b. The aforementioned condition of best response is the same for both 9 and 16 in. movements. When both the hands are involved in simultaneous motions, the speed and accuracy of the left hand is better than that of the right hand, whereas in single-hand motions, the speed and accuracy of the right hand is better than that of the left hand.

c. Force is required to change the direction of motion of an object. Physiologically, this means a lot of work for muscles. Consequently, such actions and motion result in fatigue and must therefore be avoided.

3. Use free, unconstrained motion.

4. Direction and distance of movement do have a significant effect on the speed and accuracy of single-hand motions and two-hand simultaneous motions:

a. Use free, unconstrained motion which is faster, easier, and more accurate. Motion that requires no particular precautions and can be performed without restraint is the best. Work to remove motions such as search, find and inspect. These can be improved by the introduction of guides, stoppers and jigs.

5. Avoid Unnatural Postures and Motions which Raise and Lower the Body's Center of Gravity:

a. Working in an unnatural posture (twisting your body) is tiring and dangerous and should be avoided.

b. Avoid raising and lowering the body's center of gravity, which saves moving the weight of your body.

c. It is best to adjust the height of materials to match the waste height of operators versus having to lift from the floor.

6. The hands are the most convenient and useful part of the body. Keep them free when possible.
7. In general, don't use your hands to perform work which could be done with your feet."

Spaghetti Diagram

A spaghetti diagram (see Figure 3.20) is different from a point-to-point diagram. The point-to-point diagram follows the product from point to point through the process, where the spaghetti diagram follows the operator or staff person doing the work. It is generally performed by following the operator for one complete cycle of their work. This can be done by following the operator on the floor, or in the office or by mapping it off the video.

It is constructed by hand drawing a map of the area or taking an existing CAD layout of the area and then putting in a line for each step the operator takes, even if they backtrack or do the same walk pattern over and over, and calculating their overall distance traveled. It can be a very telling pictorial. Ideally when the new cell is implemented the operator should only travel within the path of their standard work on the line.

In batch and many so-called Lean environments, you will find the operator still has to leave the line to get this or that. Even if you told them you were going to do this exercise and video them up front, we still find they miss or forget things, or someone borrowed it and they didn't realize it. Make sure you capture all of these trips in your drawing. The diagram provides a good visual of the waste operators encounter while trying to do a good job performing their work.

Exercise: Draw a spaghetti diagram

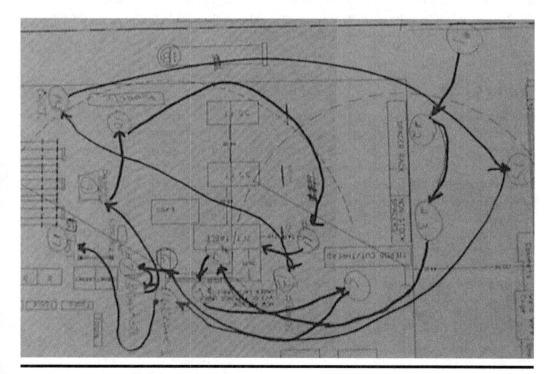

Figure 3.20 Spaghetti diagram—Following the operator.

Pick an operator and ask them to walk step by step through what they do and construct a spaghetti diagram. Now compare it to that of another operator that does the same thing on the same or different shift. Is it the same walk pattern for each operator?

Did you remember to:

- Physically go to the floor and follow the operator? You fail if you bring the operator into a room or pull them aside to just do it on a whiteboard or notepad.
- Capture all the steps, including searching or rework steps?
- Calculate the total travel distance?

After completing the spaghetti diagram:

- Is it one smooth continuous flow?
- Are there any wasted steps?
- Did the operator have everything they needed, where and when they needed it?
- Is the operator building or working on one piece at a time?
- Is there excess inventory or IT on the line?

Delineating Key Data Elements

Calculating the TLT of a process will give you a picture of how much labor and, ultimately, how many operators or staff are needed to complete one piece of whatever is being processed. The operator analysis should yield a 20%–40% productivity improvement to your overall process when compared to a strictly batch environment. In addition to capturing the labor time, the distance traveled is also captured as a baseline and future state.

World Class

Our goal with Lean and the operator is to consistently measure and strive toward world-class benchmarks. While these may seemingly be unobtainable, they provide a guard against complacency and the impetus to drive toward continually improving the process. Our goal should always be to reduce the number of operators in the process and yet continually develop them to move them to other positions. We must work to always use people wisely and safely throughout the company. We should always be working to reduce both direct and indirect labor and convert staff jobs to line jobs wherever possible and then stop distinguishing direct from indirect. (Anyone reading this book is essentially an operator, from the CEO to the person on the shop floor and everyone in between.) The indirect and direct classification of labor transition to the total labor is necessary to support the value stream. When we look at world-class percentages, we must initially distinguish between the environments in which operators work.

Operators essentially work in four environments:

1. Assembly
2. Machining/automation
3. Transactional
4. Some combination of assembly, machine, and/or transactional

In assembly operations world class should be:

- 80% VA
- 20% RW
- 0% idle

In machining/automation:

- 0% VA (machine adds the value)
- 100% RW
- 0% idle

Transactional (note most transactional processes are not VA):

- 0% VA
- 100% RW
- 0% idle

For transactional processes that are perceived to be VA, that is, service industries, banking (making a withdrawal or deposit), and insurance (cutting the check, mailing the check or electronic deposit):

- 80% VA
- 20% RW
- 0% idle

Network of Process versus Operations Defined[15]

We have attempted to expand Dr. Shingo's separation among product, operator, and changeover and take it to the next level. To our knowledge, no one has broken down these processes into the pieces of Lean thinking each one provides. We studied this for literally years before it dawned on us that each analysis tool (product vs. operator's axis plus changeover) provides different answers for Lean improvement. We would like to propose that analyzing just the operator axis will provide the following pieces of the Lean implementation:

- TLT for one piece or small lot
- Percent value added for the operator
- Percent required work for the operator
- Percent idle time for the operator
- Standard work for the supervisor
- Number of operators required
- Capacity planning when coupled with PFA analysis
- Ergonomics/safety/fatigue opportunities
- Work standards
- Motion study
- Standard WIP quantity

- Ten cycle analysis
- Line Balancing
- Operator work zones
- Scheduling flexibility/# shifts and overtime required
- Operator walk patterns
- Operator buy-in and morale
- SWIP for the operators
- Total inventory required when coupled with PFA
- Paperwork required and how the paperwork travels in the cell
- Level loading
- Proper tool and material presentation
- Baton zones (bumping)
- Job breakdown—standard work for the operator
- Training videos
- Key points and reasons for key points for each step
- Operator cycle times for each step in the process
- Percent of overhead versus direct labor
- Mistake proofing opportunities
- Opportunities to reduce variation

Chapter Questions

1. What is a WFA?
2. Why is it important to separate the operator from the product?
3. Why is it important to separate an operator from a machine?
4. What are the first things we look for in an operator analysis?
5. Why do we analyze to the second?
6. What role does ergonomics play with Lean? Are they opposed to Lean principles?
7. What is the importance of motion study?
8. How is motion study different from time study?
9. How do you calculate TLT? Why is it important? What else can you calculate from TLT?
10. What is a spaghetti diagram? How does it differ from a point-to-point diagram?
11. What does ERSC stand for? Why is it important?
12. What role does WFA play with standard work?
13. What makes a step value added for the operator?
14. What are the three types of NVA work?
15. What are the two things an operator can do?
16. What environments do operators work in?
17. Should an operator ever be idle?
18. What is a world-class goal for the operator? Should be quantified in each environment.
19. Why do we separate out material handling? What is the test for material handling?
20. When can we eliminate inspection?
21. Why should we work to eliminate inspection?
22. What is a spaghetti diagram, how is it created, and why do we create one?
23. What pieces of Lean do we obtain from a work flow analysis?
24. What did you learn from this chapter?

Discussion Question: Job Easiness Index

We asked our contributing authors the following question: We would like to create an equation for job easiness and put it in the book. Let's call it the job easiness index (JEI). Any ideas? James Bond states the following:

> With respect to JEI (Job Easiness Index) Considerations for measurement could include things that are difficult to do, see, hear, learn, train, remember, reach, lift, teach, process, overburden whether it be physical, mental or unreasonableness, excessive workload.

Measurable components of this index could include the following:

- Tracking of injuries before and after changes are made—safety always first
- Before and after steps required to perform process steps—(use of spaghetti diagram)
- Reduction of ergonomic burden resulting from reorganization of process including layout, repositioning of tools to reduce or eliminating reaching, lifting etc., excessive or repetitive use of tools, (there are programs to evaluate ergo burden) based on cycle time balance analysis—too much work allocated to process—need to rebalance process(es)
- Comparison of quality indicators before and after changes
- Attendance improvement after changes due to increased job satisfaction

Rhiddian Roach states the following:

> I'm not sure what situations you are looking to measure for Job Easiness but if it's to determine the success of an implementation (based on the fact that making jobs easier are a sign of success) then something around the rate at which operators hit standard times post implementation might work?

> What about something simple like the number of operators hitting standard divided by the total number of operators? This could then be measured at different time points after implementation.

The equation would look like the following:

> For Time T (Operators hitting std/Total number of operators) x 10 where T is the time point of the measurement. This would change over time as T2, T3, T4, etc., are introduced. As things improve, the index would get bigger, larger numbers being better.

Vincent Cao states the following:

> For the JEI does the fact that the operators hit the standard mean that it was really easier for them? I guess it comes down to how one defines the word easy. Things to consider might be as follows:

- Even though the goal is easy, there should be a safety aspect.
- Less steps should make it easier—so the number of steps should be part of it.
- I think the main one is the ergonomic component.
- There should be a DFA component as well.

- Quality ties into the mistake proofing index.
- Attendance should be a factor but it can be influenced by outside factors.
- What about the desire to maybe cross train on that job?

To the reader … What do you think?

Notes

1. Copyright: Kevin Harris 1995 (may be freely distributed with this acknowledgment).
2. *Business @ the Speed of Thought*, 1999, Warner Books.
3. *Productivity through Motion Study* by Kato, ©1983 and *Motion Study* by Gilbreth, ©1911.
4. While all of these steps are in IE books, we first learned of this breakdown from Mark Jamrog, SMC Group.
5. Contributed by Christy Lotz, CPE, Managing Consultant, Humantech, Inc., 734.663.3330 × 123, www.humantech.com.
6. ©Humantech Inc., Ann Arbor, MI, www.humantech.com, Humantech forms cannot be copied without written consent of Humantech Inc. No information can be modified, sold, or distributed without a written license. Please contact Humantech for questions regarding licenses (734) 663–6707.
7. Case study furnished in personal correspondence with Michael Gassler, LEAN/QA Manager, Creative Pultrusions, Inc., Alum Bank, PA.
8. Shigeo Shingo, *Japan Management Association Non Stock Production: The Shingo System for Continuous Improvement, 1987*, New York, Productivity Press, 1988.
9. Japanese Management Association, *Kanban Just-in-Time*, New York, Productivity Press, 1986.
10. *The Handbook of Advanced Time-Motion Study*, Sylvester, Magazines of Industry, ©1950, pp. 32–33.
11. *The Handbook of Advanced Time-Motion Study*, Sylvester, Magazines of Industry, ©1950, pp. 34–35.
12. *Motion and Time Study*, Ralph Barnes, 4th edn., p. 155, Wiley & Sons, ©1937, 1940, 1949, 1958, pp. 31, 32.
13. Tom Peters, Speed is Life.
14. Gilbreth, F.B., *Motion Study*, New York, D. Van Nostrand Company, 1911; Barnes, R.M., *Motion and Time Study*, 5th edn., New York, Wiley & Sons, 1964; Barnes, R.M. and Mundel, M.E., *A Study of Simultaneous and Symmetrical Hand Motions*, University of Iowa, Studies in Engineering, Bul. 17, 1939. Study of effect of angle and distance on the speed and accuracy of single hand and two hand Simultaneous motions in the horizontal plane By Ranveer Singh Rathore B.Sc. (engg.) Electrical, Bihar University, India, 1959, A Master's thesis.
15. Influenced by the same in Leveraging Lean in Healthcare, Protzman, Mayzell, Kerpchar, Productivity Press, 2011.

Additional Readings

Allen, C.R. 1919. The Instructor, the Man and the Job. Philadelphia: Lippincott Company,
Barnes, R.M. 1937. Motion and Time Study. New York, NY: John Wiley & Sons.
McDermott. 2000 Employee Driven Quality. *Resource Eng Journal*.
Gilbreth, F.B. 1911. Motion Study. Chico, CA: Hive Publishing.
Kato, K. 1983. Productivity through Motion Study. Productivity Press.
5S for Operators. 1996. Productivity Press, Inc.
Just in Time for Operators. 1998. Productivity Press, Inc.
Sylvester. 1950a. Handbook of Advanced Motion Study. Magazines of Industry.
Sylvester. 1950b. The Handbook of Advanced Time and Motion Study. Magazines of Industry.

Chapter 4

BASICS Assess: Setup Reduction (SMED) Analysis

The quickest way to change a tool is not to change it at all!

Shigeo Shingo[1]

The concept of setup reduction goes back to at least 1911, when Frank Gilbreth provided an example of setup reduction: "Two horse carts with horses changed from the empty to the full carts will require fewer and cheaper motions than any other methods of transportation"[2] (see Figure 4.1) This method is used today with tractor trailers. The focus of this chapter is on reducing setup times which is our third analysis tool in the BASICS® Model (see Figure 4.2).

Setup Story from P&G[3]

Word came down the line in 1953 that the company was about to introduce a second line of granule detergent called Daz. Daz would offer the housewife benefits that today could be taken for granted. The product would not be white like Tide and Oxydol but would be blue. This resulted in the need to switch over from white to blue color detergent. The horrors of having to do a changeover were obvious. Kenneth Hopper found the company determined and prepared to have his engineering staff people work with the operating staff cleaning out the equipment every few weeks.

The first changeover from Tide to Daz took days as did the changeover back from colored Daz to Tide. Flanged ducting that carried dried powder in a current of air had to be removed, cleaned by brush, by hand, and sometimes chiseled, and replaced. Then something remarkable happened. Suggestions came, largely from the hourly staff, as to how the changeover could be improved thus reducing time. Additional washing nozzles were attached to the air handling system. Spare lengths of ducting were made and substituted during the changeover. Ducting removed could be cleaned while the plant was running (external setup). Other ducting could be kept with white or blue powder in it until that color was again needed. The changeover time dropped from days to

DOI: 10.4324/9781003185789-4

Figures 4.1 Quick changeover on horse carts.

hours. The factory was, of course, working toward single-minute exchange of dies (SMEDs) ... but before the term was invented.

SMED Steps

1. Video.
2. Analyze and code the setup steps.
3. Use the omits process (eliminating, rearranging, simplifying, and combining [ERSC]).
4. Reorder the steps.
5. Create standard work.
6. Determine the machine or area's capacity.

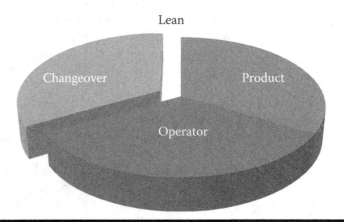

Figure 4.2 Three things we analyze—Changeover.

Changeover analysis is the third assessment tool, and it is generally performed in that order, that is, after the product and operator analysis. However, in machine shops, it may be the first tool we perform, as this is normally our biggest bottleneck and is initially prohibiting us from even entertaining implementing one-piece or small lot flow.

For now, we are going to define changeover as that encountered in the machine shop (but we will expand and expound on this later in the chapter). In machining, we find we have to change-over machines from producing one part to another. This can involve a simple quick programing change where all the tools are the same and the part is, maybe, of the same shape but different size. In other cases, it can involve a massive die changeover or several die changeovers on a progressive press line. So, our definition for changeover is going to be:

From the removal of the last good piece to the completion of the first good piece of the next lot.

This is important and is a strict definition to drive the most improvement. This means once you remove the last good piece; if there is paperwork you must do, or work order moves in the enterprise requirement planning (ERP) it all counts as changeover time! The premise behind setup reduction is embodied in the thought process required to keep the machine or machining cell producing as much as possible, assuming the demand exists to support this condition. Decreasing setup times will increase asset utilization and production capacity.

The analogy we use with Lean to improve turnover times is that of a pit stop (see Figure 4.3) How long does a NASCAR' pit stop take? Here is some history regarding NASCAR pit stops.

NASCAR was born in 1947. The original pit stops took 15 minutes. The driver would exit the car and enjoy a smoke and a cold drink while waiting for his car to be serviced. Imagine that today! In the late 1950s, the Wood Brothers (synonymous as one of the NASCAR elite families)

Figure 4.3   Changeover in a NASCAR race.

discovered if they could shorten the time in the pit, it would directly correlate to better finishing positions on the track. They discovered a better balanced cross-handled lug wrench would spin the lug nuts off and on faster. With this, there was a lot of time, research, and investment made into refining the lug wrenches. They made incremental improvements in overall time and considered it value added. The early 1960s was the advent of the pneumatic impact wrench. This dropped the pit times down another 25 seconds and was a quantum leap in the sport and a success factor for many competitive race teams. The sport embraced making a study of the pit stop and working diligently to refine/reduce pit stop times. Next, the jack, which once took three to four pumps to elevate the car, was retooled, and today's jack now does it in one pump while lowering the car in a split second through refined hydraulic release valves. To enhance the tire change, the lug nuts are glued to the tire's rim, thus eliminating the need to handle the nuts individually.

Ultimately, race teams attempted to use two jacks on a pit stop by servicing one side of the car, and immediately after lowering the completed side, hoisting the opposite side. NASCAR officials baulked at this and forced the teams to only use one jack. The fuel delivery system was once capable of ejecting excess fuel (overflow), during the fueling portion of the stop. This mandated the use of the gas catch can man. Ultimately, the fuel delivery systems were not only improved to deliver the fuel at a very high volume but were also refined in such a manner as to eliminate the overflow event. This led to eliminating the necessity of this position which is now used to remove the tear offs on the windshield and clean the rubber marbles which collect in the grill and reduce air flow to the engine. Teams continue to monitor and improve performance through standard work and routine exercises directed at measuring (filming) the stops from overhead and studying them to better align the choreography necessary to yield fast and predictable pit stops.[4]

The fastest stop recorded for four wheels was 12.4[5] seconds and only came through the efforts of the pursuit of perfection and applying the teachings of Dr. Shingo (SMED and total productive maintenance [TPM]). Pit stop cells are 5S'd to incredibly high standards with everything needed, identified, and available with backup within a millisecond's exchange.

This has always been a very effective way of demonstrating the SMED process and creating understanding with all audiences, as everyone can seemingly relate to it and quickly understand the process. On the video called *Winner's Circle,*[6] it takes about 14.7 seconds for the NASCAR Pit. It is important to note that 14.7 seconds is the clock time, not the labor time. For readers not familiar with NASCAR and racing pit stops, the local "10-minute oil change" vendor offers another good example of SMED and TPM principles. All the tools and materials are readily available, the customer never leaves their car, and an overall maintenance of the car is reviewed with a checklist. This entire preventive maintenance process is completed within minutes.

Clock Time

In Lean changeovers, we make a distinction between *clock time* and *labor time.* Clock time is the time it takes for the changeover while labor time is the total amount of labor involved in the changeover. In the NASCAR pit stop, the clock time is 14.7 seconds.

Labor Time

To calculate the total setup labor time, we need to look at how many operators are involved before, during, and after the setup. If there are seven people doing the changeover, we would calculate the labor time by multiplying seven times the 14.7 seconds clock time which equals 109.3 seconds, but this does not include what steps were done to prepare for the pit stop changeover or what work was done once the car was back on the track.

Successful Setup Characteristics

Could the NASCAR pit stop have been done with one person? The answer is yes, but how long would it take? The answer is at least 109.3 seconds, but probably longer due to travel distance and extra movements which would be required by just one person. Since races are typically won by fractions of a second, with one person doing the changeover we would lose the race.

What are just a few of the characteristics that make the pit stop concept successful?

- Everyone knows their job.
- They are dedicated to specific tasks.
- Multiple operators (pit crew).
- Doing job steps in parallel.
- Standard work for each person.
- Significant practice and training.
- 5S—that is, everything in its place prior to, during, and after the changeover.
- A constant dissatisfaction with the current changeover time until it is zero!

All these factors contribute to a successful changeover reduction formula. How many of these do you have in your setup?

Internal Time

Another concept we use is internal time versus external time. In the pit stop example, anything done while the car is in the pit is considered *internal time*. Examples would be changing the tires or refueling. In our machining operations, this translates into anything that can only be done when the machine is stopped.

External Time

Back to our pit stop example …. Anything we can do while the race car is going around the track is considered *external* time. For example, we can get the tires ready and properly located in the pit area ahead of time. For our machine, this means gathering all the tools ahead of time, dies are preset, so we basically never have to leave the machine while setting it up.

Missed My Connection—If Only He Had Used External Time!

We were waiting for a flight that had suddenly been delayed due to a maintenance problem. We decided to turn a frustrating event into an opportunity as we could see the maintenance tech working on the airplane underneath the cockpit. (It was a small jet aircraft.) The gate attendant informed us they had discovered the problem, and we had to wait for a part. After 20 minutes, the part arrived. Keep in mind right now we are all on internal time because the plane is down. The part finally arrives via a cart, and the technician removes the old part and installs the new one. Now at this point, we just need the paperwork signed off and we can board. However, instead of signing off the paperwork, the technician takes the old part back to the cart. Then he gets the box the new part came in and puts the old part in it. Ok, now let us get the paperwork signed off ... we all have connections we have to make .... He then goes into the plane to make sure the repairs worked and tests the system. We know they worked, because 5 minutes later, he comes out and buttons up the cover. Now we can get the paperwork signed off. But no, now he returns to the cart and searches the cart for some tape and then realizes he put the part in over top of the shipping label. He removes the part from the box and takes out the shipping label, puts the part back, and goes back to searching for the tape. He finds the tape and tapes up the box and puts on the return label. Ok, now let us get the paperwork signed off ... not quite. Now he takes the box over to some other vehicle. Then he returns to the cart and gets the paperwork. He takes the paperwork into the plane and gets it signed off. Yea! We could have boarded 10–15 minutes earlier, and many of us missed our connections! If only he could have packaged up the return part on external time; AFTER, he signed off the paperwork.

Internal Time and Clock Time

The 14.7 seconds time for the pit stop is only a measure of the internal time and does not include the time driving to or from the pit stop area on pit row. It does not include any external time. Why do we focus on internal time? Because this is the amount of time the machine, person, or asset is not available for use; that is, the car is not racing around the track, or the machine is down. This means our SMED or setup in less than 10 minutes really refers only to the internal time.

Four Components of Setup

The next thing needed for setup analysis is to break down each step into its component part or category. Dr. Shingo describes this in his book *A Revolution in Manufacturing: the SMED System.*[7] The four components and codes we utilize for setup reduction are the following:

1. Preparation (P) and organization:
   Preparation and organization are gathering everything necessary to minimize the internal setup time prior to starting the setup. This means all tools, dies, jigs, fixtures, measuring equipment, power and air utilities, resources, etc. are ready and in their optimum location prior to the setup. This also means we do the computer entry and other inspections while the machine is running.
2. Mounting (M) and removing:
   This code refers to mounting and removing tools, dies, jigs, fixtures, etc., necessary to run the next part.
3. Calibration (C), centering dimensioning, aligning, measurement, and testing:
   This item normally refers to setting the X-, Y-, and Z-axis points in the program. There are many books that discuss how to eliminate these steps. For example, dies can be put on sub-plates, so the Z-axis stays constant. V grooves can be setup so the X- and Y-axis for the die location are constant. Many machines will perform their own offsets, but this only speeds up and automates the waste.
4. Trial (T) runs and adjustments:
   This item normally results from having to run a first-piece inspection prior to running the parts. First-piece inspections (*first offs*) can be eliminated with technology that exists today.

SMED Process Steps

While Dr. Shingo did not originate the setup reduction concept and Toyota was doing SMED before Dr. Shingo worked with them, Dr. Shingo was able to crystallize and structure the SMED process, which took him 19 years; from 1950 to 1969. The acronym we utilize for Dr. Shingo's setup methodology is "ICE":

1. **I**dentify all steps as to whether they are performed on internal or external time.
   When first conducting setups almost all steps are not started until the machine is stopped.
2. **C**onvert as many steps as possible from internal to external.
   This is a key step in the process. Every step must be questioned and five why'd if necessary to try to convert it to external time. Many of these steps can be done while the machine is still running. This is how we get well over 50% reductions in clock time right away.
3. **E**liminate, rearrange, simplify, or combine all remaining steps, the OMITS process.
   This is our consistent ERSC approach to improving every process we analyze. Every step should be examined regardless of whether it is done on internal or external time.

Note: Keep in mind the setup step is not considered value added because we are not producing the product during the setup. So, all setup time is considered non-value-added time.

Types of Changeover or Setup Improvement

There are six generally accepted types of setup improvement:

1. SMED.
2. One-touch exchange of dies (OTED).
3. No-touch exchange of dies (NTED).
4. Zero setup.
5. One-shot (cycle) exchange of dies (OSED or OCED).
6. Eliminate the changeover completely.

SMED

SMED stands for single-minute exchange of dies. This means the internal setup time takes 9 minutes 59 seconds or one can say less than 10 minutes. This is the first improvement most companies go after (Figure 4.4).

9:59 or less	10:00
Single minute	Double minute

Figure 4.4   Single minute exchange of dies.

Zero Setup	Single Minute	Double Minute
3 minutes or less	9:59 or less	10:00 or more

Figure 4.5   Zero setup.

OTED

OTED stands for one-touch exchange of dies. The implication here is we can changeover in less than 100 seconds, or we can changeover multiple machines with the touch of one button.

NTED

NTED stands for no-touch exchange of dies. The process is totally automated with no human intervention.

Zero Minute Setup

Zero setup is generally accepted to mean setups requiring 3 minutes or less. It should be equal to setups that take less than 1 minute (Figure 4.5).

OSED/OCED

OSED stands for one-shot (cycle) exchange of dies. This means the entire cell is changed over within one cycle time *externally* (Zero internal setup time) by following the operator from machine to machine or assembly operation to assembly operation and changing the line over prior to the operator returning to the first machine or assembly operation. In some industries, this may take a setup team, a setup person or lead person to accomplish this task.

For example, as the operator finishes at machine 1 and moves to machine 2 a setup person comes in and changes over machine 1. When the operator moves to machine 3 the setup person starts to changeover machine 2, etc. This means when the operator completes their cycle and returns to machine 1, they are now producing the first piece of the next order in the cell. This means the entire setup time must be less than the total labor time (with one person) or cycle time (with more than one person) to changeover the equipment. This results in basically zero setup as all the time is external to the cell operation.

Eliminate the Setup

Every setup reduction team and machine operator should not lose sight of the goal; to eliminate a setup completely. We have successfully accomplished this many times. Sometimes it takes some rather creative out of the box thinking.

The Press Operator's Idea Story

At Company X, replacing each of these dies (Figure 4.6) used to take several hours, resulting in large batches run on the press. Based on the idea of one of the press operators we were able to mount both dies in the press and still run each part. This cut the setup time to less than 1 minute.

Figure 4.6   How to eliminate a setup - combined dies in the press.

What We Normally Find When Doing a Setup Reduction

We normally find large batch sizes in most companies that are driven by long setup times. This results in issues with scheduling equipment, scheduling labor, material availability, and floorspace needed to store all the parts batched up on the machine. In addition, accounting will want inventories of all the work in process and someone must provide status updates each day.

When filming the setup, where there are multiple presses or machines within a machine, many times the operators will batch each step of the setup. We have witnessed rotary-type presses in various industries where this was the case. For instance, the operators would first blow off any metal, dust, plastic, or fiberglass on each rotary section and disassemble the press in stages, requiring multiple turns of the press, each turn taking up a significant amount of internal time. The goal should be to utilize one-piece flow and one rotary turn of the press during the setup, where the entire section of the press is changed over prior to going to the next section. This also means presentation and organization of dies and tools must be well thought out, choreographed, and standardized.

Why Reduce Setup/Changeover Times?

We find the clock time (Figure 4.7) of almost every setup can be reduced by 50% or more the first time we analyze it and then implement improvements. By reducing setup times, we gain the ability to increase capacity in the operation and where the demand exists, we gain the ability to produce multiple products in less time or what we call mixed model cells or lines. The longer the setup times the larger the batch we want to run. For example, if your changeover is 24 hours, we are going to want to run everything for the next week or maybe even next month that is scheduled on the books today. If we have five models (let's call them models A, B, C, D, and E) and run each model for 1 week then it takes a 5-week cycle to produce a set of parts for each customer. This means even if the customer only wants one model they must wait until the week you run that model to get those parts. If they want a model A and you just changed over from Model A to Model B and all your Model A's are allocated to other customers, then they are going to have to wait 5 weeks. Normally we run the lot whether we need them or not and we produce some extra just in case someone might order more or to have some on hand until you can run that model again (see Tables 4.1 and 4.2). This practice creates inventory, both finished goods and work in process (WIP), an inherent evil of batching.

Figure 4.7 Internal time setup clock with improvement board.

"After All, the Extra Parts We Run Are Free" ... Aren't They?

Each model run in the example above is going to encompass at least 5 weeks of demand and could be much more, meaning you are violating the number one waste which is overproducing. In this environment and all ERP environments, we were taught to use the economic order quantity (EOQ) model to determine how many parts to run for each lot (see Figure 4.8).

Table 4.1 Relationship between Setup Time and Lot Size—I

Setup Time	Lot Size	Principal Operation Time per Item	Operation Time	Ratio (%)	Ratio (%)
4 hour	100	1 minute	$1 \text{ minute} + \dfrac{4 \times 60}{100} = 3.4 \text{ minute}$	100	
4 hour	1,000	1 minute	$1 \text{ minute} + \dfrac{4 \times 60}{1,000} = 1.24 \text{ minute}$	36	100
4 hour	10,000	1 minute	$1 \text{ minute} + \dfrac{4 \times 60}{10,000} = 1.024 \text{ minute}$	30	83

Source: Shingo, TPS from an Industrial Engineering Point of View, p. 35.

Table 4.2 Relationship between Setup Time and Lot Size—II

Setup Time	Lot Size	Principal Operation Time per Item	Operation Time	Ratio (%)	Ratio (%)
8 hour	100	1 minute	$1 \text{ minute} + \dfrac{8 \times 60}{100} = 5.8 \text{ minute}$	100	
8 hour	1,000	1 minute	$1 \text{ minute} + \dfrac{8 \times 60}{1,000} = 1.48 \text{ minute}$	26	100
8 hour	10,000	1 minute	$1 \text{ minute} + \dfrac{8 \times 60}{10,000} = 1.048 \text{ minute}$	18	71

Source: Shingo, TPS from an Industrial Engineering Point of View, p. 35.

Most think since we are spending all this time and money to setup the machine, any extra parts are essentially produced for *free*. If a customer wants a piece right away and is conditioned to the fact that these are long lead time parts, and you just happen to have one in stock you can charge that customer a premium to get them the part right away. The thinking is the customer is happy to get the part and the supplier is making more money on their overproduced parts. However, while this may occur some of the time, what normally happens is we end up with the following:

- A rather large stockroom of many types of parts that have been sitting for months or years, sometimes decades!
- There was still labor, run time on the machine (capacity), wear and tear on the machine, and material required to produce those parts and these costs are lost in the parts until you can sell them.
- Customers may be happy to get the part but no matter how happy they are the buyer will always remember you over-charged them for those parts. Buyers have very long-term memories for these types of things.
- Many times, there is an engineering change which now makes all those free parts obsolete. This means they must be scrapped and written off, which lowers your profit for the month.
- We spend labor to physically inventory the parts and make sure the counts reconcile.
- Some parts get damaged or lost when other parts are mixed in with them. Pretty soon it becomes easier to run more than to try to find the ones we ran previously.

So, are they really *free* parts? This is a major mindset paradigm change we must get over to start to reduce setup times.

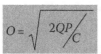

$$O = \sqrt{2QP \big/ C}$$

O = Order size units (lot)
Q = Monthly estimated demand
P = Setup costs to change a production run
C = Cost to carry per dollar of one unit in stock for one year

Figure 4.8 Economic order quantity (EOQ) formula.

What If We Can Reduce the Setup Time?

Let's say we can decrease our setup times in the previous example to 2 hours to run each model more often. The first argument we get is we are going to have to change the machine over more frequently. So, yes, we have more setups; but the setup time for all five models is now reduced from 5 days to 10 hours. We still can't run each model every day assuming we are running one shift but now maybe we can run each model every couple of days. What does this do for us?

■ Now our customers only must wait a couple of weeks for parts if they need a set of parts or place an order too late.
■ We reduced the inventory.
■ We freed up space required to store that inventory.
■ We saved on setup labor time.
■ We increase the capacity of the machine.

But we are still going to be driven by the economic order quantity (EOQ) formula mentioned earlier. Now let's say we can reduce the setup time to 10 minutes and want to run each model even more frequently. What does that do for us? Yes, again, we have even more setups but the setups for five models only consume 50 minutes of the whole day versus what used to take 5 days. Now there is time during the day to run each of the five models every day. What does this do for our customers?

■ Now they don't have to keep any inventory or wait days to receive their parts.
■ We can put a *Kanban* of parts in our customer's facility and replace it every day or two. Now where are they going to go for parts if your competitors lead times are longer than yours? Can you get a higher price if you manage their inventory for them, a value-added service?
■ You become much easier to do business with.
■ You freed up more space and eliminated the stockroom which can be used for more manufacturing.
■ You have increased machine utilization and capacity for more business and customers.
■ The overall cost of your parts has decreased and your profit increased.
■ No excess inventory to count.
■ No need for production control to keep track of the inventory since it no longer exists or a fraction of it now exists.
■ When the customer says they need to phase in an engineering change you tell them there is no impact or cost to them for the change.
■ You can now offer customers a price break on their product(s).
■ You've demonstrated the ability to meet customers' changing needs.

In this environment who will be your customer's supplier of choice? To make this scenario a reality and reduce our setup times we need to explore, understand, and implement the following concepts.

Setup Video Improvement Process

The process we use for changeover reduction is to video the changeover just like we do for the product and operator analysis. This means we need a video camera to follow every person involved during the changeover. Once we have the video, we break down each step from the video, for each person, preferably with the person we filmed, a supervisor, and someone who knows nothing about the process (who can ask why).

We initially break the analysis into what we call the *as is* or current condition. Each step is divided into either internal or external and coded as one of the four categories we outlined earlier (PMCT). We also note distances traveled where appropriate. We follow the process listed here:

1. Record baseline setup times at the equipment.
2. Video each operator(s) during the entire setup process. This may require multiple video cameras. Don't turn off the camera until you get the first good piece no matter what the operator tells you!
3. Identify steps as to whether they are internal or external and what type of setup step (PMCT) and set stretch reduction goals for both.
4. Question every internal operation and try to convert internal work to external work. Minimize or reduce to one the operator or mechanic trips around machines.
5. Brainstorm ideas to eliminate, rearrange, simplify, or combine steps and prioritize suggestions.
6. Consider minimizing internal time using parallel steps internally.
7. Create the new standard process and anticipated internal and external clock and labor times.
8. Communicate the new process to all team members.
9. Practice, practice, practice.
10. Video the new process and compare it to the standard work developed and results expected.
11. If successful, document a new process from video to use for future training sessions.
12. Analyze tape and continue to improve.
13. Keep a flip chart nearby during the new setup experiment with a large count digital clock to capture new ideas.
14. See if ideas are transferable to any other setups.

Joe's Standard Work Story

The following example shows a honing operation setup (Figure 4.9) we performed at Ancon Gear, located in Long Island, New York. The true test for any standard work is to see if someone not familiar with the equipment can follow the standard work and conduct the setup. This test came to reality one day back in 1995 when Joe, who normally performed the honer setup, was out one day and the honer had to be changed over. The standard work Joe created was located at the honer and one of the machinists was able to follow the standard work and successfully changeover the machine. With Excel, it is easy to insert pictures which can be referred to at each step.

Restaurant Setup Reduction Analysis

Example:

Let's use a restaurant changeover as an example. We will define the setup as from when the previous diners leave the table until the next diners are completely seated at the table. So, our input boundary would be first seating of diners leave the table at 6:00 pm.

From 6:00 to 6:10 the table is sitting idle. This means the table is unavailable (dirty) or what we call internal downtime for 10 minutes. There are many reasons the table may be idle. It could be the bus person is busy or is on a smoke break, but the fact remains the table is not available to us.

Operation								
Step	Omit	Description	Type Code	As Is (I/E)	To Be (I/E)	Est	Each	
Total cumulative times:						372	372	
1		Remove back cover (see Figure A)	m	I		6	6	
2		Turned stroker knob to unlatched position	m	i		2	2	
3		Pull stroker arm all the way forward	m	i		2	2	
4		Grab 6 mm wrench	m	i		2	2	
5		Loosen mandril bolt	m	i		5	5	
6		Remove mandril by turning 90 degrees and pulling out and place on rack (see Figure B)	m	i		4	4	
7		Grab the next mandril	m	i		4	4	
8		Measure the stone length	m	i	e	3	3	
9		Pull the rear tab out of the mandril	m	i	e	2	2	
10		Insert the mandril at 3:00 horizontal position and crank clockwise to 6:00 so it locks in (see Figure C)	m	i		5	5	
11		Tighten 6 mm bolt	m	i		4	4	
12		Adjust stroke length (optional - see chart) to 95% of the stone length	m	i		15	15	
13		Place parts on mandril by turning stone feed knob clockwise to minimum position. Put parts on and then turn feed knob to expand and turn stone feed knob (see Figure D) counterclockwise until reads five lines above zero on the white meter indicator (see Figure F)	m	i		33	33	
14		Attach indicator (see Figure F) on stroker feed arm with the EC stamp facing up so it can be read by operator. Move indicator lever to release (from lock)	m	i		5	5	
15		Adjust indicator over the pieces of the part. Underneath there are two bumps over the parts	m	i		11	11	
16		Adjust indicator so that it reads zero by turning the knob marked A located on the left hand side of the indicator	m	i		1	1	
17		Adjust the conical movement of the mandril by loosening the high side indicator and tighten the forward set of set screws to 180 degrees on the other side with the 4 mm wrench. Keep loosening and tightening until the Indicator is within two lines of travel	m	i		28	28	

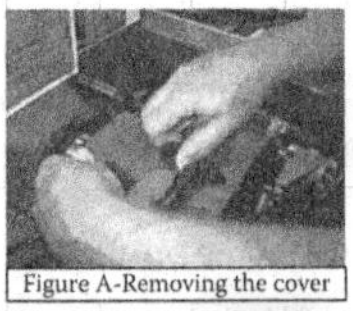

Figure A-Removing the cover

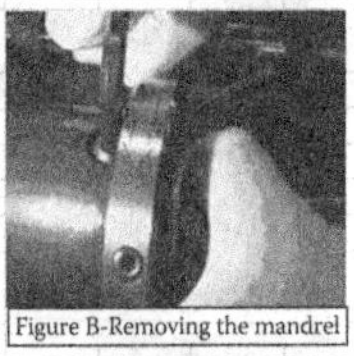

Figure B-Removing the mandrel

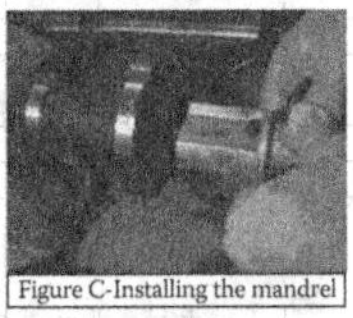

Figure C-Installing the mandril

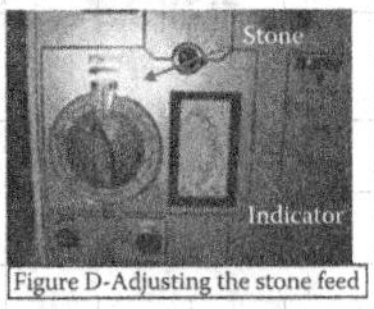

Figure D-Adjusting the stone feed

Figure 4.9   Ancon gear standard work sheet for honer setup.

If we have our guests waiting and they can see that table, what are they thinking? (i.e., "Wow we could be sitting down if they would just bus that table or we had a 6:00 pm reservation, why do we have to wait?").

Step	Omit (Enter an "X" for Omits)	Description	Additional Comments	Distance As Is (FT)	Type Code (P, M, C, T, O)	As Is (I/E)	To Be (I/E)	Distance To Be (FT)	Step Start	Step Stop	Time per Step (Seconds)
1		Table waits	Second seating guest waiting		P	I	E		6:00:00	6:10:00	600
2		Bus person arrives and sees billfolder still on table		30	P	I	I	30		6:10:32	32

Finally, at 6:10 the bus person arrives but he has a problem. Standard operating procedure (SOP) dictates he cannot bus the table while the previous bill and money sit there. Company policy is he must notify the waitress to come get it before he can bus the table.

| 3 | | Bus person leaves, looks for, finds, and tells waitress to get her billfold | Bus person could pick up for waitress | 200 | M | I | E | 200 | | 6:11:27 | 55 |
| 4 | | Waitress comes and picks up billfold | | | P | I | E | | | 6:11:34 | 7 |

The bus person returns to find the billfold gone so now he can start bussing the table. The first step is he must get his big black bin to put all the dirty dishes and silverware in. He finds the bin and clears the table. He searches for his washcloth, but he can't find it, so he must leave to go find a clean one. He finally finds it in the back by the laundry washer and dryer and returns to wipe down the table.

5		Bus person searches for bin to bus table	Bus person could have been ready	200	P	I	E	200		6:13:27	113
6		Bus person goes to table and clears dishes into bin		30	M	I	I	30		6:14:30	63
7		Bus person leaves to look for washcloth	Bus person should have washcloth ready	200	P	I	E	200		6:15:32	62
8		Bus person returns and wipes down table		30	M	I	I	30		6:16:25	53

Next, he leaves to get all the new dishes and silverware. This was a recent improvement. They used to get the dishes, set them on the table, and go back and get the silverware. They moved the silverware close to the clean dishes so they could acquire them all at one time. Then the bus person folds the napkins and puts them at each place setting. He stands back to inspect his work and finds there are two place settings not quite right and rearranges them.

9		Bus person leaves to get new setup for dishes	Bus person should have brought with him	100	P	I	E	100		6:18:12	107
10		Bus person sets out new dishes			M	I	I			6:20:22	13
11		Bus person cleans silverware as it is put on tables	Why is it dirty or spotty?		M	I	E			6:22:00	98
12		Bus person folds napkins and places at each seat			M	I	E			6:23:12	72
13		Bus person double checks place settings and rearranges two of them	Bus person should have carpet sweeper ready or nearby		C	I	I			6:23:35	23

Next, he must look for the carpet sweeper. The last person to use it did not put it back where it belongs. Once he finds it, he returns to the table to sweep the carpet. He thinks ("Glad there wasn't a baby at this table!"). Next, he wipes down the seats and notifies the hostess the table is ready once the seats dry.

14		Bus person leaves to look for carpet sweeper	Bus person should have carpet sweeper ready or nearby	150	P	I	I	150		6:23:59	24
15		Bus person returns and sweeps carpet		30	M	I	E	30		6:24:26	27
16		Bus person wipes down seats	Bus person should have carpet sweeper ready or nearby		M	I	E			6:25:00	34
17		Table must wait while seats dry			M	I	I			6:25:45	45

Next, the hostess calls and looks for the guests and finds them in the bar area and notifies them the table is ready. The guest must wait for and pay their bar tab before leaving. They are taken to the table and seated, and the hostess tells them their server will be with them shortly. They wait 2 minutes for the server to appear. While they are waiting, they have nothing to do but look at the menus and end up engaging in some conversation about how one of the guest's water glasses is dirty and has spots on it. They let the waitress know and she searches for a new glass, gets coffee for another table, and returns with the new glass and takes their orders.

18		Hostess calls second seating guests			P	I	E			6:27:00	75
19		Hostess seats them at the table			M	I	E			6:29:13	133
20		Guest complains glass is spotty			T	I	E			6:30:32	79
21		Waitress searches for new glass		200	T	I	E	200		6:31:33	61
22		Waitress returns with new glass		30	T	I	E	30		6:31:55	22

Setup Concept Expanded

While this restaurant example may not seem like a setup; it is! This table is down for almost 32 minutes and a guest had to wait all that time when they had a 6:00 pm reservation. We have coded each of the steps into their PMCT designations and internal versus external time measured in seconds. Table 4.3 shows the before results.

First, notice all this time is *internal time*, which means the table is not available for our guests. We see this all the time in offices or factories. No preparations are generally made until the machine is shut down. Then the operator gets their tools. We see this with maintenance. Maintenance obtains their ticket, goes to survey the problem or area, and then retrieves their tools. If they bring a tool cart with them half the time, they don't have everything they need to fix the problem. Landscapers will make constant trips back and forth to get tools, gasoline, line for the trimmer, etc. For a landscaper having to add gas or changing the line in a trimmer is a setup. They are on internal time. For a grocery store, the register is down when they are changing over cashiers. Many times, we are told "why does it matter? There is no one in line." If we have no demand on a machine or cash register, should we go slower because there is no demand? This is the logic embodied in the question.

Notice in our example that 53% of the time, all internal, is in preparation and organization. If you go back and look at the steps, what could be improved? So, following our SMED process, we have already identified each step as to whether it is internal or external. The next step is to see where we can convert it from internal to external. Thirty-seven percent

Table 4.3 Setup Sheet Example

	Preparation and Organization	Mounting and Removing	Calibration, Centering, Dimensioning, and Aligning	Trial Runs and Adjustments	Other	As Is (Percent of Original Time)	
	P	M	C	T	O	Internal	External
Seconds	1020.00	710.00	23.00	162.00	0.00	1,908.00	0.00
Minutes	17.00	11.83	0.38	2.70	0.00	31.80	0.00
%	53.3	37.1	1.2	8.5	0.0	1.00	0.00

Source: BIG Archives.

of the time is mounting and removing. We would want to improve these times as well. Next is centering/aligning at 1.2% and trial runs at 8.5%. Our goal for both would be to eliminate them.

Omits

We go through each step and look to see if it can be omitted, converted from internal to external, rearranged, simplified, or combined. From a coding standpoint, we end up with PIEs (Figure 4.10) that represent a preparation step that is converted from internal to external work.

Once we are done, we take all the external steps and create an external setup checklist.

Step	Omit (Enter an "X" for Omits)	Description	Additional Comments	Distance As Is (FT)	Type Code (P, M, C, T, O)	As Is (I/E)	To Be (I/E)	Distance To Be (FT)	Step Start	Step Stop	Time per Step (Seconds)	Estimated Improvement (Seconds)
1	X	Table waits	Second seating guest waiting		P	I	E		6:00:00	6:10:00	600	0

We look at step one. Could we eliminate the table waiting? What would have to happen to do this? Notice by putting an X in the omit column we set the estimated time to zero. Next is the bus person finds the billfold. Can't we change the SOP so the bus person can pick up the billfold for the waitress? Now those steps are eliminated.

Step	Omit	Description	Additional Comments	Distance As Is (FT)	Type Code	As Is (I/E)	To Be (I/E)	Distance To Be (FT)	Step Start	Step Stop	Time per Step (Seconds)	Estimated Improvement (Seconds)
2	X	Bus person arrives and sees bill folder still on table		30	P	I	I		6:10:32		32	0
3	X	Bus person leaves, looks for, finds, and tells waitress to get her billfold	Bus person could pick up for waitress	200	M	I	E		6:11:27		55	0
4	X	Waitress comes and picks up billfold			P	I	E		6:11:34		7	0

Next, we implement a new process where the bus person carries the new dishes with them along with the washcloth. We can then eliminate the searching steps. We can't eliminate cleaning off or setting up the table but when reviewing the video, the bus people came up with some ideas on how to standardize the process, speed it up, and improve the quality.

Step	Omit (Enter an "X" for Omits)	Description Check#:	Additional Comments 1915.00	Distance as Is (FT)	Type Code (P, M, C, T, O)	As Is (I/E)	To Be (I/E)	Distance To Be (FT)	Alt. Start Time (Opt)	Cumulative Seconds / Minutes	Each 1915.00 / 31.92	Est 1915.00 / 31.92
			Total Distance As Is	0		Total Distance To Be		0		Reduction /Percent of Each		0.0%
1		Table waits	second seating guest waiting		P	I	E		60000	61000	600	600
2		Bus person arrives and sees bill folder still on table			P	I	I			61032	32	32
3		Bus person leaves, looks for, finds, and tells waitress to get her billfold	Bus person could pick up for waitress		M	I	E			61127	55	55
4		Waitress comes and picks up bill fold			P	I	E			61134	7	7
5		Bus person searches for bin to bus table	Bus person could have bin ready		P	I	E			61327	113	113
6		Bus person goes to table and clears dishes into bin			M	I	I			61430	63	63
7		Bus person leaves to look for washcloth	Bus person should have washcloth ready		P	I	E			61532	62	62
8		Bus person returns and wipes down table			M	I	I			61625	53	53
9		Bus person leaves to get new setup for dishes	Bus person should have brought with him		P	I	E			61812	107	107
10		Bus person sets out new dishes			M	I	I			62022	130	130
11		Bus person cleans silverware as it is put on tables	Why is it dirty or spotty?		M	I	E			62200	98	98
12		Bus person folds napkins and places at each seat			M	I	E			62312	72	72
13		Bus person double checks place settings and rearranges two of them	Bus person should have carpet sweeper ready or nearby		C	I	I			62335	23	23
14		Bus person leaves to look for carpet sweeper	Bus person should have carpet sweeper ready or nearby		P	I	I			62359	24	24
15		Bus pers on returns and sweeps carpte			M	I	E			62426	27	27
16		Bus person wipes down seats	Bus person should have carpet sweeper ready or nearby		M	I	E			62500	34	34
17		Table has to wait while seats dry			M	I	I			62545	45	45
18		Hostess calls 2nd seating guests			P	I	E			62700	75	75
19		Hostess seats them at the table.			M	I	E			62913	133	133
20		Guest complains glass is spotty			T	I	E			63032	79	79
21		Watiress searches for new glass			T	I	E			63133	61	61
22		Waitress returns with new glass			T	I	E			63155	22	22

Figure 4.10 Setup sheet detail example as is, before improvements.

#	X	Description	Comment							Time		
6		Bus person goes to table and clears dishes into bin		30	M	I	I	30		6:14:30	63	63
7	X	Bus person leaves to look for washcloth	Bus person should have washcloth ready	200	P	I	E			6:15:32	62	0
8		Bus person returns and wipes down table		30	M	I	I	30		6:16:25	53	35
9	X	Bus person leaves to get new setup for dishes	Bus person should have brought with him	100	P	I	E			6:18:12	107	0
10		Bus person sets out new dishes			M	I	I			6:20:22	130	60

Many times, cleaning parts of the table would get missed because everyone did it differently. So, we changed our estimated times based on the bus people's suggestions while they were in the room with us. Next, we found the root cause for the spotty silverware and glasses was the dishwasher was not using the rinse aid he was supposed to use. So, we improved it by installing a new system that is attached to the wall and automatically keeps the rinse aid at the proper level in the dishwasher. We could not eliminate the cleaning silverware step because he still must put it on the table, but we eliminated the rework of cleaning the silverware and eliminated the last three steps where the waitress had to replace the dirty glass.

#	X	Description	Comment							Time		
11		Bus person cleans silverware as it is put on tables	Why is it dirty or spotty?		M	I	E			6:22:00	98	30
12		Bus person folds napkins and places at each seat			M	I	E			6:23:12	72	15
13		Bus person double checks place settings and rearranges two of them	Bus person should have carpet sweeper ready or nearby		C	I	I			6:23:35	23	5

Notice our initial setup was not over until everything in the setup process was correct. Since we now standardized the process and everyone does it the same, the bus person still inspects their setup; but no longer must rearrange it as we have a template designed to make sure everything is now properly located.

20	X	Guest complains glass is spotty			T	I	E			6:30:32	79	0
21	X	Waitress searches for new glass		200	T	I	E			6:31:33	61	0
22	X	Waitress returns with new glass		30	T	I	E			6:31:55	22	0

Next, we changed the process to have sweepers conveniently located throughout the dining room. We implemented 5S so everyone knows where they go and put them back where they belong. In the beginning, many bus persons and servers had to be monitored and coached to put the sweepers back where they belonged.

| 14 | X | Bus person leaves to look for carpet sweeper | Bus person should have carpet sweeper ready or nearby | 150 | P | I | I | | | 6:23:59 | 24 | 0 |
| 15 | | Bus person returns and sweeps carpet | | 30 | M | I | E | 30 | | 6:24:26 | 27 | 27 |

We changed the order of the steps to have the seats cleaned before we use the carpet sweeper. This also eliminated the time needed for the seats to dry as they now dried while the floor was being swept.

| 16 | | Bus person wipes down seats | Bus person should have carpet sweeper ready or nearby | | M | I | E | | | 6:25:00 | 34 | 34 |
| 17 | X | Table must wait while seats dry | | | M | I | I | | | 6:25:45 | 45 | 0 |

Now the total time to turn over the table is 269 seconds, which is less than 5 minutes. So, when our guests arrive, they are told their table is being prepared and they will be seated shortly.

| 18 | | Hostess calls second seating guests | | | P | I | E | | | 6:27:00 | 75 | 2 |
| 19 | | Hostess seats them at the table | | | M | I | E | | | 6:29:13 | 133 | 15 |

Table 4.4 is what the completed process looks like. When we eliminate the omits, it looks like Table 4.5. In our improved process, we cut the time from 31.92 to 4.7 minutes and the distance traveled from 1200 to 90 ft. We reduced the overall time by 86% (Table 4.6).

Table 4.4   Restaurant Example 15 Completed Process

Step	Omit (Enter an "X" for Omits)	Description	Additional Comments	Distance As Is (FT)	Type Code (P, M, C, T, O)	As IS (I/E)	To Be (I/E)	Distance To Be (FT)	Step Start	Step Stop	Time per Step (Seconds)	Estimated Improvement (Seconds)
1	X	Tables waits	Second seating guest waiting		P	I	E		6:00:00	6:10:00	600	0
2	x	Bus person on arrives and sees bill folder still on table		30	P	I	I			6:10:32	32	0
3	x	Bus person leaves, looks for, finds, and tells waitress to get her billfold	Bus person could pick up for waitress	200	M	I	E			6:11:27	55	0
4	X	Waitress comes and picks up billfold			P	I	E			6:11:34	7	0
5	x	Bus person searches for bin to bus table	Bus person could have bin ready	200	P	I	E			6:13:27	113	0
6		Bus person goes to table and clears dishes into bin		30	M	I	I	30		6:14:30	63	63

Table 4.4 (Continued) Restaurant Example 15 Completed Process

Step	Omit (Enter an "X" for Omits)	Description	Additional Comments	Distance As Is (FT)	Type Code (P, M, C, T, O)	As IS (I/E)	To Be (I/E)	Distance To Be (FT)	Step Start	Step Stop	Time per Step (Seconds)	Estimated Improvement (Seconds)
7	x	Bus person leaves to look for washcloth	Bus person should have washcloth ready	200	P	I	E			6:15:32	62	0
8		Bus person returns and wipes down table		30	M	I	I	30		6:16:25	53	35
9		Bus person wipes down seats	Bus person should have carpet sweeper ready or nearby		M	I	E			6:25:00	34	34
10	x	Table has to wait while seats dry			M	I	I			6:25:45	45	0
11	x	Bus person leaves to get new setup for dishes	Bus person should have brought with him	100	P	I	E			6:18:12	107	0
12		Bus person sets out new dishes			M	I	I			6:20:22	130	60

(Continued)

Table 4.4 (Continued) Restaurant Example 15 Completed Process

Step	Omit (Enter an "X" for Omits)	Description	Additional Comments	Distance As Is (FT)	Type Code (P, M, C, T, O)	As IS (I/E)	To Be (I/E)	Distance To Be (FT)	Step Start	Step Stop	Time per Step (Seconds)	Estimated Improvement (Seconds)
13		Bus person cleans silverware as it is put on tables	Why is it dirty or spotty?		M	I	E			6:22:00	98	30
14		Bus person folds napkins and places at each seat			M	I	E			6:23:12	72	15
15		Bus person double checks place settings and rearranges two of them	Bus person should have carpet sweeper ready or nearby		C	I	I			6:23:35	23	5
16	x	Bus person leaves to look for carpet sweeper	Bus person should have carpet sweeper ready or nearby	150	P	I	I			6:23:59	24	0
17		Bus person returns and sweeps carpet		30	M	I	E	30		6:24:26	27	27

Table 4.4 (Continued) Restaurant Example 15 Completed Process

Step	Omit (Enter an "X" for Omits)	Description	Additional Comments	Distance As Is (FT)	Type Code (P, M, C, T, O)	As IS (I/E)	To Be (I/E)	Distance To Be (FT)	Step Start	Step Stop	Time per Step (Seconds)	Estimated Improvement (Seconds)
18		Hostess calls second seating guests			P	I	E			6:27:00	75	2
19		Hostess seats them at the table			M	I	E			6:29:13	133	15
20	x	Guest complains glass is spotty			T	I	E			6:30:32	79	0
21	x	Waitress searches for new glass		200	T	I	E			6:31:33	61	0
22	x	Waitress returns with new glass		30	T	I	E			6:31:55	22	0

Source: Authors.

Table 4.5 Restaurant Example 16 Completed Processes with OMITS Removed

Step	Omit (Enter an "X" for Omits)	Description	Additional Comments	Distance As Is (FT)	Type Code (P, M, C, T, O)	As Is (I/E)	To Be (I/E)	Distance To Be (FT)	Step Start	Step Stop	Time per Step (Seconds)	Estimated Improvement (Seconds)
1		Bus person goes to table and clears dishes into bin		30	M	I	I	30	6:13:27	6:14:30	63	63
2		Bus person wipes down table		30	M	I	I	30	6:15:32	6:16:25	53	35
4		Bus person sets out new dishes according to new standard template			M	I	I		6:18:12	6:20:22	130	60
5		Bus person puts silverware on tables according to new standard	Why is it dirty or spotty? Fixed		M	I	I		6:20:22	6:22:00	98	30
6		Bus person places napkins at each seat			M	I	I		6:22:00	6:23:12	72	15
7		Bus person double checks place settings and rearranges two of them	Bus person should have carpet sweeper ready or nearby. Fixed		C	I	I		6:23:12	6:23:35	23	5

Table 4.5 (*Continued*) **Restaurant Example 16 Completed Processes with OMITS Removed**

Step	Omit (Enter an "X" for Omits)	Description	Additional Comments	Distance As Is (FT)	Type Code (P, M, C, T, O)	As Is (I/E)	To Be (I/E)	Distance To Be (FT)	Step Start	Step Stop	Time per Step (Seconds)	Estimated Improvement (Seconds)
8		Bus person gets sweeper from 5S location and sweeps carpet and returns to location		30	M	I	I	30	6:23:59	6:24:26	27	27
3		Bus person wipes down seats according to new standard	Seats dry. Fixed		M	I	I		6:24:26	6:25:00	34	34
9		Hostess calls second seating guests			P	I	E		6:25:45	6:27:00	75	2
10		Hostess seats them at the table			M	I	E		6:27:00	6:29:13	133	15

Source: Authors.

Table 4.6   Setup Sheet Summary Example

	Prep. and Org.	Mounting and Removing	Calibration, Centering, Dimensioning, and Aligning	Trial Runs and Adjustments	Other	As Is (Percent of Original Time)		To Be (Reduction % from As Is)	
	P	M	C	T	O	Int.	Ext.	Int.	Ext.
Seconds	75.00	610.00	23.00	0.00	0.00	708.00	0.00	269.00	17.00
Minutes	1.25	10.17	0.38	0.00	0.00	11.80	0.00	4.48	0.28
% Improvement	10.6	86.2	3.2	0.0	0.0	100.0		62	

Source: BIG Archives.

External Checklist

The external checklist lists the steps which need to be carried out prior to the machine stopping or completing the last piece of the previous order or in this case prior to the people leaving the table. Our checklist might look like this:

- Make sure silverware and dishes are prepared and ready.
- Double check for spots on glasses or silverware.
- Make sure you have a dirty bin ready, and napkins are pre-folded.
- Note: We didn't cut the overall setup time by the time it took to pre-fold the napkins, but we cut the internal time which was spent folding the napkins and where the customer had to wait for their table.
- Make sure the carpet sweeper is in the proper location.

If we make a video of the new system with the andon light to alert the bus person a minute or two ahead of time the guests are ready to leave, then we have a great training tape to go along with the new standard work we have just created. If the setup we filmed was indicative of most setups, then we just freed up 27 minutes of time per table. If the average guest spends 1.5 hours at the table, then roughly for every three guests we have freed up an extra table. So, if we have demand, we have increased our capacity by approximately 33%.

Lesson Learned: When working in most shops, we find the behaviors in the initial setup filmed are embedded in the overall system, which means all setups have the same issues. So, we counsel companies that when you have conducted one setup improvement event you should transfer the solutions throughout the shop prior to filming the next setup.

Setup Standard Work

When we complete the analysis, we end up with internal setup standard work (Figure 4.11) and an external checklist which is more of a work standard.

Dedicated Setup Teams

We find the use of a dedicated, knowledgeable setup person or teams can more than pay for themselves. At Company X, we increased the capacity by over 55%. However, for this system to work, as in all new Lean systems, there must be a process and procedure behind it with metrics, discipline and accountability, and continuous improvement built into the process.

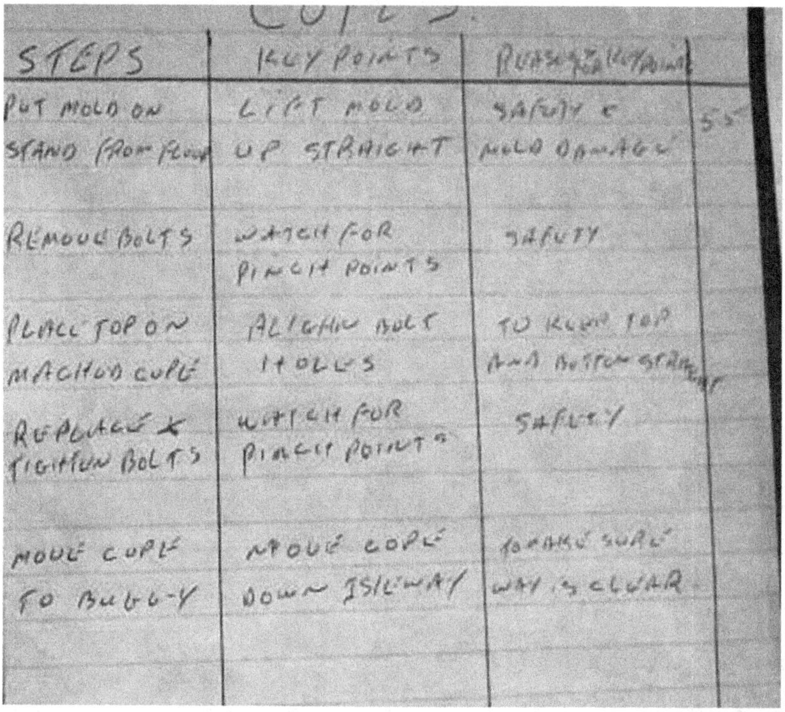

STEPS	KEY POINTS	REASONS FOR KEY POINTS	
PUT MOLD ON STAND FROM FLOOR	LIFT MOLD UP STRAIGHT	SAFETY & MOLD DAMAGE	5S
REMOVE BOLTS	WATCH FOR PINCH POINTS	SAFETY	
PLACE TOP ON MACHINE CURE	ALIGN BOLT HOLES	TO KEEP TOP AND BOTTOM STRAIGHT	
REPLACE & TIGHTEN BOLTS	WATCH FOR PINCH POINTS	SAFETY	
MOVE CURE TO BUGGY	MOVE CORE DOWN ISLEWAY	TO MAKE SURE WAY IS CLEAR	

Figure 4.11 Standard work example with key points and reason for key points.

Setup Carts

Setup carts are an interim step to improvement (Figure 4.12). The goal is to get all tools and fixtures at the machine where it makes sense (Figure 4.13). For an actual setup checklist, see Table 4.7).

External Setup Reduction Suggestions

- 5S.
- Advance preparations.
- Function standardization.
- Have all setup tools at the point of use.
- Develop checklists for external preparation.
- Investigate using setup carts and visual displays to locate all setup fixtures at the point of use.
- Ensure all tools, gauges, etc. are calibrated prior to setup and preset tools.
- Ensure all tools are sharpened immediately after the last run.
- Elimination of adjustments.
- Mechanization.
- Minimize/eliminate trial and error, tweaking, rework.
- Slots, clamps, etc.
- How many turns of the screw are required to hold it and how many screws are needed?
- Floating heads.
- Dedicated equipment.

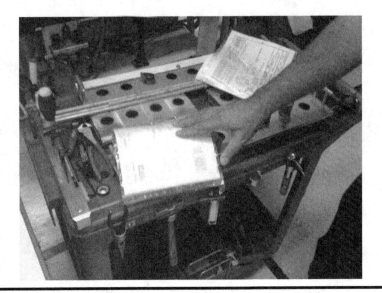

Figure 4.12   Setup cart example.

- Eliminate unnecessary tests.
- Standardize, Standardize, Standardize.
- On procedures.
- Ensure proper resources are present.
- Equipment manufacturers.
- Duplicate tools and utilize die carts.
- Preheat molds and boards.
- Collocate fixtures and dies.

Figure 4.13   Setup tools POU (point of use).

Table 4.7 Setup External Checklist Example

External Checklist for Bench 3 Setup

Step	Omit	Description	Type Code	As Is (I/E)	To Be (I/E)	Note #
		Operation				
		Total cumulative times (seconds):				
1		Unite bundles and put rope in bins	P	I	E	
2		Separate tubes and bundles	P	I	E	
3		Check method for any special instructions	P	I	E	
4		Get proper plugs, make sure they are cleaned and miced	P	I	E	
5		Make sure die pull tool is at machine	P	I	E	Have swager tool at machine
6		Make sure dies are ready and at swager	P	I	E	5S plugs
7		Clean and inspect plugs (6)	P	I	E	Supply schedule to benches with special tool
8		Get and check method	P	I	E	
9		Get and put on gloves	P	I	E	
10		Make sure dies and collars are in place for die block	P	I	E	
11		Separate tubing	P	I	E	

(Continued)

Table 4.7 (Continued) Setup External Checklist Example

External Checklist for Bench 3 Setup

Step	Omit	Operation		As Is (I/E)	To Be (I/E)	Note #
		Description	Type Code			
12		Check nozzle size at lube and have proper nozzle available if required	P	I	E	
13		Check lube barrel, fill lube if necessary	P	I	E	
14		Put away collars and dies	P	I	E	Move box closer to die block
15		Separate tubes and move in line with die	P	I	E	
16		Make sure acetone and mic are near die block	P	I	E	
17		Go to method and record	T	I	E	
19		Put old dies away after setup	P	I	E	Make sure plugs are clean before next run
18		Do test on samples	T	I	E	

Source: BIG Archives.

Internal Setup Reduction Suggestions

- Reduce or eliminate all non-value-added operations.
- Mistake proof to eliminate first-piece inspection.
- Perform setup in parallel, have operators assist.
- One-turn clamps and motions. The rule is no more than one-fourth turn in any setup.
- Automate where possible.
- Quick change tooling.
- Use multiple resources to reduce internal time.

A Couple of Other Points regarding Parts of a Setup

When you think about it, we discussed the difference between clock time and labor time earlier. The goal or target condition of the first setup reduction is normally at least a 50% reduction in clock time. So:

- Should preparation and organization steps be internal or external? The answer is it should all be done on external time. What should mounting and removing be? The answer is internal time.
- Should calibration, centering, dimensioning, and aligning be internal or external? The answer is they should go away. We need to work on eliminating them.
- Should trial runs and adjustments be internal or external? The answer is they should go away too. We need to work on eliminating them.

The final optimized setup process would only be composed of external preparation and organization steps and internal mounting and removing steps. SMED, or less than 10-minute setups, only applies to the mounting and removing steps involved in the setup, which is only internal time. Keep in mind that the overall setup time includes the external steps. We also don't want to forget the pit stop employs multiple persons doing standard work in parallel to both internal and external work. After you do the analysis and complete the omits process you can take the steps now designated as external, put them in order or split them up where they can be done in parallel and assign them to multiple persons. Be sure to make an external setup task or checklist and cut down the external setup time as well. In all our experience, we have found sustaining setup improvements to be the most difficult. If it is not driven at the Plant Manager level, it will not sustain.

What Is a Setup Really?

We said earlier in the book we would expound on the concept of setups. We often surprise people when we start to explain setup terminology and what constitutes a setup. If you think about it anytime we load or unload anything or change from one to another in any process whether man or machine it can be considered a setup. In almost every workflow analysis (WFA), see Chapter 2, we perform and find steps where the concepts of internal and external work apply. Consider:

- Changing from one person to the next in the grocery store is a setup change
- Changing over the Xerox® machine

- Changing loads in the washer/dryer
- Changing over from one patient to another in an emergency room or surgery suite
- Changing over tables in a restaurant
- Changing cashiers in a grocery store
- Changing classes at college
- Changing over presidents every 4–8 years
- Loading and unloading a part in a machine

Network of Process versus Operations Defined[8]

We have attempted to expand Dr. Shingo's separation among product, operator, and changeover and take it to the next level. To our knowledge, no one has broken down these processes into the pieces of Lean thinking each one provides. We studied this for years before it dawned on us that each analysis tool (product vs. operator's axis plus changeover) provides different answers for Lean improvement. We would like to propose that analyzing just the setup/changeover axis will provide the following pieces of the Lean implementation:

- Enabler for one-piece or one-patient flow or smaller batch sizes
- Immediately increases capacity
- Improved operator utilization
- Reduces labor costs
- Increases overall system reliability and predictability
- Enabler for *chaku chaku*
- Enabler for level loading
- Increased man-to-machine ratio
- Enabler for mixed model and ability to supply in sets
- Provides quick response to demand changes
- Less reliance on forecasting
- Capital asset utilization rate increases (if demand is there)
- Reduces material handling
- Reduced inventories
- Smaller layout footprint
- Results in standardization
- Improved operator safety
- Improved patient/product quality
- Integrates mistake proofing

Analysis Section Review

To review, we started with surveying our customers and finding out what was important to them and what challenges they experienced with the current process. We also interviewed the staff and constructed fishbone diagrams (Figure 4.14) to help categorize and determine the root cause of the problems they faced. Problem is not a bad word because identifying and bringing attention to problems needs to be encouraged. We need to surface problems by lowering the inventory, eliminating storage or waits, and reworking to uncover hidden wastes while remembering that waste hides more waste.

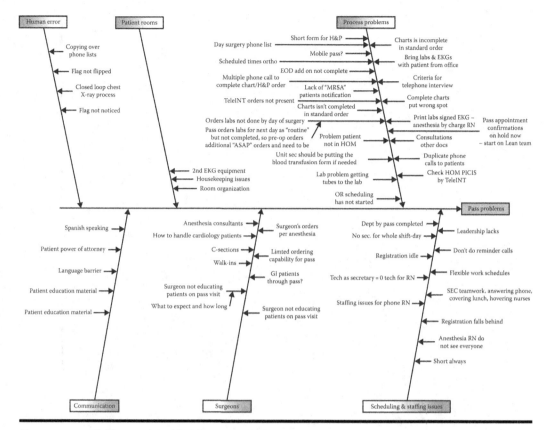

Figure 4.14   Fishbone example.

We determined our customer demand and peak demand (in some cases to the hour) and calculated our takt time. The demand is the number of products or services that need to be processed. Demand could be the number of customers who visit the restaurant at a particular hour, day, month, or year. From the pharmacy's perspective, they would be more interested in the number of medications they need to fill in 15 minutes, 60 minutes, or daily, so the demand from the pharmacy's perspective might be medication fills per given time frame. Takt time is equal to the available time divided by customer demand or the beat to which we need to construct our new system.

Next came the value stream map (VSM) (Figure 4.15) which provided a high-level systemic view of the overall process, identifying process versus non-process-based activities and a baseline view of throughput for the overall process. Part of our calculations included determining value-added versus non-value-added time, cycle time, and throughput time.

The findings and opportunities identified through the analysis helped us to gain insight into what areas needed improvement and where to focus the next level of tools. Our assessment tools included the process flow analysis (PFA), operator analysis (WFA), and changeover analysis. It is optional at this point to go back and update the VSM with the analysis-based data.

Utilizing the PFA tool, we looked at how the products or services flowed within and throughout the process. Information was gathered on the time and distance it takes to go through the process or service. We used the eight wastes to identify the value-added percentage along with the process steps that could be eliminated, rearranged, simplified, or combined. We now look at the remaining steps to see which ones can be done in parallel. The PFA also gives us the total

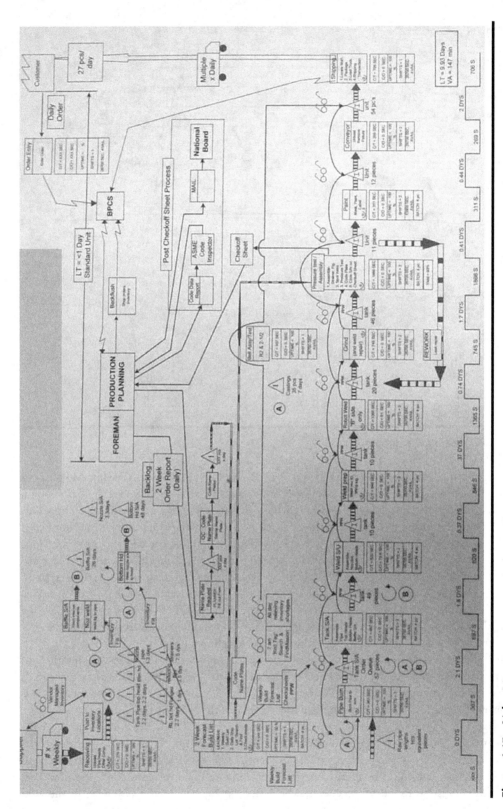

Figure 4.15   Value stream map.

throughput time, which we can use to calculate how much inventory (product or paper) needs to be in the system to meet the takt time. The ability to measure and track throughput as a metric is key to improving processes. Throughput is a key metric in Lean and should be a key metric for every department in every organization.

We also pointed out that just because we must perform a step does not make it value added. Determining the new flow and new layout begins with the knowledge gained from the PFA analysis. The next step was performing the operator analysis, which looked at the process from the operator's or staff's point of view and provided a baseline for *total labor time*. We were able to eliminate, rearrange, simplify, or combine the steps as they relate to the staff member doing the work.

This helped streamline the work of staff persons to make sure the activities being performed were value added based on what is really needed to achieve the results. Observations during this process provided opportunities to make sure the staff person had been provided with the right tools or parts at the right place to get the job done with the least amount of effort, thus the least amount of wasted motions and activity while, again using the eight wastes as a guide. This provides the basis for standard work and balancing our operation steps. The operator analysis gave us the total labor time that we can now use to calculate how many staff we will need in our newly designed process and area layout.

We performed the changeover analysis, which looked at the setup between parts and the opportunities that existed to convert internal steps to external steps. Reducing changeover time frees up capacity throughout the system.

The overall goal is to achieve a new process flow, free of waste, and non-value-added activities. Remember, it is essential to ensure we have clear definitions of each metric. These include precise starting and ending points for the process, how, when, where, and who is collecting it, and over what time frame. It is important that consistency in the metric collection process is obtained.

The definitions need to be discussed and clearly understood by all stakeholders to avoid downstream confusion of what exactly is being reported. To summarize, we have the following key process metrics coming out of the analysis phase: available time, takt time, throughput time, total labor time, and changeover time.

Lesson Learned: The real key with Lean is figuring out the product axis versus the operator axis; analyzing the changeover axis separately and developing the solution for all of them together.

Total Process Optimization

As we move through the utilization of Lean tools to reach a Lean process to deliver the customer a quality product, each tool discussed provides another piece of the puzzle required to achieve total process optimization. Using Lean tools enables one to understand and optimize what the operator does to the product as they move through the process. Just looking and fixing the operator axis piece of the network can yield as much as an additional 20%–40% productivity improvement. When combined with the product piece which yields a 20%–40% productivity improvement one can attain a 40%–80% improvement when converting operations from a pure batch environment to flow. The changeover improvement process is sometimes critical to being able to achieve these results.

Analysis Results As True One-Piece Flow Is Attained with Zero Setup

When one obtains true one-piece flow the product and operator pieces become essentially the same analysis. Take the following example: The operator reaches for a part, grabs, moves the part to the assembly and inserts it into the product, and repeats this pattern several times slowly moving the product down the assembly line.

From the products point of view, the TIPS analysis looks like this:

B	VA	T	B	VA	T	B	VA	T

B = Between process storage while the operator reaching, grabbing, and transporting the part to the unit should take no more than 1–2 seconds.

VA = When the part is added to the unit (unit is having value added to it).

T = Transport—when the unit is moved to the next spot at the station (or to the next station).

From the operator's point of view, the WFA looks like this:

P	VA	RW	P	VA	RW	P	VA	RW

P = Reaching for, grabbing the part, and moving it to the unit should take no more than 1–2 seconds.

VA = When the operator inserts the part in the unit (operator is adding value to the unit).

RW = Required work—moving the unit to the next spot at the workstation (or to the next station). So, when placed on top of each other it looks like this ....

B	VA	T	B	VA	T	B	VA	T
P	VA	RW	P	VA	RW	P	VA	RW

Notice the value-added steps align perfectly.

Lesson Learned: Initially the product and operator analysis are very different steps. When one truly becomes Lean, one will find as the product and operator get closer to one-piece flow, the analysis begins to converge into the same steps. Table 4.8 shows the results of the analysis for each piece of the Lean network. Figure 4.16 shows a summary of the three parts of the process we analyze.

Determining Potential Total Savings

As we review the analysis process, it is not unusual to stumble on many small improvements and some rather large opportunities to improve the process. However, some of these opportunities may require some expense or capital investment. For instance, many times just the introduction or addition of some simple power tools or duplicate jigs and fixtures may be required. In this case, once we know which steps can be omitted or improved, we can take the labor time associated with those steps and convert it to dollars and develop a quick return on investment (ROI) to justify the improvement to management. In some cases, the improvements relate to safety and ergonomics and should just be implemented regardless of ROI. The WFA times can also help us to calculate the required staffing along with any labor savings and improvements at the end of the project (understanding that improvement never ends) to calculate the productivity realized through the Lean initiative. However, labor savings are not fully realized until such time as the personnel are removed from the area and put to work on something else. It is important prior to

Table 4.8 PFA, WFA, and Setup Analysis Results

Product Process Flow					
	VA		*NVA*		*Total*
	Time	*%*	*Time*	*%*	*Time*
Valves	3,900	8	42,925	92	46,825
Hopper	65	2	4,092	98	4,156
Final Assy	5,943	28	15,590	72	21,533
Totals	9,908	14	62,607	86	72,514
Goal is 80% or more value added					

Full Work Analysis					
	VA		*NVA*		*Total*
	Time	*%*	*Time*	*%*	*Time*
Dryer Bed	1,014	34	1,964	66	2,978
Valve Assy	1,414	32	2,985	68	4,399
MD50 Test	279	0.7	87,752	99.3	88,031
Totals	2,707	3	92,701	97	95,408
Goal is 80% or more value added					

Setup reduction analysis (seconds)					
	Before		After		%
	Int.	Ext.	Int.	Ext.	Improve
Weld bottle	423	0	25	0	94
Punch press	491	0	95	25	81
Press brake	428	0	148	0	65
Goal is less than 10 minutes (SMED)					

Projected results were obtained 100% increase in output with same census. Throughput time is currently estimated at 3 days or less for final assy. Value added can be increased to close to 80% for product and operators
Improvement identified and prioritized
Analysis is 100% complete

The Source: BIG Archives.

the implementation to determine where employees who are freed up are going to be moved and put the appropriate plans in place.

Lean Office Example

At Company X, during an office implementation, we freed up two out of two and a half accounting clerks within the weeklong effort. It became obvious during the implementation they had nothing to do. We initially had them work on 5S'ing their area while the assistant controller found a new home for them.

In an assembly operation at Bendix which became part of AlliedSignal (now Raytheon Technologies), we advised the manufacturing manager we were going to free up 14 of their 28 people on the Monday we implemented. They literally laughed at us and refused to believe it. On the following Monday, we ended up with 14 people against the wall watching the new line run. We rotated them in during the day for cross-training purposes until the manager who was no longer laughing, but, now in shock, figured out how to move people around and eliminate most of her temporary labor. We also ended up bringing several operations back in from Mexico which made the Union Leaders ecstatic!

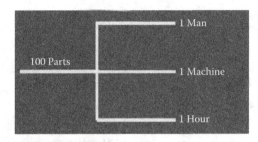

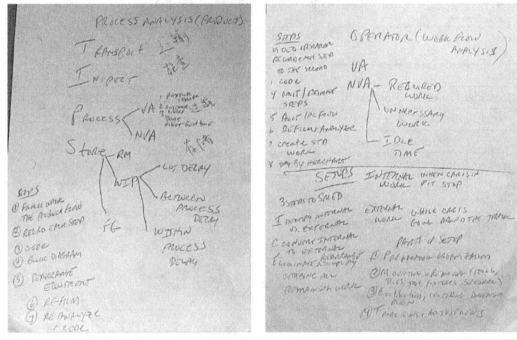

Figure 4.16 Three parts we analyze on flip chart example.

Chapter Questions

1. What does SMED stand for?
2. What does OTED stand for?
3. Describe OSED.
4. What are the four parts of a setup?
5. Explain external versus internal work.
6. Where else can it apply other than traditional setups?
7. Give an example of something we don't normally think of as a setup.
8. Why is standard work important in a setup?
9. What is an external checklist? How is it used? Does it ever change?
10. What pieces of Lean do we obtain from a setup?
11. What is world class for a setup?
12. How should we analyze potential savings from implementing SMED processes?
13. Why is SMED important to the Lean implementation journey?
14. What did you learn from this chapter?

Notes

1. Shigeo Shingo, A Revolution in Manufacturing: The SMED System. Portland OR: Productivity Press, ©1985.
2. Frank Gilbreth, *Motion Study*, 1911.
3. Story From Kenneth Hopper
4. NASCAR Pit Stop Detail furnished in Personal correspondence with Michael Gassler, LEAN/QA Manager, Creative Pultrusions, Inc., 214 Industrial Lane, Alum Bank, PA 15521, Phone: 814-839-4186 Ext. 229, Fax: 814-839-4276, http://*www.creativepultrusions.com*
5. http://www.chacha.com/question/what-is-the-fastest-pit-stop-in-nascar-history—I don't believe there is a stat for the fastest pit stop ever. I can tell you a FAST pit stop is in the 12.0 second's range.
6. Winner's Circle, Tier One Communications.
7. *A Revolution in Manufacturing: The SMED System*, Shingo, Productivity Press, 1985.
8. Protzman, Mayzell, Kerpchar, *Leveraging Lean in Healthcare*, Productivity Press, 2011.

Additional Readings

Arai, K., Sekine, K. 1992. Kaizen for Quick Changeover: Going beyond SMED. Portland, OR: Productivity Press.

Shigeo, S. 1985. Quick Changeover for Operators: The SMED System. Portland, OR: Productivity Press.

Shingo, S. 1985. A Revolution in Manufacturing: The SMED System. Portland, OR: Productivity Press.

Chapter 5

Lean and Change Management

All progress comes from change, but not all change is progress.

Unknown

The Change Paradox: "The only thing which won't change in life is change itself, i.e. The process of change is the only thing that stays the same. Therefore, Resistance to change is ultimately futile!"

Charlie Protzman

Change Happens! Get over it!

Dilbert[1]

The best way to predict your future is to create it.

Abraham Lincoln

Introduction

As a current or future Lean practitioner, you will probably find yourself at some point talking with someone and thinking these words. "Change happens, why can't you just accept it?" "Don't you understand? What we are doing is going to save your job!"

But wouldn't it be great to hear, "Ok, I'll do it!" "I can't wait until our culture is transformed to one of ongoing continuous improvement!" Ah, if only it were that easy! We thought a good way to start this chapter would be reviewing the adage that states 10% of us are early adopters, 10% are never going to go along with the change, and 80% of us wait to see which way the change is going to swing before picking sides. If you are going through a Lean organizational change now and you are already a change agent, please feel free to skip this chapter. The rest of you please read on: Dealing with and managing change is the most difficult part of any Lean transformation. There are no easy recipes, no slam dunks, and no ideal solution, which works in any organization. As of this writing, there are over 15,000 books written on dealing with some type of change or change management.

DOI: 10.4324/9781003185789-5

This chapter explores a variety of change tools including paradigms, the change equation, change management observations, and barriers along with techniques to overcome them and closes with thoughts on implementing suggestions systems (the core of change management systems). This suggestion system is at the heart of the Lean Culture we are trying to create. Since every company is different, there is no cookie cutter solution for implementing culture change. Suffice it to say, to be successful and to truly sustain, the change must start and be driven with a pull from the very top level of the organization and driven (and at times pushed) through the line leadership. A roadmap for Lean implementation is depicted in a book called The Leadership Roadmap.[2]

This change may take the form of a new way to do the process, technological innovation, or a new way of working. We frequently must introduce change into the process to meet these goals. It is not always easy to change and may be more difficult for some, more than others. Ironically, the only constant in the world is change. There is no escaping it! Our goals in Lean are to:

1. Increase customer and employee satisfaction
2. Reduce costs
3. Increase capacity
4. Improve quality (zero defects)
5. Reduce WIP (work in process) inventory
6. Shorten lead times
7. Improve safety and ergonomics
8. Maximize efficient use of all resources
9. Reduce/eliminate waste from all areas in the organization
10. Improve communication and information flows
11. Develop accountability within all systems and processes to ensure sustainability of change
12. Improve the process—reduce complexity, overburden, and difficulty in terms of learning, teaching, doing, and reaching

These goals will no doubt drive change in every organization. There are many change tools out there to choose from and we have selected a few we use across virtually all implementations. The first concept of change management we explore is paradigms.

Paradigms

What got us here ... won't get us there![3]

Do not underestimate the power of paradigms! How many times have you had a great idea for improving a process? How many of you had trouble implementing your new idea? This is the concept Joel Barker explores in his video series, Business of Paradigms.[4] He states: "paradigms are sets of rules and regulations that do two things: First, they establish boundaries ..., second, these rules and regulations then go on to tell you how to be successful by solving problems within these boundaries."

We all have paradigms and they are easy to slip into without realizing it. Mr. Barker goes on to say that "... In his book, The Structure of Scientific Revolutions[5], Thomas Kuhn discovered that paradigms act as filters that screen data coming into the scientist's mind. Data that agrees with the scientist's mind has an easy pathway to recognition ... but Kuhn also discovered a startling negative effect. With some of the data, scientists had substantial difficulty. Why? Because that data did not match the expectations created by their paradigms. In fact, the more unexpected the data was, the more trouble the scientist had perceiving it. Sometimes the scientists would ignore the data, in

Figure 5.1 Change saying in Rotterdam, Netherlands.

other cases the scientists would distort the data to fit their paradigm rather than acknowledge it was an exception to the rule. In some cases, the scientists literally, physiologically were incapable of perceiving the unexpected data. For all intents and purposes that data was invisible."

Paradigms are good because they help us filter out unneeded data, but they can be bad when our paradigm becomes "the" paradigm or the only way to see things. The real challenge lies in recognizing and dealing with them. We are all full of great ideas on how to improve; but all great ideas tend to meet some resistance. To implement new ideas implies change and therefore resistance, which we and others meet as we work to change their paradigms. Many times, those great ideas come from outsiders because they are not vested in your paradigms. The first step we take in change management is to educate those participating in the change about the benefits and potential traps of paradigms. This serves two purposes:

1. It helps to open their minds and to see their natural resistance to the Lean changes coming (Figure 5.1).
2. It lets them know people in the rest of the organization will not be so open-minded to the changes we will be making.

Change Tools

Change Management and Lean

Change management is not only a large part of Lean; it is an essential part of becoming Lean. As you move from accepting new ideas and then transitioning ideas into reality, one should not underestimate the importance of this component to successfully disseminate, deploy, and sustain

$$D \times V \times F > R_{change}$$

Figure 5.2   Original change equation.

Lean. We have a saying when implementing Lean: 50% is task related and 50% is people. The first 50% is applying the Lean tools to any process, which is the scientific management part of Lean. The other 50% is what we call the people piece or change management. There must be a balance between these two pieces. If the Lean scale swings too much to the scientific management side, we can end up with low morale and discontent among our team members resulting in the lack of sustaining any changes and ultimately unionization. If we swing too far on the people side, we end up with no discipline on the floor or in the office and no chain of command. People in this environment do whatever they want to do, are not accountable, hoard their knowledge (to protect their job), are literally out of control, and again there is the lack of sustaining any significant beneficial changes. Therefore, striking this balance before, during, and after the ongoing improvement phase of Lean is so important.

Change Equation

The change equation is a critical tool we use with every company. It was originally developed by Gleicher, Beckhard, and Harris[6]. Their equation was Dissatisfaction × Vision × First Steps must be greater than the Resistance to change (Figure 5.2).

We have modified the equation as shown in Figure 5.3. Over many years of implementing Lean, we have found we always come back to this equation with every implementation of kaizen. We will review each letter of the new equation and explain why we chose to modify it from the original.

R = Resistance to Change

Notice there is a multiplication sign between each letter. This is because if any of the letters equal zero or are not addressed, we will not overcome the R_{change}, which stands for resistance to change, thus effective change will not occur. In addition, each step needs to be followed in order.

C = Compelling Need to Change

We have learned Lean is generally not proposed in most companies unless there is a perceived need to change. The question to ask is, Is there really a compelling need to change? If we could say this 1,000 times louder, it would not even come close to how necessary this is for change. We have traded the D for dissatisfaction with the C, which stands for the compelling need to change (Figure 5.4). While we agree dissatisfaction is important and Dr. Shingo said, "Dissatisfaction was the Mother (relationship) of all improvement,"[5] we feel dissatisfaction by itself is not a strong enough statement or motivator for change. Most people are dissatisfied

$$C \times V \times N \times S > R_{Change}$$

Figure 5.3   BIG change equation.

$$\textcircled{C} \times V \times N \times S > R_{\text{Change}}$$

Figure 5.4   Compelling need to change.

with the current system, process, or even with things in their personal lives but for one reason or another they never change. Many times, we become comfortable with the inefficient processes because we know how to work around them or we feel they will just never change. We all love to complain about them, in fact, some of us thrive on the constant whining because in essence we really do not want it to change. Until your dissatisfaction reaches the level of a compelling need to change, it is not strong enough to force changes to individual or organizational behavior.

> With the right to criticize comes the responsibility to recommend
>
> **Mark Jamrog**[7]

Change is hard. This is an understatement. If we do not have a compelling need to change, all efforts will be futile and ultimately, nothing will change. If change does occur and it is not driven or supported by the Leadership, it will have no chance of sustaining. To be successful with Lean, we need more than just dissatisfaction with the way things are today. We must literally have so much passion that we eat, live, and breathe waste reduction and continuous improvement.

A great example is weight loss or exercise. Look back to New Year's Eve. What is one of the major resolutions? I am going to lose 20 pounds by summer. I am going to hit the treadmill every day! Sound familiar? After all, I must fit into that bathing suit. Then January comes and goes, February comes and goes, and we are no closer to losing 1 pound much less 20. Next thing you know it is the end of April. One month to go. At this point, some of us may move from dissatisfaction to a compelling need to change. We have an entire multibillion dollar industry built around diets and losing weight. Good thing for the industry, we are all just dissatisfied but not enough to really change our daily living habits.

There are two ways to incentivize change:

1. One is to have an actual crisis or business case, where without change, the organization will not survive. The crisis dictates a true compelling need to change but can be dangerous if it leads to a totally reactive approach.
2. The other way is to invent a crisis or to set very high goals (challenges or stretch targets) for the organization that cannot be achieved by doing it the way it has always been done. This creates a healthy fear or paranoia that keeps the organization changing and improving. While this can be done at a department level, it is most successful when led at the most senior executive level.

As Lean CEOs, we must find a way to drive Lean improvements and implement employee ideas every day. Only the CEO can create this compelling need to change for the organization. So, this means not only do we go through the change equation but also the CEO must figure out a way to continuously repeat the change equation cycle to create a systemic way to drive continuous improvement every day.

Why Change?

When faced with this question, our answer is "What is the option?" Ask yourself these questions:

- Can we afford to continue to work with the level of waste in our current processes?
- Have past improvements worked? Remember, all the solutions put in place over the years have gotten us to where we are today!
- Is your department or company world class?
- Do you want to be world class?
- Are other departments you impact satisfied with your performance?
- How many of you are satisfied with your current processes?
- Have we always met all our customers' expectations in terms of cost, quality, and delivery?
- Do we have too many people/redundant processes or systems? (Are we a fat organization?)
- Are our competitors catching up or are ahead of us in terms of competitive advantage?

In many organizations, change is driven by a leader who is not satisfied with the status quo, has the desire to transform the company from Good to Great,[8] but must create the need and vision to get there.

Hedgehog Concept from "Good to Great"[9]

Jim Collins in his book, Good to Great, introduces his Hedgehog concept, which is doing one thing and doing it well. He tells the story of the clever, devious fox, and the simple hedgehog. The fox keeps coming up with new ideas to eat the hedgehog, but the hedgehog defeats him each time by doing his one trick, which is rolling into a thorny ball.

This concept requires the reader to consider three questions. Your answer must meet all three of these criteria:

1. What are you passionate about?
2. What can you be the best at?
3. What can make you a living?

These three questions help to focus on the organization's priorities. Can your company or department survive in the future? The impact of globalization has required many organizations to become nimbler and the ability to change effectively is more critical than ever. Industries such as manufacturing are dynamic, so not changing is the equivalent of regressing because the rest of the world is moving against you. This also applies to people. In the book, Miller's Bolt, the author Thomas Stirr states, "Once people stop learning on the job, their effectiveness slowly starts to erode, and often they become layoff statistics."[10] The only way to progress is to continually learn and add new skills sets to make yourself more marketable.

Exercise: Do you or does your company have a compelling need to change? If so, what is it? Write it down. Answer the change questions: Why are we making the change? What is in it for us as individuals and as an organization if we make this change?

V = Vision

I can't get there if I don't know where I'm going.

The next letter in the change equation is V for vision. Vision is important in the change equation because without a vision how can you chart a course? People must understand the vision and

Figure 5.5 V= vision.

the change required to support the vision, including the how, when, and what their contribution will be as well as their role in the change. This will make the change easier to sell and become adopted thus reducing the resistance to change. Communicate, communicate, and communicate. It is critical when you begin deploying Lean that team members communicate clearly as to why a Lean transformation is needed. This should be at the project level, departmental level, and organization level. Creating a shared vision of why Lean is important, the desired goals and achieving buy-in from all levels will result in a clear understanding of the vision. This will help the cultural transformation occur at all levels (Figure 5.5).

Part of our vision is to seek out the true north. Keep in mind a compass can point you to magnetic north but not necessarily true north. True north is ultimately defined by our customers and their value-added (VA) proposition. In addition, a compass will not show you the obstacles that have to be overcome on the journey. It only points one in that direction. There will be many obstacles on your Lean journey toward the true north. Only a real leader can lead everyone on the journey to true north. Are you that leader?

Exercise: Take a moment and write down your vision of true north. What obstacles will have to be overcome? How will you communicate this path to everyone? Answer the change questions: What is our vision for the change? How will it benefit every employee and the company overall? Write the answer down.

N = Next Steps

N stands for next steps (Figure 5.6). Once we know we have a compelling need to change and know and understand the vision, we need to determine the next steps (not just the first) to get to the vision. These steps come from assessing where we are currently relative to the vision. If the roadmap of how we are going to achieve the vision is communicated and people gain an understanding of it, this will help diminish the resistance to change. If your company has gone through a history of adopting quality improvement programs, outlining a clear roadmap will help deflect the notion of the flavor of the month view. There are many Lean tools that help with this letter of the equation.

Exercise: What are the next steps we need to take? Write down a high-level plan of how and where you would start. Answer the change question: How are we going to make this change? How will we know if we have made the change? What metrics will we utilize? What training will be required? How will we embody our corporate values into the change? What resources will be required to make the change? Write down your answers to these questions.

Figure 5.6 N= next steps.

Figure 5.7 S = sustain—You have to keep improving to sustain!

S = Sustain

The final letter, S, stands for sustain, which we have added to the original equation (Figure 5.7). Once we have implemented our steps, we must sustain ongoing improvement. This is the most difficult step of all. Sustaining is the true test of whether there was a compelling enough reason to change and a sign if the other letters were implemented properly. One can only sustain by creating a culture of daily improvement. The only way to truly sustain is with top management leadership and drive (not just support). The leadership must be unwavering and totally committed to sustain and continually foster the compelling need to change and ongoing improvement. When you stop and think about it, the change equation resembles plan–do–check–act (PDCA). It is really a problem-solving model for change.

Exercise: How will you sustain these changes? Who will resist you in the organization? How will you handle the resistance? Are you prepared to let someone go if necessary? What type of infrastructure or resources will be required to sustain the change?

Change Observations

We Cannot Change Other People

No matter how hard you try you cannot make other people change. Someone once told me, trying to make people change is like pulling a dead horse. There are many divorces built around this theme. We must realize only people can change themselves. Therefore, the change equation is so important. We must have the deep down, internal passion to do Lean. If there is no passion then this system may not be right for you. We must figure out a way to make them want to change. As Lean practitioners, we can help:

- Communicate the compelling need to change
- Create the vision
- Create a positive framework for the change
- Help people to make the decision to move to the new Lean system

Is What I Am about to Say Going to Help Me Get Where I Want to Go?

We all run into people we perceive to be difficult. Sometimes we cannot always overcome their objections right away. It is very easy to get frustrated during the change process. Many times, we need a way to just vent or find someone to vent to. It is good to find someone you can trust and talk to as you go through this process. Sometimes it helps to write a letter or email to the person you are frustrated about, put it aside for a day or two, and then come back to it and see if you still want to send it. But it always pays to ask yourself at the peak time of frustration: "Is what I am about to say (to this person) really going to get me the result I am looking for?" If not, do not say it or figure out a better way to say it. Remember, the first rule of a change agent is to survive. Always figure what you say or write will show up on the front page of the newspaper tomorrow. Remember, e-mails and phone calls can be saved, forwarded, and blind copied.

I Do Not Have Enough Power or Authority

I wish I had a dollar for every time I have heard this from a Lean practitioner. It is a special skill to learn how to get things done through people who do not report directly to you. One must be able to build a good case as to why things need to be done and what is in it for them if they do it. Everyone can accept changes they perceive as positive very quickly. We have always used the rule that we have as much power as people give us or until our boss says you cannot do that. If you are a good leader and have supplied the vision, people will follow you. If you do not believe you have the power, you will not have it! Believe it. As Yoda[11] said, "there is no try ... only do!"[12]

The Power of the Word "We"

As change agents, it is important in just about all conversations to shy away from using the word "I," and replace it with the word "WE." When people overuse the word "I," others think it is all about them. It becomes a barrier for change as people start to ignore what they are saying. It also replaces the word "You," which is a natural progression from the word "I." Instead of a conflicting relationship of "YOU" versus "I," or the colloquial "US versus THEM," if we use "WE" instead, it sets us up as a team, making people less defensive. By saying "WE," it implies a unified working relationship where people involved can say they worked together. A suggestive "WE" beats a demanding "I" anytime ... it is amazing what difference a simple pronoun can make.

How Do We Sustain the Lean? Who Should Own It? The Three-Legged Stool for Lean Implementation

While working at a factory in China, we were asked the question, how do we sustain Lean and who should own it? We developed this example (see Figure 5.8). We compared it to a three-legged stool. The first leg is the change equation. The second is the developing Lean practitioner skills and the third is establishing the pull for Lean:

1. Everything starts with the change equation. If we do not have a compelling need to change, and the passion for Lean, the stool will fall.
2. The next two items require a balance. The pull for Lean and the ownership must come from and be with the top of the organization, board of director level, president, or general manager, etc. The pull for Lean creates the need for Lean resources. However, pushing Lean on an organization normally results in much resistance. Therefore, making the Lean leader be responsible to implement Lean does not normally work very well unless it is combined with line ownership. Otherwise, everyone will just say it is the Lean leader's job to do Lean, not them.

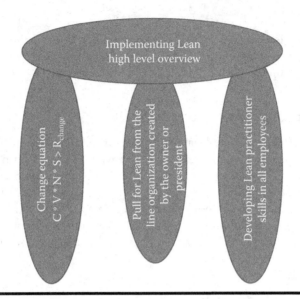

Figure 5.8   Three legged stool high level Lean implementation overview.

3. If there is a pull for Lean, there must be Lean resources trained to meet the demand. Initially, the Lean team, which should be composed of both Lean practitioners and team members from the floor (future Lean practitioners), need to learn the Lean tools while working on several projects. Six to nine months is a normal amount of time to really learn the fundamentals of the Lean tools. This does not mean just learning how to run a kaizen event which can be learned very quickly, maybe after two or three events. We are referring to a thorough grounding in the tools and exposure to the different environments for Lean implementation (i.e., assembly, machining, transactional). Once they are trained, we can create the pull for them from the line organization.

Eventually, everyone in the organization should become a Lean practitioner!

Building a Good Foundation: Changing Too Fast

A Chinese proverb states: If the tree grows too fast and gets too tall too quickly, the wind will knock it down![13] The moral is you must have a good foundation for your idea, proposal, and life in general for people to support you. In our world of Lean, it can mean if one just starts making improvements without thinking them through, and without a proper foundation and support, people will work to make it fail. When one makes changes too quickly, they may not consider impacts to upstream or downstream processes. Changing something in your process may make downstream processes unable to perform their functions/processes. One must ensure all affected personnel and departments are involved in the decision with consensus before the change is made. This results in extensive discussion and agreement prior to making the change so the change can be implemented quickly.

Another way to look at the boiled frog syndrome is in reverse. As you make small, gradual changes, the frog either doesn't notice or adjusts get comfortable.

Casey Weems

Lean Team Leaders

We normally start making Lean changes where the process is closest to the customer. For manufacturing companies, this means we are normally starting on the final assembly line. Therefore, if you are the team or group leader of the production line, by default, you must become a Lean leader! If not, how will you run the new Lean system? It is imperative the production leaders be on the implementation teams full time (this is true in hospitals and clinics as well) or it is virtually impossible to secure the buy-in necessary to sustain.

It's the Way, We Have Always Done It![14]

Start with a cage containing five monkeys. Inside the cage, hang a banana on a string and put stairs under it. Before long, a monkey will go to the stairs and start to climb toward the banana. As soon as he touches the stairs, spray all the monkeys with cold water. After a while, another monkey will try with the same response—again all the monkeys are sprayed with cold water. Keep this up for several days. Turn off the cold water. If, later, another monkey tries to climb the stairs, the other monkeys will try to prevent it even though no water sprays them. Now, remove one monkey from the cage and replace it with a new one. The new monkey sees the banana and wants to climb the stairs. To his horror, all the other monkeys attack him. After another attempt and attack, he knows if he tries to climb the stairs, he will be assaulted. Next, remove another of the original five monkeys and replace it with a new one. The newcomer goes to the stairs and is attacked. The previous newcomer takes part in the punishment with enthusiasm. Replace the third original monkey with a new one. The new one makes it to the stairs and is attacked as well. Two of the four monkeys that beat him have no idea why they were not permitted to climb the stairs, or why they are participating in the beating of the newest monkey. After replacing the fourth and fifth original monkeys, all the monkeys which have been sprayed with cold water have been replaced. Nevertheless, no monkey ever approaches the stairs again. Why not? "Because that's the way it's always been done."

Change Is a Funny Thing

Change is part of the very fabric of our everyday lives. It is ironic the only constant in our lives is change. Everyday something or someone we know has changed. Each day we get one day older! Often, when we go on vacation for a week, we come back home only to notice something has changed somewhere on the ride home. There are different parts to this equation. We must deal with the change itself, the rate of change, and the repercussions of the change. To be successful, we need to give people as much control over the change as possible. We need to over communicate why we must change, train people in the changes, and show how the changes will help them and the organization. We need to be sensitive to the fact that change is uncomfortable for most of us and deploying Lean can literally turn people's worlds upside down. We may not necessarily change what they do, but we may change when or how they do it, with the added expectation that everyone does it the same way. We need to create an environment that is change friendly and train and coach people on how to deal with change and practice the new change until we can meet the objective of the change.

There are many change models available to facilitate the change management process. It is critical to have a well thought out plan to follow in guiding people impacted by the change to ensure acceptance and adoption. Having a plan will enable you to mitigate the risks of nonacceptance and identify areas that need to be addressed along the way. Managing change and expectations will increase the probability of achieving success in the change you are trying to implement and will give you the best chance of sustaining.

Change Acceleration Process[15]

The change acceleration process (CAP) model was popularized by General Electric (GE) and used at AlliedSignal (now Honeywell). The model is

$$\text{Quality} \times \text{Acceptance} = \text{Effectiveness or } Q \times A = E.$$

This model looks at the message content (quality) of the change, the message being communicated, and assesses the potential level of resistance (acceptance) for the change (soft skills) to create a shared need for the change (effectiveness). If the change you are trying to deploy is not accepted, you will not achieve an effective result. One must understand (leverage stakeholders analysis tools) and deal with resistance from key stakeholders, build an effective influence strategy and communication plan for the change, and determine its effectiveness. Again, the relationship in the equation is multiplicative, which suggests if any of the components are zero, the change will not be effective. For example, if you have a great process in quality "10" and cannot articulate the message and have it accepted "0," the result is the change will not occur. There are many great tools that can be leveraged to facilitate change management in the GE CAP model.

This process involves building a predictive model by assessing each key stakeholder's anticipated resistance to change and building a strategy to increase their acceptance. In some ways after ensuring a robust message (quality), the acceptance part of the equation is like performing an FMEA (failure modes and effects analysis) for the change rollout process. By measuring the effectiveness, it forces the practitioner to not only develop but also implement some way to monitor and report on the progress of embedding the change in the organization. Leveraging change processes can be extremely beneficial and critical to a successful change effort. These processes help to define and clarify scope; set the direction; affirm the need to change, enhance communication, garner support; facilitate adoption and the ability to sustain; and become a determining factor in what is ultimately accomplished. Following a more formal change, roadmap will help ensure the success of the change. The roadmap will help by deploying and aiding risk mitigation with ongoing communication and barrier removal throughout the effort. Ironically these steps that walk one through the change process are again very similar to the change equation itself, which is a problem-solving model. So, if we were to relist the acceleration process with the change equation, BASICS® model, and PDCA, it would look something like that shown in Table 5.1.

Six Steps to Change Acceleration Process at Allied Signal (Honeywell)[16]

I've never seen a company that was able to satisfy its customers which did not also satisfy its employees. Your employees will treat your customers no better than you treat your employees.

Larry Bossidy
Former CEO Honeywell

Table 5.1 Change Acceleration Model Comparison to Other Models

Steps	CAP	Change Equation	BASICS	PDCA	DMAIC
1	Creating a shared need	Compelling need to change	Baseline	Plan	Define, measure
2	Shaping a shared vision	Vision	Analyze	Plan	Analyze
3	Mobilizing commitment	Next steps	Suggest solutions	Control (Shingo)	Implement
4	Making change last	Next steps	Implement	Do	Implement
5	Monitoring progress	Sustain	Check	Check	Control
6	Changing systems and structures	Sustain	Sustain	Act	Control

Source: BIG Archives.

The CAP is outlined below (see Figure 5.9):

1. Creating a shared need
2. Shaping a shared vision
3. Mobilizing commitment
4. Making change last
5. Monitoring progress
6. Changing systems and structures

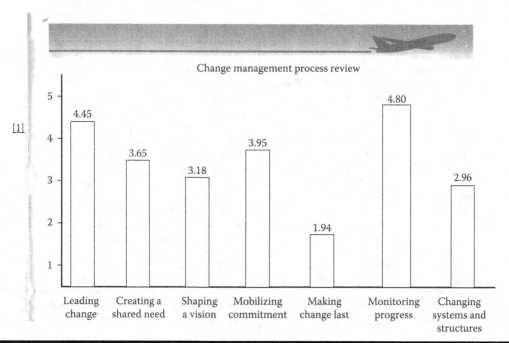

Figure 5.9 CAP = change acceleration process steps.

1. Creating a Shared Need

One must create a shared need or belief among the key players that there is a need and logic for change, critical to the company at that time. The need for change must be greater than the resistance to change and framed in such a way where people are ready and anxious for change (Table 5.2).

Key Questions to Assess Creating a Shared Need

- How well do we currently perform on the issue we want to change?
- In the eyes of the customers?
- In the eyes of the employees?
- How critical is improved performance on this issue for business results?
  • Because of competitive threat?
  • Because of growth opportunities?
  • Short term or long term?
- How widely shared is the need for change?
- To what extent is the need for change greater than the resistance to change?
- Once the need for change is assessed, one must determine the optimal way to rally the need to change. There are several key actions one can take.

Table 5.2   Adopting Change Roles

Change Acceleration Process			
Change Process	*Change Sponsor*	*Change Agent*	*Process Owner*
Leading change	Supports change	Champions change	Must make changes
Creating a shared need	Questions status quo, encourages risk taking	Builds case for changing status quo, takes risks	Defines status quo, absorbs risks
Shaping a vision	Integrates change with strategy	Translates change to be consistent with strategy	Makes changes to ensure it fit strategy
Mobilizing commitment	Shares ownership, involves others, buffers upper level conflicts	Accepts ownership, networks with others, resolves conflicts	Owns changes, informs others, manages day to day conflicts
Making change last	Provides resources for change, integrates change initiatives	Assigns resources, persistently pushes change initiative	Uses resources, gets results from change initiatives
Monitoring progress	Monitors results, shares credit	Measures results, receives no credit	Achieves results, earns credit
Changing systems and structures	Works to design and align systems and structures	Makes systems and structures practical and real	Implements new systems and structures

Source: BIG Archive—AlliedSignal TQ Training Materials.

Actions Necessary to Create a Shared Need for Change

- Set high expectations of others (e.g., devil's advocates, bold statements)
- Get data—generate external or internal data to induce change (e.g., external visits, reports, surveys, benchmarks)
- Demonstrate by example, lead the change (be a role model)

Depending on the change and the culture within your organization, it is important to understand potential common failure points in cultivating the recognition that change must occur.

Failure Modes Common to Creating a Shared Need

- Assume need is obvious to all
- Not meaningfully characterized
- Crying wolf
- They just do not get it
- Fuzzy diagnosis
- Underestimate the resistance to change

2. Shaping a Shared Vision

To create a shared vision, we need a clear statement on how the outcome of the change effort will be articulated in both emotive (visual, enticing) and pragmatic (numerical) ways. It starts with asking questions to make sure the vision is clear and everyone is on the same page. As a picture speaks a thousand words, the ideal would be to create a picture of an improved state, which is

- Challenging
- Easy to understand
- Not just one person's dream but indicative of team's commitment
- Not fixed or static but evolving
- Actionable

Questions to Ask to Assess Shaping a Vision

- To what extent has a vision been clearly articulated?
- What is in it for customers?
- What is in it for employees?
- To what extent is the vision simple and understandable?
- To what extent is the vision shared and known in the business?
- To what extent is the vision motivating and energizing?
- Test the vision statement and make sure it meets the following objectives.

Actions Necessary to Shaping a Shared Vision

- See the world from the customer's point of view (What would the customer like more/less of?).
- Articulate a vision that others can readily embrace.
- Create a bold and clear sense of purpose that energizes others.

- Create enthusiastic support for business objections.
- Once it is created and meets the objectives, ensure the following to mitigate risks and that shared support and vision have been achieved.

Failure Modes Common to Shaping a Vision

- No single statement of a vision; everyone has their own version.
- No buy-in that this is the direction we want to move; everyone does not support the vision in private talks.
- No continuity; the vision changes too often.
- No tie with customers; the vision focuses too much on what we want, not what the customer wants.
- No simplicity of vision; the vision is too complex to be easily understood and translated into practice.

3. Mobilizing Commitment

Mobilizing commitment ensures support of change effort throughout the organization.

Outcomes of Mobilizing Commitment

- A coalition/network of relevant and committed individuals who are buying into the change effort and visibly supporting it
- An ability to manage conflicts inherent in change and engage in appropriate problem-solving
- An extended commitment to change throughout the organization

Questions to Ask to Assess Mobilizing Commitment

- To what extent have we identified the key individuals who must support and be involved with this change for it to be successful?
- Inside the business?
- Outside the business?
- To what extent do we have extended buy-in for the change to happen?
- Among employees?
- Among customers/suppliers?
- To what extent have champions/sponsors been identified?
- Outlined in the following are activities to help identify challenges related to having the right people onboard to achieve a successful change effort.

Actions to Mobilizing Commitment

- Form a coalition of key players who will be change advocates, sponsors, and agents.
- Leverage sponsors to form a network of support.
- Determine who will resist and the causes of resistance, so that resistance can be overcome.
- Recognize ways of dealing with conflict to build commitment.
- Engage in appropriate problem-solving activity.

Failure Modes of Mobilizing Commitment

The following activities should be cautioned against to prevent a breakdown in commitment.

- No political sensitivity in change
- Not sharing the glory of the success
- Assume that a technical solution is sufficient (e.g., I have the right answer, why is everyone else not smart enough to see it)
- Not enough involvement and sharing responsibility
- Depends on conflict resolution style all the time
- No effective communication

4. Making Change Last

One of the significant challenges is sustaining the new change put in place. This is generally easier if there is a layout change or an equipment relocation, removal, or new installation. It is best to mistake proof the changes wherever possible so they cannot regress to the old way. Outlined here are questions that should be asked before, during, and after the change effort:

- Have we identified implementation barriers that could jeopardize success?
- What transition structures have we put in place? Transition manager, transition team's networks, control center teams, pilot teams, cross-functional committee, communications, and run control centers? To what extent do people believe this change will last? Have we eliminated all the tell-tale signs the change will not last?
- Are we communicating and celebrating successes?
- Are we significantly rewarding/recognizing the people who have driven the change and taken significant risks?
- Are we rewarding progress against milestones?
- To what extent are we tolerating refusal to change and change blockers?
- Are we consistently reinforcing desired changes in behavior?
- Are we integrating change initiatives to ongoing work patterns where possible?
- Are we helping people acquire the skills, tools, and other resources to sustain the change implementation?
- Are we encouraging learning from mistakes?
- Are we managing competing distractions?
- Are we passing on the success of this change to other areas of the organization—sharing best practices?

5. Monitoring Progress

Monitoring is a vital component of ensuring successful change and can provide an opportunity or an early identification in a potential breakdown. These are questions that could be asked to determine if there is appropriate attention on monitoring the change progress:

- Are we continuously clarifying expectations?
- Are we aligned to customer expectations?
- Are we validating our metrics with our customers, end users, and the next process?
- Do we know what success looks like?
- Are the metrics understandable and clearly related to change goals?

- Do they provide direction about what is important?
- Have we set milestones and do we check progress against them?
- Are we communicating measures and performance against them?
- Are we using personnel monitoring to foster learning and continuous improvement?

6. **Changing Systems and Structures**
   What formal aspects of the organization will be impacted and how?

   - Mission/strategy
   - Culture, values, norms—organizational structure
   - Work processes and systems
   - Leadership behavior/style
   - Skills and competencies
   - Roles and jobs responsibilities
   - Management process
   - Physical structure and technical infrastructure
   - Personal working space
   - Reward systems
   - Communications systems. Are we acquiring and placing properly the talent to manage and sustain change?
   - Are we developing our people and building the bench strength to sustain change?
   - Are the systems and structures flexible and robust?
   - Are there clear connections between the communication system and the desired change?
   - Are we developing leaders through change?

As the organization takes on initiatives that require change, there must be an appreciation that change impacts many facets of the organization. How to assess and ways to address these are outlined throughout this chapter and the book.

Leading Change

Taking charge and having a clear plan to identify and mitigate risks in the change effort is critical to acceptance. Leading change can be difficult and we will go through the challenges one may encounter; however, the outcomes if done methodically will enhance the process with the understanding that each challenge will need to be addressed and resolved as it surfaces to help ensure a successful change effort.

Outcomes of Leading Change

- Demonstrate management commitment to making change happen.
- Visible, active, and public support for accelerating change.
- Willing to take personal initiative and support other's initiatives in changing the status quo.
- Risk taking, self-confident, and empowered behavior exhibited by individuals at multiple levels in the organization.
- Conflicts and paradoxes inherent in change are identified and resolved.
- Clarity around roles for accomplishing change.
- Leaders are known as change advocates.

- Change can happen with a good roadmap/plan and a positive belief in the system.
- Improved communication.
- Demonstration of scientific approach (PDCA) to facilitate change.

Questions to Ask to Assess Leading Change

To what extent do we leaders:

- Seek and support process innovations that improve productivity?
- Clarify roles and responsibilities for accomplishing change?
- Vigorously question status quo?
- Lead by example?
- Find opportunities in change rather than excuses for avoiding change?
- Pay attention (focus time, have passion) to change?
- Demonstrate personal competencies of a change advocate?
- Assign critical roles for change?
- Involve the leaders in the change? (servant leadership)

Actions to Lead Change

- Master the processes for accelerating change
- Manage, time, energy, and focus
- Demonstrate personal leadership competencies required for change
- Articulate roles of change sponsor, agent, and target

Failure Modes Common to Leading Change

- Leaders fail to engage in behaviors necessary for change
- Leaders are transferred too quickly before change has occurred
- Leaders try to do it all alone without involving others
- Leaders shift to other goals before completing initiative
- Leaders not trained in leading change

Change efforts are not for the light of heart. An assessment should be performed to gain a full understanding before, during, and after, and the appropriate level of planning in relation to the gravity of change is proactively in place to ensure positive impact to the organization.

Change Management—Barriers and Techniques to Overcome Them

Impact of Barriers: Removal Degree of Difficulty

Whenever implementing change, we run into barriers. We classify these barriers as cultural, process, and technical.

We describe these below:

1. Cultural barriers result in entrenched habits, behaviors, and attitudes. They have a degree of difficulty = 100×.
2. Process barriers directly prevent reaching the process entitlement (3 × VA). They have a degree of difficulty of 10×.

3. Technical barriers are those specific to machines or the industry. They have a degree of difficulty of 1×.

Examples of Cultural Barriers

1. No incentive to improve.
   - No cycle time reduction mind-set. It's already good enough!
   - Lack of interest.
   - Lack of knowledge and skills.
2. Organizational structure—bureaucracy.
3. Poor problem-solving skills.
4. Lack of a problem-solving model.
5. There is a culture of sitting on the assembly floor.
6. Accounting measurements, controls, and incentives.
7. Poor resource allocation.
   - Resources must be allocated based on facts, not whims or opinions.
   - Employees get away with doing what they want versus what needs to be done.
8. Lack of balanced sense of urgency.
   - Constancy of purpose toward improving products, or services, that is, +QDIP.
9. Cultural blindness.
   - Organizations think they know themselves well, but do not.
   - Sacred cows are never acknowledged or challenged, but everyone knows they exist.
10. Data integrity.
    - Poor data collections systems that lead to bad decisions.
    - Focusing on the wrong vital few metrics.
11. Lack of discipline when it comes to following procedures.
12. Lone ranger—hero syndrome.
    - One person cannot lead the change.
13. Lack of accountability.
    - Forcing accountability is not negative.
14. Communication.
    - Poor communication of company goals.
    - Lack of reporting daily progress.
    - No voice of the customer reaches the shop floor.
15. Poor or no training.
16. Lack of management direction/input or indifference.
17. Management lack of action on poor performers.

Most cultural barriers can only be modified, replaced, or removed by a realistic cultural behavioral assessment by the senior leadership team. Senior leaders must be able and willing to take the time to critically assess their organization's strengths and weaknesses. These barriers take some change to the overall reward and recognition system.

Process Barriers

1. Process capability.
   - The process is not capable of meeting the spec requirements.

2. Poor training systems.
   - Lack of cross-training.
   - Lack of standards.
   - People do the jobs differently by shift.
3. Poor housekeeping.
   - The process requires the operator to get their own parts.
   - The operators must search for items needed to do their work.
4. Inspection.
   - We inspect quality into the process (vs. designing it in).
5. Rejects and rework are part of the process.
   - We don't want to take the time or don't know how to do it right the first time.
6. Maintenance: unplanned versus planned downtime.
   - Machines constantly and unpredictably go down.
7. No synchronous flow.
   - There is a lack of uniform flow across operations.
   - When people are out, the work gets convoluted.
8. Disrupted flow-excessive transportation, distances, and floor space.
9. Setup/changeover—not flexible—waiting time.
   - Tools are not pre-set prior to using them in the machine.
   - Operators are idle while the machine is being set up.
   - Operators do not know how to program their machines.
10. Inventory.
    - Inefficient materials management
    - Too many suppliers
    - Lack of supplier controls and reporting systems
11. Push scheduling production for the internal supplier.
    - Batch and queue internal replenishment systems between departments.
12. Engineering change process.
    - Design variances.
    - Engineering changes after production has begun.
    - Late engineering release—generally already within the allocated purchasing lead time—means purchasing cannot possibly meet customer delivery requirements.
    - Slow response by engineering on changes—engineering change notices.
13. Suppliers.
    - Offshore sourcing suppliers have their own cultural, process, and technical barriers.
    - Constantly short parts.
14. No total productive maintenance (TPM) program.
15. Parts stored away from POU (point of use).

Process barriers are best removed by using cross-functional teams and championed by senior leadership. These barriers normally cross departments and are very difficult to remove. These are good candidates for Lean system-wide kaizen projects or in some cases point kaizen events. Administrative processes are typically much more difficult to implement than shop floor activities.

Technical Barriers

1. Parts received don't meet the print or the print is wrong.
2. Parts come in packaging that must be removed prior to assembly.

Baseline... Entitlement.... Benchmark...

Figure 5.10   Baseline versus entitlement versus benchmark.

3. Lack of work instructions.
4. Problems with equipment on the front line.

These barriers can normally be removed by individuals or cross-functional teams.

Barrier Removal Process

1. Identify the barrier and ask if there is a compelling need to change the barrier.
2. If there is, categorize the type of barrier and choose the appropriate method or approach to deal with the barrier.
3. Pick and charter the appropriate team or individual to attack and remove the barrier using plan–do–study–act (PCDCA).
4. Have the team map the process and identify the critical metrics. Then see if the process is at entitlement and needs a paradigm shift to a new process or standard (Figure 5.10).

Lean and Change Management

Does Your Organization Have Sacred Cows?[17]

As organizations begin to implement change, they often encounter sacred cows (Figure 5.11). Sacred cows are outmoded, generally invisible, beliefs, assumptions, practices, systems, or strategies that inhibit change, are ineffective, and prevent responsiveness to new opportunities. If not

Figure 5.11   Sacred cow—Rotterdam, Netherlands.

recognized and addressed, the transition to a Lean organization may be challenging. Sacred cows are an example of cultural barriers. They are the most difficult to overcome as they tend to be embedded in the organization and are systemic. They can only be removed at a very high and sometimes the highest level of the organization.

Exercise: List four sacred cows at your company. How would you overcome them?

Complete the following sentences and answer the following questions:

- This job would be great if I did not have to …
- What a nuisance it is to …
- It is a waste of time to …
- I could be more productive if I did not have to …
- We could save a lot of money if we stopped …
- What frustrated me today?
- What took too long?
- What was the cause of any complaints?
- What was misunderstood?
- What cost too much?
- What was too complicated?
- What took too many people?
- What was just plain silly?
- What involved too many actions?
- What was wasted?

These questions will help to surface the sacred cows and other barriers to change.

Which Comes First? Lean Culture Change or Lean Tools?

Which route is the best way to take? We think the answer is neither and both. We have seen companies go the culture change route first and others the tool route. Both have their pros and cons. Our approach is to tailor the roll out to the company and culture. We recommend doing both in parallel if possible. Lean tools without the culture will result in improvements but sustaining will be difficult. Lean culture without the tools will make the culture difficult to sustain because there is no real improvement being implemented. This reinforces the theme of 50% people and 50% tasks required for successful continuous improvement culture and business models.

People mainly fear changes they perceive as negative. None of us resist changes we perceive as positive. Would any of you object to the change of increasing your pay by 10%? Even if the change was made without telling you ahead of time? We would all view this increase in pay as positive. Positive changes or changes which fit our paradigms pass through our filters easily. It is only the changes we perceive as negative which generate resistance.

Change and What's in It for Me

Change can be a difficult adjustment for many individuals, despite the fact there are those that walk around complaining about the barriers that surround us daily as we try to do our day-to-day work. However, as soon as there is change in the wind, the tone shifts and an uneasiness of the unknown begins as people try to understand the impact to their local microcosm. We developed this tool knowing each employee is going to ask, "What's In It For Me" (WIIFM) and how is it going to affect me and my future in this company? When challenged with a new initiative, it is important to answer these questions, and they must be addressed from multiple perspectives. For example, an office manager is in the middle of a Lean initiative that will reduce cycle times enabling more output utilizing the same or less staff with no need for overtime. Now, let us look at this from different perspectives:

1. Employee 1 is silently concerned she will no longer be paid for the 5–10 overtime hours per week she is accustomed to; therefore, the project will potentially impact her current lifestyle and is perceived negatively.
2. Employee 2 is a working parent who has struggled over the past year to pick up her children on time at daycare; from her perspective, the project is a positive one. We find the WIIFM question applies to changes even in our personal lives.

Management must be ready with the answers to address both positive and negative impacts from the employees' perspective. If we do not answer the tough questions, employees are left in the dark creating an unnerving void. They will fill in any gaps not clearly communicated with the worst-case scenario, often creating, or spreading rumors that will run rampant in the office and potentially on the Internet. Think about the proverbial call from the school nurse. The nurse leaves a message on your voicemail asking you to call her back. What starts going through your mind? You start to think the worst things which could possibly happen to you child.

The key is to answer the following questions using WIIFM from the point of view of the employee each time they are impacted by a change. What do they really want to know and why? It is crucial not only to know the answers to the following questions, but also to be able to frame them in a positive fashion. Everyone on the management team should be aligned and have the same answers. These questions must communicate to the organization the compelling need to change and provide the impetus to work together and marshal all resources toward this common goal.

1. What is the change we are making?
2. Why are we making the change?
3. How will it affect the employees? Now and in the future?
4. How will it affect the company? Now and in the future?
5. What is in it for the employee if we make the change?
6. What is in it for the company if we make the change?
7. Share as much of the implementation plan as possible to provide the when's, where's and how's the change will be implemented. People feel much more secure knowing there is a plan in place and that they have a future role in the company.

We suggest scripting answers to the above questions prior to starting the Lean journey. Once scripted, it is important to communicate the answers with the staff in each department prior to rolling out the Lean implementation. This tool forces leadership to think through each of these questions. The answers must be compelling enough to support the big "C" in the change equation. The biggest concern people will have been how it will affect them and what is in it for them.

Lesson Learned: Remember communicating this once will not be sufficient. One cannot over-communicate. Remember, when people are tired of hearing it is when they have just begun to listen. Additionally, it will be important as changes are made when concerns arise and/or changes are challenged, each concern must be addressed to mitigate the resistance.

Homework: Script out your answers to the questions prior to implementing your Lean initiative.

"Right Seat on the Right Bus"[18]

As you go on the Lean journey and paradigm shifts in thinking are required to transform the organization, you may find not everyone can or is willing to make the adjustments necessary to move the organization forward in this new direction. You need to assess if you have the right people in "the right seat on the right bus." This concept is from the book, Good to Great,[19] which we have found invaluable in our change management toolset. The goal is to find out if your employees are on the right bus or, in other words, supporting our change initiative and then assess if they are in the right seat on the bus (in the organization chart) to help us get to the next level of change. To implement this tool, we take the organization chart and review the persons in each position. This is a very difficult process and should be taken very seriously from an extremely critical and realistic point of view.

The other dimension in this tool is time. It is possible for a person to be in the right seat on the right bus during one time frame, but not for the next. One may not have the necessary skills required to implement the changes required in the next phase. Do not underestimate the importance of having the right people in the right seat on the bus as it will impact the success of your organization especially as you go through a Lean journey. One must decide what time frame to use, but generally it pays to review the organization every 6 months.

Note: This tool can be combined with other tools such as the CAP process.

The goal of the evaluation is to determine the developmental needs required to keep the person in the same role but which will enable them to help the company achieve the next level. Consideration must be given to determine if the manager or staff member is the right individual but may have not received the appropriate level of training. The leadership team and the change agent will need to determine if this is a valued employee and if there is enough time to coach and mentor to ensure needed skills are received to achieve the desired results.

This should be a collaborative process. The persons being evaluated should also be given the opportunity to determine if they have the skills to take them to the next level. They should be asked to write down what they think are their strengths and weaknesses. These should be compared with the evaluator's perception of their strengths and weaknesses. Differences should be discussed. If we determine someone is not going to be in the right seat but is on the right bus, there are a couple of options. Either the person needs to be moved to another area of the organization where they can be successful or they need a clear plan to receive coaching, mentoring, and skills to stay in the same seat. Sometimes, they are just not the right fit for where the organization is going. This takes us back to the question, if we were hiring someone for life, would we still have this issue? The result should be either to agree on a move or on what steps should be taken to raise the level of skills for the individuals to stay in the same roles.

Lesson Learned: During any culture change, there are some individuals, even sometimes at high levels, after coaching and mentoring who honestly believe the changes will never work. The longer you hold on to these individuals, the more adverse it will become for the organization.

Top Ten Signs People Do Not Get It (Affectionately Known as Concrete Heads) (Figure 5.12)

1. Just wait until it breaks and then we can replace it.
2. We are too busy to implement Lean now. We must make the end of the month.
3. We need to cut indirect labor!
4. We need more inventory and more space.

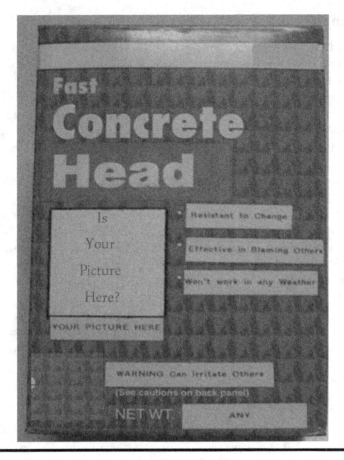

Figure 5.12 Are you a concrete (close minded) head?

5. Tell me what I need to do. When will you get to us?
6. We have improved enough already. Why should we improve anymore? Is there any return on investment (ROI)?
7. We do not want to invest in teams or training; we would rather lay them off.
8. We do not need to benchmark other companies; besides, we need to cut back on the travel budget.
9. We must make double-digit returns on sales. We cannot get there with Lean!
10. What does get-it mean? Do I have it?

It is important to identify and determine the best course of action to take when encountering concrete heads. If not addressed, they may negatively impact the ability of the organization to achieve Lean success.

Leaders as Change Agents

Lean can be brought into the organization at many different levels; however, for Lean to take hold, permeate, and sustain with the organization in a significant manner, it requires leadership at all levels. Leaders must act as change agents and support their change agents in their efforts. Identifying leaders and individuals within the organization that exhibit the behaviors of good change agents can develop and can facilitate your change initiatives. It is not unusual to see totally unexpected leaders emerge from the "woodwork" who thrive in this new Lean environment.

Leading Change: Leader Characteristics[20]

There are several attributes that make a successful Leader change agent:

1. Resourcefulness—Knows how to adapt to challenging and often ambiguous circumstances, can both think strategically and make good decisions under pressure, can set up complex work systems and engage in flexible problem-solving behavior, and can work effectively with higher management in dealing with the complexities of the change.
2. Does what it takes—Has perseverance and focus on the face of obstacles; takes charge, knows what is needed, and moves forward; and can stand alone yet is open to learning from others when necessary.
3. Is a quick study—Quickly learns new management and technical skills.
4. Decisiveness—Prefers quick and approximate actions to slow and precise ones in many management situations.
5. Developing subordinates—Delegates to subordinates effectively. Broadens subordinates' opportunities, acts with fairness toward subordinates, and is not intimidated to add talented subordinates.
6. Sets a developmental climate—Provides a challenging climate to encourage subordinates' developments.
7. Confronts problem subordinates—Acts with fairness when dealing with problem subordinates.
8. Team orientation—Team is key. Does not have to do it all alone, accomplishes tasks through managing others.
9. Hiring talented staff—Hires/surrounds self with talented people.
10. Building and mending relationships
    a. Knows how to build and maintain working relationships with coworkers and external parties.
    b. Can negotiate and handle work problems without alienating people and understanding others.
    c. Can get their cooperation in non-authority relationships.
11. Compassion and sensitivity—Shows genuine interest in others and sensitivity to subordinates' needs.
12. Straightforwardness and composure—Is steadfast, relies on takt-based positions, does not blame others for mistakes, and is able to recover from troubled situations.
13. Maintains and embraces work/life balance—Balances work priorities with personal life so that neither is neglected.
14. Self-awareness—Has an accurate picture of strengths and weaknesses and is willing to improve.
15. Putting people at ease—Displays warmth and a good sense of humor.

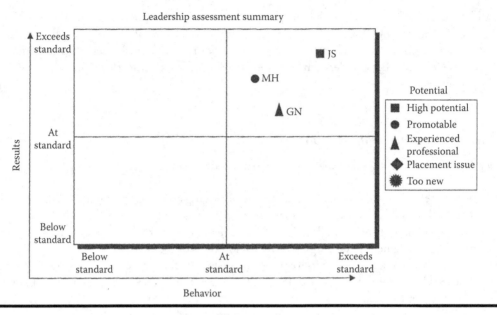

Figure 5.13   Leadership assessment 2x2 matrix.

16. Acting with flexibility—Can behave in ways that are often seen as opposites, can be both tough and compassionate, and can lead and let others lead.
17. Has high energy—Displays sense of urgency and displays high energy levels, which become contagious within the team.

Succession Planning

We find many organizations do not have succession plans in place. As leaders, we need to be prepared in the event someone leaves or is unable to continue in the position assigned. Our daily routine should include developing our people to be able to take our place (see Figure 5.13). If there is no one there to take our place, it is much more difficult for us to advance since there is no one to replace us. Therefore, it is in our own best interest to ensure we are constantly developing a successor(s). This also helps to prove if people are truly in the right seats. Once a potential successor(s) is selected, a process for fostering growth and continually evaluating their progress is needed. If it is determined that the successor selected does not have the ability to take over your job or cannot either physically or mentally do the job, we need to re-evaluate the future and what role that person will be playing.

However, a former mentor of mine was correct in saying that not everyone can be the boss and not everyone can be A players (see Table 5.3). We need people to efficiently complete the work every day with the recognition some people will reach their limit or do not want to move further in the organization. We call these folks seasoned/experienced professionals. We always need some C level people as they provide a significant contribution to the organization doing the everyday tasks required.[21]

Lesson Learned: It is difficult to do, but we need to constantly assess our bench strength to complete our work each day and develop those who are going to take us to the next levels of growth and continuous improvement.

Table 5.3 A Player Grid

Characteristics	A	B	C	D
1. Change				
2. Leadership				
3. Manager				
4. Trust/credibility				
5. Initiative				
6. Team focus				
7. Flexibility				
8. Speed/urgency				
9. Priority				
10. Continuous learning				
11. People developer				

Note: This is a blank form where we rate the individual in each area of the grid.
Source: BIG Archive—AlliedSignal TQ Training Materials.

A Players

The questions everyone should be asking in an organization at any level are:

- Is what I am doing right now VA to the customer?
- Am I an A player? (See Table 5.4).

If you are a manager, you are there to support and assist the frontline person to help them do their job better. Middle managers tend to be particularly threatened by Lean as are frontline supervisors. Our experience is that 40%–60% in the beginning do not cut it and cannot make the change from cop to coach. Imagine an environment where the goal of every manager is to try to improve their area to the point where you work yourself out of a job. One should not be afraid to go to their boss and say, "You do not need me any more in this position." Every time we have seen this happen; the person has been promoted to a new position with more responsibility in the company. At first glance, most people think this is crazy. But at second glance, if you were the boss who would you rather keep: the person who worked themselves out of a job or the person who creates busy work, creates work for others, or harbors information so they are perceived as valuable and must be kept around? We must create more adaptive and more responsive organizations with good real-time evaluation and teaching processes, good developmental tactics, succession planning, and constant development of new skill sets to take us to the next level, whatever that may be. We need adaptable A team players, open minded, and always looking for the next best way to do something. We need to develop counter strategies to constantly fight complacency and big company disease.

Table 5.4   A Player Grid Detail

Characteristics	A	B	C	D
1. Change	Innovator/agent	Accept	Slow	Resistant
2. Leadership	Motivator	Team player	Follower	Disruptive
3. Manager	Closer/delivers on commitments	Meets commitments generally Willing to restate expectations	Well organized, may require follow-up	Requires continual monitoring
4. Trust/credibility	Admired	Respected	Accepted	Tolerated/ suspected
5. Initiative	Self-starter	Implementor	Maintains status quo	Lagger / blocker
6. Team focus	Committed to company objectives	Supports company objectives	Works well on team	Self-serving, struggles with mine versus ours parochial
7. Flexibility	Easily adaptable	Adaptable	Copes/ adapts	Rigid
8. Speed/urgency	Anticipates	Responds	Reacts	Stalls
9. Priority	Perceptive	Consistent	Needs focus	Wrong agenda!
10. Continuous learning	Self-continuous improvement	Responds enthusiastically	Trainable	Knows it all
11. People developer	Personal investment Recognizes potential and grows it Plans to do, committed to the process	Recognizes potential and grows it	Routine/ cook book approach	Does not value but uses people
12. Coach	Mentor/coach	Advisor (guide)	Teachable	Intimidator micromanager
13. Diligence/ perseverance/ passion	Drivers/intense determination/ contagious	Persistence personally intense	Focused	Easily distracted

(Continued)

Table 5.4 *(Continued)* **A Player Grid Detail**

Characteristics	A	B	C	D
14. Communicator	Knows audience Recognizes needs and versatile/ multimedia (written and oral)	Delivers well and effective	Mechanical messenger	Avoids/stifles miscommunicates
15. Listener	Feedback sensitive Creates environment that is open	Listens to feedback when offered and acts receptive	Hears but does not always listen	Appears to listen, or ignores or shuts off access
16. Customer focus	Walks-the-talk Knows the center of the universe-customers Customer's advocate Long-term partner	Considers important Will support	Lip service Neutral depending on the forces	Internally focused Manipulation/ short sighted
17. Business perspective	Cross-functional Contribution to whole organization Influences beyond area of expertise	Primarily influences within the area of expertise Understands interrelationships	Vertically oriented Directly related functions	Myopic Narrow
18. Judgment	Astute	Analytical	Procedural	Trite/shallow

Source: BIG Archive—AlliedSignal TQ Training Materials.

Change: Threat or Opportunity?

Resistance to Change

We are all guilty when it comes to resistance to change, some of us more than others. We all resist change to some extent. Sometimes resistance to change is good. We say, "Skeptics are good, cynics are bad." Skeptics keep you honest by asking very good questions. Cynics on the other hand will never go along with the change and become concrete heads/blockers during the culture transition. It helps to surface problems and valid objections to the anticipated change. It is important to realize we do not have to always view change only as a threat. We can view change as an opportunity. Our experience, when implementing culture changes, is that the company must get 20% of the people on board to start the flywheel moving and journey down the path to internalizing the Lean change. Figure 5.14 shows some Leadership Characteristics. It's all about changing our behaviors to drive effective Leadership. "Leaders don't create followers, they create more leaders." - Tom Peters

Resistance[22]

While working with Company X, I was on the workshop floor with an operator who consistently opposed any changes and was very negative. We were looking at the flow and process elements and as we identified waste together. Every time I said something … the operator said, but that won't work because. … This continued for an hour or so. After all the "buts," I said let's just try the initial work sequence we all discussed, arrived at consensus, and agreed upon. The new process resulted in a reduction in process cycle time of 45% simply by changing the flow and removing some additional waste. The operator was amazed how easy the new process was. At this point, the operator became more open and supportive of the Lean initiative. He is now talking to others promoting the change initiative.

Lesson Learned: With open-ended questions, a bit of empathy, and patience, there may be an opportunity to turn a naysayer or concrete head into a Lean believer who can influence others in a very positive manner.

Team members, who view change as a threat, only focus on the negative, which many times results in a self-fulfilling prophecy. The person is moved, or let go, because they simply could not

The product supply way

Driving performance excellence through effective leadership

Long term philosophy and commitment	• Exemplify the credo values in thought, word, and action • Always remember the customer in everything we do • Maintain a strategic, long term mindset • Drive a quality – oriented, continuous improvement culture
Leadership engagement	• Cultivate strong leadership skills across the organization • Develop a learning organization through active involvement in real life opportunities • Anticipate and prepare for tomorrow's challenges • When problems occur, get the facts first hand at the source
People development	• Teach, coach, and challenge • Empower employees with accountability and authority • Recognize and reward performance • Involve and respect our extended family of partners
Performance alignment and management	• Align goals and challenging targets across the organization • Lead with facts and data • Mobilize the workforce around specific business issues/opportunities • Communicate clearly and decisively
Lean production system	• Create standard, simplified processes • Deploy Lean principles and build them into the very fabric/infrastructure throughout the organization • Recognize that today's standarization is the foundation for tomorrow's improvement

Figure 5.14 Selected leadership characteristics.

adjust to the change. This is part of what is called the expectations theory where everything fits their expectation or paradigm, making them believe, the change would not succeed; therefore, they would not succeed. There is a quote in the book Miller's Bolt that supports this theory: "Once you put a label on someone or something your brain goes on scan, looking for evidence to support your belief."[23] Those who embrace change and see it as a positive not only succeed but also have fun doing it and they tend to advance in their organizations. Some people are just naturally early adopters for change, while others wait and sit back to see what will happen. We need to remember, in any given area of the organization, you will find all types of people, at all levels, who respond to change differently and we must be prepared and have a plan in place to deal with each of them.

When communicating expectations for change, everyone should recognize process changes will not roll out perfectly. In general, a rule of thumb in Lean implementations is the Pareto rule, 80% will be operationally correct and the remaining 20% will need to be tweaked when moving from concept to pilot to real world. It is critical to set appropriate expectations, and to ensure that team members and staff realize most changes in the process as they are implemented will require some initial adjustments. Processes implemented today should not remain the same for months or years. A continuous improvement plan should be in place, with processes revisited periodically per the business plan and revised based upon changes that occur to the business over time. Change can be emotional; people will say things that sometimes might be out of character. The key is not to overreact to what you hear or what you hear other people say they heard. Try to understand their concerns and ask them for solutions. It is not unusual for people to say they heard you (the Lean Practitioner) say things you really did not say. It is all part of the change process.

An operator from a subassembly area totally refused to do one piece flow. He was so convinced batching was better he continued to batch despite coaching, group training, and one on one training. He even walked off the line a couple of times and refused to work. (In my younger days, we would have written the operator up for insubordination and he probably would have been fired!). We figured once we combined his subassembly area with the final assembly line and integrated the processes, he would see the benefits of one-piece flow and why it was necessary. On his first day working in the new combined line, the operator continued to batch. Suddenly, the final operator did not have his sub assembly because he was still batching. The final assembly operator disciplined him saying you are making me wait while you batch those ten pieces (which fortunately was all he could fit in the new workstation). The operator finally relented but only after his team member made it clear he could not batch. The line set a record that day for the highest output and halted 3 weeks of 12-hour overtime days. At a company function, he (unsolicited) came up to us and apologized for his behavior and said it would not happen again. After working on the new combined line, he finally realized one piece flow was the way to go. In this case, patience and coaching paid off.

Language Barriers to Change

The number one barrier to change is your mind! The following words/phrases should raise a big red flag:

- I cannot …
- It will not work …
- I already know …
- It will not work here …
- I tried that before …

- I do not want to run it that way ...
- It is not our way ...
- We need more data ...
- How do you know it will work?
- I only have a few more years until I retire ...
- We are already Lean ...

We have a saying,

> When you say, 'I can't' you admit your own ignorance![24]

Our other saying is,

> If you tell me, you CAN'T, I will agree with you that you CAN'T and then I will go find someone who will!

Most Loved Words

A favorite story book growing up was The Little Engine that Could.[25] The little engine in the story kept saying, "I think I can, I think I can."
The most loved words with Lean are the following:

- What if we could ...?
- What if we tried ...?
- How can we ...?
- I know we can ...
- I saw someone else doing it ...
- Why didn't it work the last time ...?
- When was the last time we tried ...?
- Maybe the manufacturer can help us ...
- Let us benchmark a company that is doing it that way ...
- Let us take the best from your way and my way and make it our way ...

Leading a Horse to Water Analogy

During our Lean system implementations, we find people at all levels resist change. Some people just seem physically incapable of changing their paradigms. As stated in Thomas Kuhn's, The Structure of Scientific Revolutions,[26] "It is as though some scientists, particularly the older and more experienced ones, may resist indefinitely, most of them (eventually) can be reached in one way or another." Our analogy is
We lead the horse to water. The horse drinks the water. The horse likes the water but then refuses to drink it again.

> Sometimes you just want to ask the simple question: Would you rather have $10 or $20? It is amazing how many companies take the $10.

Joe Thompson

We find it odd when we implement the new process and people like it! They get great results but, if allowed, will go back to the old way of doing it. How can this be? How often as a Lean Practitioner have you experienced this in your organization? It all comes back to the change equation and although they might have been dissatisfied with the way things were, they obviously did not have a truly compelling need to change!

Sometimes You Have to Unlearn What You Have Learned[27]

At a Company in South Carolina, we installed a new Lean line with a two-bin system. The line was very successful, and everyone loved it. The plant manager, however, had a prior history with another company where they kitted the parts prior to assembly, which was also very successful. He insisted on using his kitting system. With a two-bin system, there is no need for kitting. The only exception might be where there is a special job requiring parts that are not on the line. The Lean practitioner explained kitting would require additional personnel and slow down the line; however, the plant manager did not care. Since one must pick the hills, they want to die on, the Lean practitioner implemented the kitting system. When the line performance decreased, the plant manager blamed the Lean practitioner. The two-bin system was removed, the kitting system was installed in its place, and the Lean practitioner was removed from the line.

Lesson Learned: Most employees are resistant to new process changes; however, leaders need to help the team embrace change and see it as a positive.

We Are All Interconnected but Not Typically Measured That Way

We are all interconnected, so it is important if we change a process, we ascertain its impact on other interrelated processes to avoid unintended consequences. There is no value to a stakeholder to make one area better at the expense of another area. How can we work together to improve the total system and enterprise? It is critical that changes are not made in silos but support cross-departmental views and evaluate value streams with the appropriate stakeholders to ensure all are engaged as the process changes. Any proposed changes should be performed through collaboration, agreed upon, and then communicated to all staff involved.

Sometimes People Need to Vent!

One of the first steps we take in implementations is surveying or interviewing people in the area, department, company, etc. The object of this exercise is to allow people to vent and get out their frustrations. People cannot move forward in terms of actions or thinking without the opportunity to voice what is bothering them. In training, we utilize an exercise called hopes and fears. We ask participants based on the pending initiative to record their greatest hopes and greatest fears on a flip chart using a drivers/barriers chart format. We find the answers are similar across all organizations across the world.

Top three fears are generally as follows:

1. It will not sustain
2. Management will not walk the talk (lack of support)
3. Loss of jobs

Top three hopes are generally as follows:

1. Will be successful and increase profitability
2. Will improve job security
3. Will improve customer satisfaction

Again, remember it is critical to take a pulse of the reaction to change during a Lean deployment and individually address any concerns to mitigate resistance to change and improve the success of the implementation. Lean is about making sure the frontline staff have the right tools at the right time at the right place and are doing the right thing for the organization. It is often helpful when making a change to have a post-it board on an easel in the area where the change is occurring so staff can write down challenges, concerns, and ideas. This gives the staff a mechanism to provide feedback and let them feel they have a say in what is happening.

Keep Things the Same or Similar Where Possible

We were implementing Lean in a hospital emergency department (ED) that required us to change how certain rooms were being utilized. The team decided to re-label the rooms based on the new usage of the rooms. So, room S1 became exam room 2 and room S2 became exam room 1. Well, you would have thought the world was going to end. No one objected to the new usage of the rooms, but no one could keep straight which rooms were which. When the team looked back at what they had done, they realized it really did not matter how the rooms were labeled and switched S1 to exam room 1 and S2 to exam room 2. This simple change helped everyone accept the new process with no negative impact to the results.

Bumps in the Road

We all fall victim to this tendency as we tend to get caught up in the excitement of implementing and making things better. When we find out we have inadvertently upset someone (especially at the executive level) and need to take a step back and take a breath. No matter how big a deal it seems initially it too will pass. Once the problem is smoothed over, we need to step back and look at these as just bumps in the road. We move forward with the improvements and persevere with the change. Make no doubt, there will be those who will feel threatened by the changes and they will work against you at first outwardly and then covertly. They will eventually expose themselves and will need to be dealt with. We work hard to coach them and motivate them to see the advantages of the new system and to seriously listen to their concerns. The more people you can involve up front the less people who can say you never told me about this or they did not ask me.

Lesson Learned: We always tell our teams, do not worry if you make a mistake, there will always be someone who will be more than happy to point it out to you!

Manage Expectations: Highs and Lows

As we implement improvements, the teams, individuals, as well as organizations tend to go through highs and lows. For example, highs are when the team is elated about improvements made or positive feedback from a CEO are received and lows are when the team's changes are not accepted or they receive negative feedback from their peers or an executive. This is totally normal. However, we have found it is important to monitor and work to manage people's expectations and to minimize the highs and lows they experience. If the team cannot recover from the low, the implementation can fail. If expectations get too high, the team may feel they cannot meet them and will feel like they failed.

Rule of Unintended Consequences

Part of systems thinking is the rule of unintended consequences. No matter how much we plan, we still run into unexpected problems or situations. Again, this is normal. If it is not a safety-related issue, it is very important not to overreact to these unintended consequences or to how people initially react to change but to resolve the unintended consequence.

2 × 4 Story[28]

I walked into the manager's office. He told me what a great job we were doing, to keep up the great work, and keep him informed of our progress. He was going to order the items we needed right away. As I walked out of the office, the manager picked up a 2 × 4 (piece of wood) and hit me in the back of the head with it. I said to myself "I think I just got hit in the back of the head by a 2 × 4, but I know he would never do that, he told us what a great job we were doing, but boy did that hurt." The next week I met with the manager again. Again, he told me what a great job the team was doing and to keep up the great work and keep him informed of our progress. Oh, and by the way, he had just gotten around to placing the order we needed and he was going to follow up on it next week. As I walked out of the office, the manager picked up a 2 × 4 and hit me in the back of the head with it. I said to myself "I think I just got hit in the back of the head by a 2 × 4, but he wouldn't do that, he told us how great we were doing, but boy that hurt." The next week I met with the manager again. He still had not placed the order but continued to tell us what a great job we were doing. I guess he did hit me with that 2 × 4 after all.

Lesson Learned: 2 × 4 is not always easy to recognize. Eventually, we wake up and realize we are getting hit in the head by the 2 × 4 and we start to duck as it is coming but sometimes, we still cannot get away from it. They are thrown at the best of us and many Lean practitioners have ended up leaving their companies.

Lesson Learned: Document the baseline condition prior to making change as people forget the way it used to be and hold meetings as needed, which go through the original process, changes, and improvements over time so people can track forward progress.

Complacency: The Arch Enemy of Lean

The paragraph title says it all. We must be vigilant never to be content with the status quo or feel we have improved enough or cannot improve any more. There is always room for improvement. There is always a better way to do something. We may not know what it is yet, but we know it exists.

Exercise: Think about how you can build safeguards into the organization so you are always driving continuous improvement. How can we keep the healthy paranoia that will keep us on our toes? Make sure your vision and audits always settle for nothing less than perfection. If you are concerned you might be getting complacent, take the following test:

- When was the last time you made an improvement to your process?
- Do you only make a change in reaction to something occurring externally (to your organization or department)?
- Do you have a mechanism to receive and implement suggestions?

- Do you track the number of suggestions implemented from your employees per month?
- What is your average implemented suggestions per month from your employees?
- Do you often receive the 100 reasons why something cannot be done?
- How often do you say?
- "It can't be done."
- "Management won't let me …."
- "I can't get money …."
- "We tried that before …."
- "We don't need to get any better …."
- "My department's metrics look great …."
- "What does it matter if we impacted the other department … that's their problem."
- "I'm tired of hearing about customer satisfaction issues."
- "We know we have problems … we will fix them when we get that new facility with more space."
- "We can wait on that improvement …."
- "The new software we are installing will solve all our problems!"
- "I can't make any changes because …."
- "It's not my area or my job …."
- Do you celebrate when you hit your goals?
- Do you set your audit standards so people will feel good instead of driving continuous improvement?
- Do you tell people they are doing a good job when they are not?
- Are you complacent?

People Forget Quickly How It Used to Be

People will quickly forget how things used to be. You will hear comments like "Things have not changed much around here." When you confront these folks and start reminding them of how it used to be, they quickly backtrack and realize they were wrong. For this reason, we recommend creating a visual display of before and after pictures, along with improvements made during the implementation, near the line, department, or in the cafeteria or conference rooms to remind people how it used to be.

Comparison to Where We Are Today

Many times, as we introduce new Lean concepts, people will dismiss them out of hand. We hear things like: No way that will work here. Or you don't understand how things are or It's impossible! This is because they are comparing and trying to apply what they are learning to their current work environment. In most cases, the transition to Lean thinking and Lean practices is so different that it is impossible to imagine what is possible when compared to the current work environment.

Lesson Learned: Even though we try to help people see the vision, sometimes it is difficult for them to see it or get it until we implement the changes and they experience it.

Let's Try It

A process in Company X required a product to be square, which resulted in a significant amount of time presetting tools, measuring and re-measuring. We discussed this with the operators and one of them had an idea. He suggested creating a fixture to set inside the part to make it square and then secure it. The other employee doing the job was very negative saying it would never work. We said let's try it. After trying this, it produced the desired result. The product was square. The negative employee said we were just lucky. We said let's try it several more times. After six consecutive successes, the negative employee finally agreed that our trial was successful. The idea to square up the product saved 15% of the time in their process. We then witnessed the employee happily telling several other employees about the successful change he had made to the process and that it was the first time anyone listened to his ideas!

Lesson Learned: As a leader, one must have the patience to help lead the employees on a journey of idea generation and self-realization using a hands-on approach.[29] Another example was at a hospital. We explained that no patient would wait longer than 20 minutes to see the Emergency Room physician. The nurses told us that was not possible as they had very complicated patients, not just earaches and sore throats. Of course, they were right! In their current environment, full of waste and systems not built for patients to flow they were correct; it was not possible. Once we worked together to identify the waste and streamline the process, we achieved the goal.

Objections Are Good!

Many people feel if they object or want to discuss proposed Lean ideas, they will be perceived as negative. This could not be further from the truth because we need people to ask the difficult questions. People who appear negative, skeptics, are not always against you! Just because people ask difficult questions does not mean they are negative. But once the questions are answered, are they on board with the changes? To start the discussion, one needs to understand the true nature of an objection. There are three answers one encounters when trying to sell an idea: yes, no, or what about this?

If someone objects to an idea, they have not said no. Objections come from our paradigms we discussed earlier. Objections are a way for the person who is being told to change, to try and buy-in to the change. If we can satisfactorily answer all the objections, we get the sale, that is, we get the person to accept the change. Therefore, we look forward to objections. Objections are good! When someone does say no, we normally respond with why? The question why is designed to solicit the objection. Once we have the objection, we must work to overcome it. Sometimes an objection can be overcome quickly, while other times it may take training, a series of long discussions, or showing the person an example of where their objection was overcome, that is, benchmarking. Some of us just need to see it to believe it. Once we see it, there is no stopping us from going after it. Once we overcome all the objections, we need to go for the close.

Lesson Learned: We must patiently solicit and overcome every objection and take away every excuse to get people to buy-in to the change. This can be a very painstaking process but with perseverance pays off in the long run. It is important each objection is individually addressed or you will not be able to gain complete buy-in or closure.

Overcoming Objections—Types of Closing Questions

Closing techniques can be leveraged to help overcome CI objections and facilitate change. In essence, it is another form of our overall Lean problem-solving system. Objections represent a "problem" the customer (stakeholder) is having with the change. We need to identify the problem (objection) and then work to determine the root cause (source of the objection) and then work together to develop a solution (win-win) to the problem and eliminate the need for the objection.

Once the objection is addressed, we should be able to follow it up with what we call in sales "a closing question" to see if we have "sold" the person on the change or if there remains some objection.

Continuing the sales analogy, once we overcome the objection, we need to find out if we have succeeded in convincing the person to "buy" our idea. This is the same as selling any product and is called "closing the sale." If the person answers our closing question with a sincere "yes" then we have done our job. If we get a "no" then we have more work to do. We must find the next objection and work to overcome it and then go for the "close" again. This process is no different than in any other type of sales. There are several closing processes taught in retail sales. Some of them are the following:

- The direct close
- The indirect close
- The positive-negative close
- The assumed close

These techniques work well with change management because we are trying to sell the change, or in this case, Lean Thinking, to the organization.

The most important thing to remember is most of us are only good at selling something we really believe in. If you really believe in Lean principles and have seen it work repeatedly, it becomes an easy sell. When someone does object to implementing Lean in their area, the first thing we try to ascertain is the objection. If the objection is that it is "going to make my job more difficult," our response might be, "So what you are saying is, if we could show you how it would make your job easier, you would buy into the change? OK, let's show you how it will make it easier to do your job in the long run." Once the discussion is complete, we are ready for the closing question: "so now we have shown how much easier your job will be to manage in the new Lean environment, are you willing to work with us on the change?" Then be silent because he who speaks first loses.

Badgering and the Closing

Why is it important to be silent after asking the closing question? Have you ever been to a store where the person asks the closing question "Would you like to buy the carpet tonight?" While you are thinking it over, they say, "Well, you know it is very good carpet and it will last a long time and we have free installation, and it is the best carpet in its class." Before you know it, all you want to do is get away from this person. By the salesperson continuing to speak, he/she now gives you more cause for objections and reasons to walk out. This behavior translates into "begging" you to buy the carpet and the person appears "desperate" to get the sale. We see this same behavior with ideas and change.

Lesson Learned: Do not badger. Sell your case based on data and facts, not what other people think. Be confident, believe, and be passionate in your responses, back them up with data and past results, answer the objections, and close the sale! Teach team members to value and work with the strengths of others.

"Just the Facts, Ma'am"

Many times, we will be touring an area and spot a problem. It is not uncommon for the person taking us on the tour to get defensive and start making excuses for the situation. Their sentence normally starts with something like: Well maybe they had to … or It is probably because of …. After a while, it gets old and reflects very negatively on the person doing the tour. Excuses are like bad breath … no wants to smell it.

Lesson Learned: As a Lean Practitioner, never make excuses for others. Just stick to the facts. There is nothing wrong with agreeing with the observation. If you have the facts and know why something is being done then present the facts accordingly but don't start off with the word "maybe" or "I think."

Toyota Kata[30]

In the book, Toyota Kata, the author Mike Rother suggests we start with a production vision. The production vision should come from the senior leadership team. The thought process here is most often we only spend time discussing how things are going relative to the specific departments, key measures or metrics, and always seem to miss how our department is connected to the rest of the plant or organization. This gets back to our earlier discussions on the importance of systems thinking. Otherwise, we get lost in the day-to-day firefighting activities. A good vision statement helps to align where everyone should be headed and it gives us that connection of purpose and desire. Examples of the production vision from his book are:

■ Zero defects
■ 100% VA
■ One-piece flow
■ Security for people

There is a significant difference in how most of us have been taught on how we approach setting targets. As an example, when we construct value stream maps (VSMs) which identify the current state and then create a future state map based upon what opportunities or ideas are known to fix the problem. Their future state goals are typically tied to what they think they can accomplish with the current information in our possession.

In the kata approach, we identify what the future state should be or what we want it to be. We then figure out a way to make that happen. The target conditions in the kata are those things that we set as the condition we want to achieve. Therefore, we brainstorm an ideal state during our VSM process. At the time, we may not have an idea of how we will achieve it so we set out on small incremental experiments with the intent on learning. The result may be that the experiment did not move us any closer to the target condition but learning did take place and now we can apply the PDCA cycle and plan for the next experiment. Our traditions in manufacturing taught us that all experiments must be successful initially, and if they did not work then we must be failures or we lacked a good plan.

With kata, we learn that we do not spend a lot of time creating a plan. It is more about doing and learning from doing. We often have heard comments from people who say they have tried a particular fix before, but it did not work so they never try it again. The kata approach focuses more on what we learned from those failures and how can we adjust and do another experiment and then keep on experimenting until we get closer to our target condition. The target condition keeps changing toward the desire for greater improvement as we move further and further toward our vision. Another significant issue we see in the difference between a kata approach and some traditional models is in the target condition. The kata target condition is viewed as a state of being. As an example, we want to be processing products in one-by-one flow.

In our traditional model, we would phrase that as a result outcome of a part of xx amount of seconds. Our natural tendency is to make target conditions "result-based outcomes" because that is what our bonuses are typically based upon (i.e., we need to make so many parts per labor hour or reduce the parts per million (ppms) defects. The best analogy to set a target condition is to think of it as if we are on the ceiling of the building staring down at the plant. What would we see happening? Would we see products flowing in batches or would we see one-by-one processing? Our target is to see one-by-one flow.

Another significant learning with kata is the coaching aspect. There is always a coach and a learner. Guy Parsons and Alan Milham explore this in their book called Out of the Question, How Curious Leaders Win. Often, the coach is also a learner from someone at a higher level. For example, consider someone who is learning karate. A brown belt may be a coach to a green belt but also learning from a black belt. The idea is we should always be learning from our experiments and taking time to reflect on our targets, actions we are taking to move closer to the target, and the results. We should reflect on what we learned because whether it was a good or bad result, it is still a learning experience. Our traditional manufacturing methods focus on short-term objectives and are not tied to a vision. When we implement kata, we have methods for tracking progress on those traditional objectives, which many times are posted on story boards throughout the plant. We also have glass walls or storyboards that focus on experiments or target conditions, which are items that we are working on to move us closer to our vision.

If you are like most of us in manufacturing, you are working long hours and are probably consumed by the day-to-day demands on your time. With the kata approach, we reserve time out of each day to spend working on one of our experiments, which are moving us closer to our vision and target condition. We often look back at the end of the day and wonder what we accomplished in today's firefighting battle. With the glass walls, we now have a method to review and discuss our efforts in working toward a longer term plan. Our coach then discusses the next step and we agree upon when to get back together to review the results of the next step and the cycle continues.

Coaching Reward

It is amazing once the Lean paradigm becomes clear how some people make such a 180-degree reversal from total resistance to total sheer unadulterated surprise at the resistance they now receive from others. It is so fun to watch! They so quickly forget how resistant they were at the beginning of the process. We have even seen physicians (almost as resistant as machinists to change) go from completely fighting us during the entire Lean implementation spanning several months to writing a book about their Lean journey.

The transformation, once people buy in and now see Lean as just common sense, is astounding and helps keep us coming back to repeatedly start the process repeatedly at each company. We already know, going in, all the resistance we are going to get, all the questions we are going to receive, and all the meetings and coaching and mentoring required each time we start the process over again. The only analogy we can think of is with golf. The frustrated hacker, ready to wrap his club around a tree, suddenly has a great tee shot, scores a par or birdie on one hole, and this makes the entire 18 holes worthwhile and they cannot wait to come back again. This is kind of what implementing Lean is like. Professor James Bond states, "When these AHA or WOW moments occur it is most gratifying. Which brings up a couple of questions:

- Where do you see these moments first occurring in your organization?
- Everyone in an organization is resistant to change albeit at different levels. How do we as Lean Practitioners move them out of their comfort zone into one where managed risk is the accepted norm?

Indeed, much of what we do can be gathered and expressed as a commonsense approach. This is not meant to oversimplify what we do as Lean Practitioners. These aha moments occur when they make that transition from an area of comfort to one where there is some risk, albeit structured and manageable and it is at that point this transformation occurs. I believe this transformation and these moments can be accelerated by the organization's leadership creating an environment of trust and respect."

Change: Are You Empowered? If So, How Much? The Freedom Scale

Leading Lean initiatives requires a level of comfort with delegation. Engaging frontline staff in problem-solving and supporting them in the initiatives requires managers to be able to empower and delegate activities they may not have in the past for a variety of reasons. Managers or supervisors may choose not to delegate because they do not think anyone else is as qualified to do the task, could not do it as well or as fast as they could, or the right person was not hired. Some managers just like to do everything themselves because they do not trust other people or because there is an innate comfort for some in knowing and managing every detail and making every decision, micromanaging, as it were. The manager may not be proficient in coaching or mentoring. Delegating is not something we learn in school. How do we overcome delegation challenges? It is done through empowerment. To help with this, we use a tool called the empowerment or freedom scale.[31] The scale is composed of the following five levels:

1. Told what to do
2. Ask what to do
3. Recommend, then take action
4. Take action, notify at once
5. Take action, notify periodically

These levels represent the comfort levels between a manager/supervisor and their direct reports or team they are championing. The scale can be utilized for individual tasks, job descriptions, and team projects. Let us discuss each of these levels.

Level 1

An example of Level 1 begins on the first day of work or when the staff member is presented with a new task. The staff member is so new they may not even know where the bathroom is yet. At which level will he/she be working? The Level 1 employee does specifically what they are told, normally nothing more or less. In this mode, one may find the employee standing around with nothing to do because he/she has completed their assigned task. If asked why they did not tell someone they were idle, they will respond, "I wasn't told to do that!" In some cases, this phase and Level 2 are good opportunities to ask the employee if they see any "waste or stupid" things we seem to be doing that could be improved.

Level 2

As employees progress at the task or job, and gain a better understanding, their manager's comfort level with the employee or team increases. Additionally, the employee in turn feels more comfortable in the task. The managers will now tell the employee to start asking what to do next.

Level 3

At this level, managers are much more comfortable with the employee and the employee is much more confident and competent with the task. Now the employee is told to recommend what they think should be done next. If they present a problem, they should be asked to think about what the answer might be prior to providing the answer. The problem and the solutions are discussed and decisions are jointly made on a course of action. This forces the employee to start to think on their own and is the first step to moving the employee out of the micromanaging mode. This will also increase the morale of the employee because they are now contributing their ideas and recommendations to the organization.

What Happens When You Always Answer Everyone's Questions?

During a visit to a manager's office, the conversation kept getting interrupted by phone calls. During each phone call, he listened to the problem and gave the caller the answer. When this was brought to his attention, he was totally unaware of what he was doing. He had always done it this way.

Lesson Learned: This is a sure sign of a micromanager. Every decision must go through them! We all get a certain satisfaction of being the boss, the person who does it best and can make all the decisions. But every decision we make is stifling our employees and endangering the organization. Why? Because we are not developing our people and the bench strength needed for the succession planning.

Exercise: Tie your hands together (or someone who works for you) behind your back for a day to force yourself (them) to delegate. At the end of the day, you will not believe how hard it was and how ingrained your old behaviors are.

Exercise: Keep track of how many times a day someone comes to you or your phone rings for an answer or status and how often you give them the answer.

Every employee in a Lean environment should be moved to Level 3 as quickly as possible. This requires ongoing training and mentoring (kata) to be successful. Managers who have trouble with this level stick out once you know the tell signs. When an employee comes to a manager with a problem and does not come prepared with a solution or recommendation and the manager simply answers the question or provides the solution, employees are forced to stay at Level 2. Most of the time, this is done unconsciously. But when the answer to the question or the solution is provided to the employee, what will happen the next time they encounter a problem? Managers will be asked again for the answer. Some employees enjoy this, as it keeps them from ever taking any accountability or responsibility for their actions. They see this as job security because they can never make a mistake, they can never be blamed for making a bad decision. As a result, they are never afforded an opportunity to make a mistake and therefore never forced to learn from a bad decision. As a manager, you find yourself not being able to get everything done because you are constantly answering everyone's questions or solving problems. Many organizations reward this behavior as the hero of the day, week, or month. The manager becomes the fire chief and is awarded the firefighter's hat. While there is a certain joy or satisfaction, some of us may experience with this, it is not supportive to the growth of employees. We are denying them their ability to develop and prosper. We are rewarding them for not thinking and are encouraging a non-learning organization. In some cases, these managers see this as job security because in their minds, there is no one who could possibly replace them. On the other hand, they may have difficulty moving up in the organization because there is no one to take their place.

Homework: The next time an employee comes to you with a problem or question, the most important rule is to ask them, "What do you think we should do? What recommendations do you have for me?" Force them to think! And move them to empowerment Level 3.

Level 4

At this level, managers are very comfortable with the employee, and the employee or team is totally competent with the task(s). Employees are told, "From this point on, I am going to trust you to take the appropriate action and implement the correct solution to solve the problem or complete the particular job or task at hand." The manager, however, also tells the employee(s) to notify them immediately of the actions taken. This is just in case they missed a step or did not totally think things through, to mitigate risk. Employees are trusted, but managers may want to make sure things were done properly or provide damage control if necessary. We call this "trust but verify." Managers must make sure that employees at this level are on a professional growth plan to move up within the organization, so employees can develop to their full potential.

Level 5

At this level, the manager and the employee are very comfortable with each other and the process; the employee is competent and can be trusted implicitly. Employees are told to make whatever decisions are necessary and report back via a weekly, monthly, or quarterly report.

Change Your Hiring Process

HR systems play a critical part in helping to establish the Lean culture. The analogy here is to engineering. If engineering "designs" Lean into the product as well as into the manufacturing processes for the product, we eliminate much of the current work we as practitioners must do on the manufacturing shop floor. We then must design our hiring process to identify change agents and set the expectations for Lean Team Members, up front, so we can offset as much of the resistance as possible we currently meet as Lean Practitioners. HR should design a system to check to make sure potential team members have the physical ability and dexterity necessary to do the job by using an assessment tool. HR also needs to ensure new recruits can work as a team with other employees, have an openness to new ideas/suggestions, and can work in a team or group environment, that is, getting the right people, from the start, in the right seats on the bus as outlined earlier in the chapter. The Lean concepts and principles should be introduced as expectations during the interview process, that is, the need to follow standard work, leader standard work, the expectation for suggestions each month, the need for discipline (getting back from breaks on time), accountability, and the ability to coach and mentor fellow team members. This hiring process should be used for team members working in the transactional world as well.

HR, like all functional leaders, must wear multiple "hats" when it comes to implementing Lean and creating the Lean culture. Not only does HR need to identify, hire, orient, and monitor our new employees' ability to exist and thrive in a Lean culture, but they must also (2nd hat) work to "Lean out" their hiring processes by eliminating non-VA and wasteful steps. This initiative is a great activity to remove waste as well as checking for Lean understanding within this group. An opportunity to also fine tune Lean skills exists in this area. The (3rd hat) next step is to develop systems to embed and measure the Lean culture within the organization.

At Company X, every job advertisement included the words "Experience with Lean and Six Sigma preferred." Many candidates do not currently work for an organization that practices Lean but using good behavioral guidelines can assist HR in determining fit for their organization. HR should develop these behavioral anchors that identify desired characteristics necessary for their Lean thinking organization. This could include anchors such as motivation, adaptability, teamwork, personal responsibility, and initiative on a graduated scale, to name a few. Using this approach will help target those change agents.

Lesson Learned: If we can design "Lean" into our hiring process and embed these new desired behaviors into the organization's systems, we can eliminate the need for most of this chapter on change management.

Author's Note: The books Toyota Culture and Toyota Talent by Liker delve significantly into this topic.

Company Suggestion Systems

Employee suggestion systems if deployed correctly can foster a culture of continuous improvement, which can facilitate rapid change acceleration. In fact, this is the crux of the Lean system. To put this in perspective, the suggestion system at Toyota is owned by a Board of Directors Member! Who owns your suggestion system? In 1988,[32] the Toyota suggestion rate was four suggestions per month per employee with a 96% implementation rate, resulting in 20 million ideas over a 40-year period (Table 5.5).

In comparison, the typical US company averages about one-sixth of a suggestion per month per employee.[33] Toyota is not a normal type of suggestion system. There is no suggestion box which

Table 5.5 Toyota Suggestion System

Year	Number of Suggestions	Number of Suggestions/Person	Participation Rate (%)	Adoption Rate (%)
Number of Suggestions at Toyota Through 1988				
1976	463,442	10.6	83	83
1977	454,552	10.6	86	86
1978	527,718	12.2	89	88
1979	575,861	13.3	91	92
1980	859,039	19.2	92	93
1981	1,412,565	31.2	93	93
1982	1,905,642	38.8	94	95
1983	1,655,868	31.5	94	95
1984	2,149,744	40.2	95	96
1985	2,453,105	45.6	95	96
1986	2,648,710	47.7	95	96
1987	1,831,560	—	—	96
1988	1,903,858	—	—	96

Source: 20 Million Ideas in 40 Years ....

Figure 5.15   Suggestion box.

gets reviewed by management prior to implementation. Suggestion box (see Figure 5.15) systems normally use up significant amounts of time in the review, ROI analysis, and approval cycles. The employee may or may not hear back on their suggestion, which can negatively impact the employee's perception of the solicitation of request or actual suggestion. Toyota, on the other hand, budgets 50% of the team leader's time to implement and encourage employee suggestions. They try out the suggestion prior to submitting it for approval. This is how their implementation rate is so high.

Look at Table 5.6[34]:

■ Japan receives an average of 24 suggestions per person per month per employee, 60% participation rate, 82% adoption rate, $100 per suggestion received, amount awarded per suggestion adopted $4.40.

Table 5.6   Comparative Idea Data from the United States and Japan in 1989

	Japan	The United States
Number of ideas per employee	37.4	0.12
Participation rate (%)	77.6	9
Adoption rate (%)	87.3	32
Average net savings per adoption ($)	126	6,114
Net savings per 100 employees ($)	422,100	22,825
Average reward per adopted idea ($)	2.83	602

Note: American companies were paying more than 200 times greater than their Japanese counterparts, but getting less than a 300th of the number of ideas? How was it that nine out of ten Japanese ideas were used while less than a third of American ideas were used?

■ The United States receives 0.16 suggestions per month per employee, 13% participation, 22% adoption rate, $5,500 per suggestion received, amount awarded per suggestion adopted $550.

What do you notice about these stats? Two things become immediately obvious. The first is the United States has much fewer per capita suggestions. The second is the United States is only going after the big wins. Toyota realized the key was to go after every suggestion regardless of size and scope as you are bound to get some big wins here and there. The other thing that becomes apparent is the United States is basically bribing its employees for ideas where Japan has a small level loaded monetary reward system. The modal payout for Toyota in 1988 was $25 per suggestion, which was shared with the other team members.

Developing a Suggestion System

We worked with a company called ETG in Baltimore which wanted to establish a suggestion system. We called together several groups of employees to have them work through a problem-solving exercise on creating a lasting suggestion system. In every case, the employees wanted to establish some type of review committee and large payout system even though they complained about exactly that type of system during their discussions prior to developing recommendations.

We instructed the teams to come up with another process. Only one team recommended a system even remotely like what Toyota was doing at the time. As a sideline, this was a union company. When we rolled out Lean, eventually after several years, we were able to introduce a bonus program shared equally between the union and management employees. One year when business was off a bit the bonus had dropped from 10% to 7%. The union objected to the drop in bonus saying the 10% the prior year was a precedent and should be met every year. The issue was taken to court where the Union not only lost the battle but also lost the bonus!

The bottom line is there must be a system behind the suggestion system for it to work. The system must include time for the team members and management to implement the ideas. Our biggest struggle when implementing Lean at any company is addressing and implementing all the ideas coming from watching the videos with the employees.

Three Stages of the Suggestion System[35]

1. Encouragement. In the first stage, management should make every effort to help the workers provide suggestions, no matter how primitive, for the betterment of the worker's job and the workshop. This will help the workers evaluate the way they are doing their jobs.
2. Education. In the second stage, management should stress employee education so employees can provide better suggestions. For the workers to provide better suggestions, they should be equipped to analyze problems and the environment. This requires education.
3. Efficiency. Only in the third stage, after the workers are both interested and educated, should management be concerned with the economic impact of the suggestions.

Idea System Flow Should Look Like This

Small ideas lead to big ideas. We then look to see if they are transferable within a similar system and if they can be utilized in a dissimilar system in some other way? Can we take these ideas and?

■ Transfer them to other sites/plants
■ Further them and generate new ideas

- Apply the ideas to another area or process
- Utilize them for people development and discriminator for advancement
- Understand which team members are not suggesting ideas and why

Small ideas (especially if they are implemented by in-house personnel) are the best ideas because they cannot be easily copied by other companies unless they have identical processes and equipment to yours. For example, poka yoke on machines, speeds and feeds, total productive maintenance changes, etc. are difficult for someone else to copy. Keep in mind, if you can buy it from a catalogue, so can your competition!

Ironically, sources of ideas come primarily from things we normally look at negatively, that is, customer complaints, production problems, paperwork issues, and mistakes. Remember ideas have no value until they are implemented. Every organization should provide training on how to develop better ideas and realize every suggestion is a development opportunity. We have found for suggestion systems to work; organizations must make implementing ideas part of every managers' job and align the organization to support idea development and implementation. In essence, the employee reward should be the implemented idea not some dollar amount. However, we have found that implementing organization-based bonus systems tend to work well if they reward the right behaviors. "Unfortunately, the far greater number of ideas that are discouraged by the same reward scheme can go unseen and unmeasured."[36]

"Free Lunch" Program

At the end of our 5-day Lean seminars, we ask each participant to write down one idea they are going to go back and implement and then we follow up to see if it was implemented. There are stipulations the ideas must meet which include the idea must be something simple and easy and take no more than an hour to implement. We encourage soliciting help from other team members and they must have proof of implementation via before and after photographs or some other type of documentation. We suggest the company hold a pizza lunch where all the participants get together a week or two later to present the ideas they implemented.

Jim Greco states:

> "Our site chose to carry this process on calling it the 'free lunch' program. Each month employees who participated were encouraged to go out the next month and get someone else involved in implementing an idea and come back and present it. As each person concludes, they receive a warm round of applause. At the end of the presentations, each person is asked to make another improvement but, in addition, they are asked to have another person in the company work with them. As the site leader I attended every meeting. Eventually, to provide even more recognition, we started inviting the president of the division to attend. Not only did we start making some simple but great improvements but morale increased as well." These lunches are held every 4 weeks or so. Of course, there is no such thing as a free lunch: the price of admission is a small improvement.

When eliciting suggestions or ideas, it is critical it is done without judgment or emotion. Listed below are 20 things a team leader or group leader/supervisor should never say to someone suggesting an idea[37]:

1. Everyone understands that.
2. We have never done that before, there is no point in trying it.

3. I tried to do that before, and I know it will not work.
4. This is not up to date enough.
5. Is this within budget?
6. There are just too many plans being made I will look at your opinion when I have time.
7. Let us talk about this some other time.
8. Let us wait a while and see how things turn out.
9. Why do you want to change? Are things not going, okay?
10. There is no rule on this, so it is no good doing it that way.
11. I do not think it is technically feasible.
12. This idea is really off the wall, the manager will never agree to it.
13. This is just not done at this company!
14. Might work somewhere else, but certainly not here!
15. The real world is more complicated than that.
16. You do not really understand the situation, do you?
17. Your suggestion is good, but the company cannot afford it.
18. This will create problems later.
19. Even if I give you advice, there is still no way.
20. What is this suggestion? Can't you make it a little better?

Implementation Tips

Ideas should be encouraged by the team leader and group leader/supervisors every day. Once the idea is proved out, it is submitted to the suggestion system tracking process. Ideas should be implemented as quickly as possible as delays result in lost opportunity cost. However, resources must be available to implement the ideas or the system will fail. The system should be led and driven by the CEO and board of directors. The suggestion system should not be undertaken lightly. It is so critical to the Lean culture and should be well thought out and resourced at the highest levels. It may require a significant reorganization. For example, most companies successful with this type of system have no more than five or six direct reports per supervisor and supervisors and managers have 50% of their time dedicated to continuous improvement and working with the team members to implement their ideas.

Quick Wins Formula

We want to implement every idea. But when first starting out we find there are so many ideas, that it is best to score them as low cost or high cost (Figure 5.16). Pick the dollar value of what is considered high cost and rank the ideas accordingly. Then look at which ideas provide low benefit and which provide high benefit. It is best to determine benefit as either pertaining to improving something that will result in increasing your end customer satisfaction or helps to meet a hoshin or strategic planning goal or objective. Rank each idea accordingly.

Quick wins = low cost + high benefit solutions

Implement them now! Do not wait.

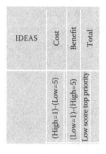

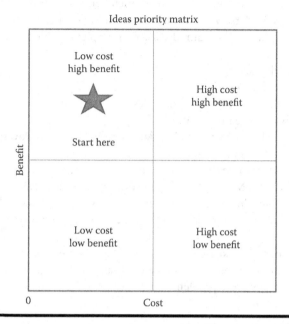

Figure 5.16 Idea priority 2x2 matrix.

How to Test an Idea

When presented with an idea, it should be reviewed by the team leader and the rest of the team members together. Does the idea positively impact any of the following?

- Safety
- Quality
- Delivery
- Inventory turns
- Productivity
- Customer satisfaction
- Will it reduce waste and improve VA?
- Will it make us more competitive?
- Will it make the job easier?

To see if your idea system is driving the right behaviors, it must pass what we call the bonus test:

- Is the bonus site wide?
- Does the bonus drive the Lean behaviors we are trying to reward? To answer this question, we must first define the right and wrong behaviors that exist in the organization.
- Will it result in a better workplace, more advancement opportunities, more money, job security, recognition, and more idea participation?

Most ideas should come from those doing the jobs. We need to educate and train team members to be able to see waste (using the video) and learn the Lean principles. Leadership should lead the teaching and work with team members on an improvement activity. We need to get ideas to the team leaders, which means the team leaders need to become facilitators for implementing and tracking ideas. The team idea systems' implementation process should look something like this:

- Pilot/test out idea.
- Does it work?
- Does it meet Lean principles?
- Can it be improved?
- Collect before and after data to validate the improvement.
- Implement the idea.
- Incorporate the idea into standard work.
- Use VSM or some other measurement to keep track of progress.
- Build the standard work into your system and audit the standard work to sustain results.
- Reflect on the idea and the process. Can we transfer the idea to a similar or dissimilar area?

Looks a lot like PDCA, doesn't it? Suggestion, idea, and reward programs can facilitate participation in improvement from all levels across the organization and provide great ideas to management to solve core problems needed to propel a company from good to great.

Putting a Reward System in Place

Change is hard; the uncertainty surrounding change felt by individuals can be very stressful and must be managed. It is extremely important that attention is given to reward the participants who are impacted by a successful change effort. Thoughtful consideration must be given to the development of a reward system. Putting a reward system in place can provide incentives for participation in the current change process and reinforce willingness for staff to participate in future change. Outlined here is a list of attributes to take into consideration as you develop or review your current reward system. There is a good book on this called Carrots and Sticks Don't Work[38].

Rewards: Some Characteristics of a Good Reward System[39]

- Availability: The extent to which a particular reward is available for distribution within the organization.
- Eligibility: Whether classes of employees (e.g., hourly, nonexempt) are eligible to receive a particular reward.
- Visibility: The degree to which a reward is visible to the recipient and to other organization members.
- Performance contingency: The extent to which the receipt of a reward, and the size of the reward, are based upon the recipient's performance.
- Flexibility: The extent to which a reward can be tailored to the needs of individual employees.
- Timeliness: Whether a reward can be distributed soon after the decision is made to distribute it, as opposed to being delayed by calendar dates, employee anniversary dates, or one-over-one approvals.
- Reversibility:
  - Whether the reward, once given, can be reclaimed.
  - Whether the decision to give the reward can be reversed so the reward need not be given again.

Note: All reward systems have pros and cons. Make sure you understand these prior to implementing the system. Sometimes it helps to do an FMEA on your proposed system. Also, remember rewards do not have to be monetary. Recognition can be used as well.

Kaizen-Teian 改善 (Kaizen): Improvement, 提案 (Teian): Proposal[40]

Kazan-Teian embodies the soul of Lean, which fosters small improvements every day at the shop floor and departmental level. Kaizen-Teian focuses on a team of collaborators within the work area who engage in implementing a series of small local improvements. It can facilitate executing on suggestion programs as it empowers the workers who are closest to the process to drive the changes of improvements. These are not led by experts and may inherently contain flaws with the new processes created. It can aid in nurturing the cultural transformation as the kaizens are led by the local departments and become the building block of a typical Lean organization. It must be recognized they do not typically lead to large-scale global transformations as they focus on the local level. It is this process that is our goal for Lean.

The OODA Loop and Change Management

The OODA Loop (see Figure 5.17) was created by Col. John Boyd. It has many implications for change management. We will not go into a detailed explanation here. The Loop goes from Observe to Orient to Decide and then Act. There are many feedback loops. We will just concentrate on two of them. The feedback path from Orient to Act is called Implicit Guidance and Control. This means that we just act without really thinking. For example, there is a fire, so what do we do? Based on our training and experience encompassed in the ORIENT block, we throw water at it or we run out of the building etc. This is a very low energy pathway and it can save us or kill us. If we have the wrong orientation and it's a grease fire and we throw water on it, what will happen?

We hypothesize that when it comes to problem-solving 80%–90% of us take this pathway. The Acts we perform are to ignore the problem or throw a solution at the problem. This is human

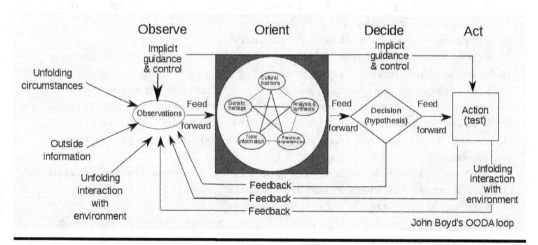

Figure 5.17 OODA loop—John Boyd.

nature. The problem with this is that if we ignore the problem what will happen? If we throw a solution at it four things can happen:

1. It gets better
2. It gets better but then comes back
3. Stays the same
4. It gets worse

It is this path that creates and sustains the firefighting we do every day.

The next pathway is the pathway utilizing Decide and Act. This is the PDCA pathway. This pathway takes energy to root cause and solve the problem. This assumes we are in the Cynefin Ordered Domain. Because this pathway requires a much higher energy level, it is difficult to get people to really perform PDCA and root cause analysis.

What Toyota has done, over the last 60–70 years, is through their ongoing training in team member accountability and ownership of the job and improvement of the job, along with problem-solving used daily as part of on-the-job development, is create an Orientation where standard work and the PDCA path becomes the default path for daily improvement and problem-solving. In other words, they train in standard work which becomes the implicit guidance and control path for team members doing their job. When they do problem-solving, the implicit path is PDCA. They don't think about it, they just default to that thinking based on their training and orientation. As problems are solved, standard work is updated. This way the improvements are process based versus people based. The more problems we root cause and solve using PDCA thinking, the less firefighting we have to perform. This is the only way to get out of the firefighting vicious cycle.

Chapter Questions

1. What is the change equation? Why is it important?
2. What is the CAP process?
3. Is it important to understand the personality traits of Lean team members? Describe why.
4. What process should be used to implement suggestions for establishing quick wins?
5. Concrete heads can cause problems during a Lean implementation. How do we identify a concrete head? How do we deal with them?
6. Describe how to empower a Lean team for success.
7. Why do firms need to change and what processes can be used to accelerate changes?
8. Name five characteristics of a good reward system.
9. What is the quick wins formula, and how would we use the formula in a manufacturing environment? Can we use the formula in an office environment? If so, provide an example.
10. What are the different types of closing statements? Why are they important?
11. What is the danger with complacency? How do you know if a person or company is complacent?
12. What makes a good idea system? Why has the United States struggled with idea systems?
13. What is the problem with a suggestion box system?
14. What are the three stages of the suggestion system?
15. If an employee gives you an idea, what is the most important thing you need to do?
16. What are some of the barriers to change?
17. What is the importance of WIIFM?

18. What should you script prior to making a change?
19. What is the difference between a skeptic and a cynic?
20. Should you look at change as a threat or an opportunity? Why?
21. What did you learn from this chapter?

Notes

1. Dilbert Cartoon, http://search.dilbert.com/comic/Change%20Happens, November 19, 2000.
2. Baumgardner and Scaffede, *The Leadership Roadmap*, Great Barrington, MA: North River Press, 2008.
3. Article title in INC. Magazine, http://www.inc.com/author/greg-wittstock, December 18, 2007, http://www.inc.com/pondemonium/2007/12/what_got_us_here_wont_get_us_t_1.html, seems to be adapted from the title of a book from Marshall Goldsmith, What Got You Here. Won't Get You There.
4. Video—Business of Paradigms, Joel Barker.
5. Thomas S. Kuhn, The Structure of Scientific Revolutions, University of Chicago Press © 1962.
6. This equation was taught to Charlie Protzman by Coopers and Lybrand as part of the AlliedSignal TQ training http://ezinearticles.com/Change-Guided-By-A-MathematicalFormula&id=260182, April 21, 2009. Gleicher, Beckhard, and Harris have found an equation that shows the relation to overcome resistance to change. The formula is modeled in the following way: $D \times V \times F > R$.
7. Saying by my sensei Mark Jamrog, SMC Group.
8. Jim Collins, *Good to Great*, New York: Harper Business Press, 2001, ibid.
9. Jim Collins, *Good to Great*, New York: Harper Business Press, 2001, ibid.
10. Reprinted with permission from Miller's Bolt by Thomas Stirr. Available from Basic Books, an imprint of The Perseus Books Group. ©1997.
11. Yoda is a Star Wars character. The reference for this is in another chapter.
12. Yoda is a character in the Star Wars movies.
13. Kefan Chen.
14. Source: www.jimrosenbaum.com/humor/humor212.txt. Public domain?
15. http://bvonderlinn.wordpress.com/2009/01/25/overview-of-ges-change-acceleration-process-cap/. In 1989–1990, under the direction of Jack Welch.
16. AlliedSignal Training Manual.
17. www.gembutsu.com/articles/leanmanufacturingglossary.html. Robert Kriegel, *Sacred Cows Make the Best Burgers*, New York: Warne.
18. Jim Collins, *Good to Great*, New York: Harper Business Press, 2001, ibid.
19. Jim Collins, *Good to Great*, New York: Harper Business Press, 2001, ibid.
20. AlliedSignal Training Manual.
21. Fred Haley, Former Director of Materials AlliedSignal.
22. Contributed by Professor James Bond.
23. Reprinted with permission from Miller's Bolt by Thomas Stirr. Available from Basic Books, an imprint of The Perseus Books Group. ©1997.
24. Taiichi Ohno.
25. The Little Engine That Could, Piper and Ong, Grosset and Dunlap, ©1930.
26. Thomas Kuhn, *The Structure of Scientific Revolutions*, Chicago, IL: University of Chicago Press, 1996, p. 162.
27. Yoda saying from Star Wars movie.
28. A 2×4 is a piece of wood used for framing walls and which is 2 in. $\times$ 4 in.
29. Story provided by Professor James Bond.
30. Toyota Kata, Mike Rother, McGraw-Hill, 2009, 40 Million Ideas in 20 Years Book, Yasuda, Productivity Press, ©1990, www.artoflean.com.
31. Coopers and Lybrand. Allied Signal TQ Training Course 1994.

32. Ideas Are Free, Alan D. Robinson, Dean M. Schroeder.
33. Yuzo Yasuda, *40 Years, 20 Million Ideas: The Toyota Suggestion System*, New York: Productivity Press, 1990.
34. Ideas Are Free, Alan D. Robinson, Dean M. Schroeder.
35. Source of Information: Japan Human Relations Association, http://www.1000ventures.com/business_guide/processes_kaizen_suggestions.html
36. Ideas Are Free, Alan D. Robinson, Dean M. Schroeder.
37. *40 Years, 20 Million Ideas: The Toyota Suggestion System, Productivity Press*, ©1990 Yuzo Yasuda.
38. Carrots and Sticks Don't Work, Paul L. Marciano, McGraw Hill; 1st edition © July 5, 2010.
39. AlliedSignal Training Manual.
40. Kaizen-Teian Improvement Systems Module 10.1 Yue Cathy Chang (LFM '06), Johnson Wu (LFM '06) ESD.60—Lean/Six Sigma Systems MIT Leaders for Manufacturing Program (LFM).

Additional Readings

Beitler, M.A. 2003. Strategic Organizational Change. Greensboro, NC: Practitioner Press.

Blaha, R. 1995. Beyond Survival. Colorado Springs, CO: Air Academy Press.

Buckingham, M. 2001. Now Discover Your Strength. New York: The Free Press.

Cameron, E. and Green, M. 2012. Making Sense of Change; Third edition, London: Kogan Page.

Carr, D.K., Hard, K.J., and Trahont, W.J. 1996. Managing the Change Process. New York: McGraw-Hill.

Champy, J. 1996. Reengineering Management. New York: Harper Business.

Conner, D. 1992. Managing at the Speed of Change. New York: Villard Books.

Frost, C. 1996. Changing Forever the Scanlon Principles. East Lansing, MI: Michigan State University Press.

Gladwell, M. 2002. The Tipping Point. Boston, MA: First Back Bay.

Haines, S.G. 1998. Systems Thinking and Learning. Amherst, MA: HDR Press.

Harvard Business Review 2002. Harvard Business Review on Culture and Change. Boston, MA: HBR Press.

Hutton, D.W. 1994. The Change Agent Handbook. Milwaukee, WI: ASQ Quality Press.

Nikkan Kogyo Shimbun, Japan Human Relations Association 1989/1992. Kaizen—Teian 1—Developing Systems for Continuous Improvement through Employee Suggestions. Portland, OR: Publishing/Productivity Press.

Jennings, J. and Haughton, L. 2002. It's Not the Big That Eat the Small … It's the Fast That Eat the SLOW. New York: Harper Business.

Kotter, J.P. 1996a. Leading Change. Boston, MA: Harvard Press.

Kotter, J.P. 1996b. Meeting Change. Boston MA, HBR Press.

Kuhn, T. 1962. Black Body Theory and Quantum Discontinuity. New York: Oxford Press.

Kuhn, T. 1978. The Structure of Scientific Revolutions. Chicago: University of Chicago Press.

Lencioni, P. 1998. The Five Temptations of a CEO. San Francisco, CA: Jossey-Bass.

Lencioni, P. 2004. Death by Meeting. San Francisco, CA: John Wiley & Sons.

Mann, D. 2005. Creating a Lean Culture. Portland Oregon: Productivity Press.

Manzoni, J.F. 2002. The Set-up-to-Fail Syndrome. Boston, MA: Harvard Business Press.

Miller, K. 2002. The Change Agent's Guide to Radical Improvement. Milwaukee, WI: ASQ Press.

Peter, S. 1994. The Fifth Discipline Fieldbook. New York: Doubleday.

Sweeney, L.B. and Meadows, D. 1995. The Systems Thinking Playbook. Hartland, U.K.: Sustainability Institute.

Waterman, R.H. 1990. Adhocracy. Knoxville, TN: Little Books.

Appendix A - Study Guide

Chapter 1 Questions and Answers

1. The elimination of what main waste drives the conversion from batch to flow production.
   - The waste of overproduction is the number one waste in the Toyota production system (TPS), the one Ohno worked on the most, and we find it is the hardest to remove. This is what drives the conversion from batch to flow production. This waste focuses on the following:
     - Making only the customer driven amount of product
     - Making it only when needed—Eliminate the just in case mentality
2. What are the six levels of waste?
   - The first level is obvious waste: low-hanging fruit.
   - 5S wastes: the easiest wastes to see.
   - The seven (eight) wastes: discussed earlier.
   - Boiled frog waste: the waste that is hard to notice because it is old and we pass by it every day.
   - Tribal waste or sacred cows: untouchable waste in our culture and systems.
   - Hidden unseen waste: waste we don't typically see, as it is hidden behind or masked by other wastes and is the hardest waste to find and yet the most dangerous.
3. What is the Ohno circle?
   - Taiichi Ohno was known for drawing a chalk circle around managers and making them stand in the circle until they had seen and documented all of the problems in a particular area (sometimes an entire shift or longer). Today the stand in a circle exercise is known as a 30-30-30 and is a great first step to train someone's eyes to see waste and to provide structure for the group leader/supervisor or manager to carry out daily improvement or for the busy executive with limited time to go to the Gemba and see what is really happening. The exercise entails telling the person to stand in a circle for 30 minutes or more and just watch and look around to capture at least 30 wastes and then spend 30 minutes fixing one of them.
4. What is the best way to find waste?
   - The best way to find waste is to systematically look for it, i.e., Gemba Walks, or Video Analysis. There are processes to help identify wastes such as value stream mapping and filming a process.
5. It is easiest to find wastes in the area you work in. Is this statement true or false? Why?
   - False. Fresh eyes and utilizing outside support are beneficial in locating waste. Beware of the Boiled Frog Syndrome. Utilizing outside resources brings a new perspective and does not fall into the trap of "that is the way we always did it."

6. What was the P course?
   – The P Course (P was for production) was taught by Shingo as part of the industrial engineering training. The question he would ask the class is:
     • If one man and one machine in 1 hour can make 100 parts, how can they make more parts?
     • The normal answers were of course to:
       ■ Add people
       ■ Add machines
       ■ Add more time
   – These were all unsatisfactory answers because they all add cost to the system. A fourth answer was often given such as "work harder," which was also unsatisfactory since it could not be sustained. When the class was stumped, he would inform them the right way was to improve the overall method by which the elements work together and produce more efficiently.

7. What is the difference between apparent and true efficiency?
   – By reducing the steps and complexity in the process, we also reduce the opportunity for defects in the process. The wastes of overproduction and overprocessing are violated all the time. Toyota differentiates this by highlighting the difference between apparent versus true efficiency. True efficiency occurs only when we increase efficiency without overproducing or overprocessing.

8. What are the eight wastes? Give an example of each.
   – **Waste of Overproduction**
   This is the number one waste in the Toyota production system (TPS), the one Ohno worked on the most, and we find it is the hardest to remove. This is what drives the conversion from batch to flow production. This waste focuses on the following: Making only the customer driven amount of product and making it only when needed. An example is making too many hamburgers at a fast-food restaurant and then storing the cook food until an order is placed.
   – **Waste of Time on Hand (Idle)**
   When employees are idle, this is waste. There are many examples of waste of time. One example is waiting for late attendees in meetings. First one needs to examine if the needed is actually needed, which is another waste.
   – **Waste in Transportation**
   Moving materials, employees, or information is a waste. In a manufacturing plant, moving subassemblies around the manufacturing floor is an example of transportation waste.
   – **Waste of (Too Much) Processing**
   We define this as doing more to a part or paperwork (electronic or paper) than necessary to meet the customer-defined specifications or perceived quality needs. An example in manufacturing is machining a part to a tighter tolerance than is required by the design or function.
   – **Waste of Stock on Hand (Inventory)**
   This includes not only excess stock, which is nonproductive inventory (excess and obsolete—E&O) or which we will never use, but also the following: work in process (WIP), parts stacked in a stock room, material stacked to the ceiling on the manufacturing floor, and cabinets full of excess office supplies.

- **Waste of (Worker) Movement**
  We define this waste as follows: whenever someone has to reach outside their normal path of motion while sitting or standing, including having to get their own supplies. This includes getting up and down from a chair.
- **Waste of Making Defective Products**
  This is making products, which do not meet the customer's specifications or perceived quality characteristics. Any rejected or defective item in a company such as a rejected invoice, scrap hardware, or a returned item that fell apart after being shipped to the customer.
- **Waste of Talent (An Organization's Most Valuable Asset)**
  We see this waste when organizations do not tap their employees' brainpower, ideas, and experience. The engagement of an organization's talent is critical in making Lean initiatives successful. The talent in your organization will drive innovation and change by identifying and eliminating all waste.
    Whenever we don't fully utilize/recycle our resources or we dump waste into a land-fill. Another example is having an engineer perform clerical duties.

9. What are some root causes of the eight wastes? Can you think of anymore?
   - Batching.
   - Lack of standards and standardization at the work instruction level.
   - Inefficient layouts.
   - Complacency—no compelling need to improve, need paradigm shift.
   - Centralization—most of it is hidden and is paramount to and synonymous with batching.
   - Poor hiring practices.
   - Results only driven metrics creating shoot from the hip solutions.
   - Lack of voice of the customer (VOC).
   - Lack of leadership—inflexible—no constancy of purpose—fear-based environments— lack of clear ownership, responsibilities, discipline, and accountability.
   - Lack of pride in one's work or one's workplace.

10. How should we eliminate the need to feel defensive when ideas/suggestions are challenged/ changed? Describe your approach.

11. What are the principles of efficiency? Are they in any way related to Lean principles? How do they relate to companies today? What lessons can we learn from these principles?
    - Many of the fundamental concepts of Lean as well as the cultural considerations can be found in the 12 principles of efficiency which were published in 1911 by Harrington Emerson. We have provided quotations and ideas from his book. We have found Emerson's definitions of companies, and these 12 principles still apply today:
      - **Principle 1: Clearly Defined Ideals**
        Organizations must have clearly defined "high ideals" with very specific targets.
      - **Principle 2: Common Sense**
        The difference between near common sense and supernal common sense, which looks at every problem from a lofty versus a near point of view.
      - **Principle 3: Competent Counsel**
        Emerson suggests we all need competent counsel. For example, most companies have a VP of legal, finance, materials, operations, or engineering.

- **Principle 4: Discipline**
  The word discipline has three if not more meanings:
  - The spirit of discipline where the institution is greater than the individual, for example, railroad schedules...
  - The discipline of the rich man who makes his servants wait until his convenience in spite of a definite program arranged by himself...
  - The discipline of life, which leads us, almost compels us, from intimate contact with the existing order. In the narrowest sense, we use the word to denote the act of punishment inflicted on a bad boy with the object of encouraging observance of prescribed conduct or rules...
- **Principle 5: The Fair Deal**
  "In practice it is difficult to put up a fair deal unless there are three qualities, and these are rarely found in the same person. The qualities are as follows:
  - Sympathy
  - Imagination
  - Above all a sense of Justice"
  Note: Wages are a small part of the fair deal but are critical.
- **Principle 6: Reliable, Immediate, and Adequate Records**
  The object of records is to increase the scope and number of warnings, to give us more information than is usually received immediately through our senses... Records are anything which provides information.
- **Principle 7: Despatching**
  Despatching (now we say dispatching) is equivalent to execution of the work plan or production schedule as well as the logistics encountered within and outside the company.
- **Principle 8: Standards and Schedules**
  There are two kinds, physical and chemical... We use instruments to measure, and physics, chemistry, and mathematics to establish standards and schedules for material things.
- **Principle 9: Standardized Conditions**
  There are two distinct methods of standardizing conditions:
  - To standardize ourselves so as to command the unalterable extraneous facts, earth, water, gravity, and wave vibrations
  - To standardize the outside facts so our personality becomes the pivot on which all else turns
- **Principle 10: Standardized Operations**
  Determines the operational method of standardization, in order to improve work efficiency. There are two elements to consider:
  - Standardizing the work itself
  - Individual skill: One man may have laid 8,000 bricks and the other only 800 a day
- **Principle 11: Written Standard-Practice Instructions**
  Makes the written manual the standard course of action. The best results are obtained using the 'ratchet' process, by holding onto every gain and by never allowing any slip back; these results being secured by a voluminous book of instructions and suggestions.
- **Principle 12: Efficiency-Reward**

12. What is the concept of strenuousness versus efficiency?
   - The difference is working hard (strenuous) and smart (efficient). Strenuousness demands one put forth extra effort, bringing about greater results with abnormally greater effort.

For example, piece rates that are paying workers based on the number of pieces they produce per hour or per day are based on the theory of strenuousness. A destructively offensive company is based on strenuousness. An organization based on efficiency is diametrically opposed to strenuousness. Efficiency brings about greater results with lessened effort. Standard times and bonuses are based on the theory of efficiency. The differences between the two types of companies are both philosophical and physiological.

13. Which are the differences between the destructively offensive or constructively defensive company? How are they like plants versus mammals? Which type of company is better? Why?
   - Emerson begins by defining two types of companies: the destructively offensive and the constructively defensive. He notes the two types of organizations are radically different leveraging primitive examples to show the differences. He describes the constructively defensive as a plant and the destructively offensive as a mammal. The constructive defensive type or plant trusts the generous, often enthusiastic, cooperation of forces outside of itself and it therefore draws strength of a wide and unlimited range. Plants trust all nature and draw help from everywhere and see the view from 400 ft. The destructively offensive or "mammal" trusts the occasional, often grudging, cooperation of powers identical in kind; animals trust none but their own kind and "grow through destruction" and have a view of the tallest animal, the elephant that stands at 12 ft. Contrasting the two reveals the difference in spirit, effectiveness, and methods. Most organizations choose to operate as mammals, limiting their ability to apply the efficiency principles effectively, rather than operating as constructively defensive.

14. What did you learn from this chapter?

Chapter 2 Questions and Answers

1. What are the four things the product can do?
   The four things a product can do are:
   - Transport
   - Inspect
   - Process
   - Store (to signify a delay)
2. What is the world-class goal for the product?
   - World-class goals for the product should be 75%–80% value added noting most products start out around 1%–3% value added and many times less than 1%.
3. What are the three types of storage?
   The three types of storage raw material (RM), WIP, and finished goods (FG):
   - RM is considered any part that has not had any direct labor added to it.
   - WIP is defined as any RM received with direct labor added to it.
   - FG is defined as the completed product, ready for sale to the customer.
   - What are the three types of WIP?
   There are three types of WIP storage **Between-Process Storage (B), Lot Delays (L), and Within-Process Storage (W).**
4. Explain the difference among a between-process delay, lot delay, and within-process delay?
   - Between-process storage is defined by products sitting and waiting individually or as an entire lot for the next process, that is, they are stored in-between two sequential processes.
   - Lot delays are where we are waiting for the rest of the batch to be processed.

Within-process storage (delay) is a new type of delay that occurs after a process is started on a part or a lot where the part, person, or lot is delayed because the process is interrupted for some reason. It could be a machining operation interrupted for lunch break or a machine that breaks down or a tool bit that breaks, and the piece has to wait while it is repaired. It could be someone stuck in an elevator or a requisition being placed but having to stop the process to check the status of that or another part in a different screen or window.

5. What is the network of operations?

Dr. Shigeo Shingo described manufacturing as a network of operations and was the first who realized that they were not on the same axis; they were on two separate axes composing a network of operations. This network is composed of two pieces:
- Process (product) flow
- Workflow of the operator or those functions carried out by the person(s) doing the job

6. What are the three criteria for VA for the product?
- The customer must care about the step. If the customer doesn't care, there is no value added. We used to say the customer had to be willing to pay for it, however there are times when it can be value added but the customer is not willing to pay for it. For example, a dring in a casino is expected and valued added but as a friend of mine, Mark Caponigro, pointed out.
- The step has to physically change the thing going through the process whether a product or paper: form, fit, shape, size, or function.
- The step must be done right the first time. If the step is not done correctly, it must be reworked and rework is not value added. A step can only add value when it is done correctly the first time and any prior or subsequent rework is by definition non-value added.

7. What is a process wall map? How do you construct it?
- To create a process wall map, we first layout either flip chart paper or a roll of paper on the wall. Decide what we are going to follow or become since we are now the product. We begin in a conference room with each of the participants that actually do the jobs on the team and ask them to write down on yellow stickies step-by-step what they do in the process. The wall map:
  • Shows what is happening to the product
  • Shows all the details of every step the product goes through, including transport, storage, and inspection, no matter how small (TIPS)
  • Shows the number of activities and the time required for each activity
  • Shows who touches the product and does each step
  • Shows overall length of the process (throughput time) by having each yellow sticky represent a standard amount of time
- Have the team start by putting yellow stickies on the left-hand side with who or what position does the job. We then start by having each person write each individual step in the order that they perform on a different sticky with a magic marker. As soon as they write the first step, for example, we have them break the step down into finer detail of the details involved in the step. It is important to follow up the PFA wall map exercise performed in the conference room with actually following the product through each step on the floor or through the office for a transactional process with operator participation.

8. What is the difference between flowcharts and process flows?
- Flowcharting is not the same as PFA analysis. Flowcharting lacks many pieces the PFA provides. Flowcharting generally doesn't give you times, what type of step it is, what the value-added content is in the process when you are done, or all the delays a product will encounter. Flowcharts simply don't capture all the steps and times within a process. They do give us a high-level view of the process and decision points but do not nearly provide enough detail to expose all the steps or waste in the process.

9. What is a point-to-point diagram? Can you draw one?
   – Point-to-point diagrams are utilized to show the path of the product through the layout of the area. This differs from the spaghetti diagram we use for operators. It is utilized to identify only product flow patterns and to guarantee the product always moves forward in a point-to-point fashion. The product should never move backward in a process. If any stations are out of order, they will immediately show up as you draw the point-to-point flow of the product. Stations out of order will force the product to move backward and must be corrected in future revisions to your layout.

   From the product's perspective, the point-to-point diagram assists in creating a logical grouping of operations or machines based on the flow of the product.
10. What is the importance of ERSC?
    – ERSC is important because it represents the steps needed for the analysis of VSMs, PFAs, WFAs and Setup reduction. They are in hierarchical order of application. i.e., eliminate, rearrange, simplify and combine. We always try to eliminate the step first. Without these steps there would be no improvements.
11. What is the importance of following the product?

    Following the product through each step on the floor or through the office for a transactional process with operator participation is very important and fundamental. No matter how good the person is at doing the job, there will be steps missed when just listing them out and you will find things to improve by walking and videoing the process you can't possibly come up without following the product.
12. What are the four of the things the product gives us toward a Lean?
    – Total throughput time
    – Flow, flow, flow
    – Layout and workstations
    – In hospitals it shows where rooms should be in relation to the activity that is occurring
    – Where the workstations should be located
    – The proper sequence for equipment and supplies
    – The location of where standard WIP (or number of rooms in hospitals) will be needed
    – Machine times (running time of the process within a piece of equipment)
    – Routings: which are the paths or sequence of steps the product or patients follow as they progress through the process?
    – Percent VA for the product
    – Percent of storage for the product
    – Percent time inspecting the product
    – Capacity analysis when combined with operator and setup analysis
    – Travel distance for the product
    – Point-to-point diagram: numbered steps the product follows
13. What is the total throughput time of the process, and how do we determine it?
    – The total time from raw material to finished goods. It is the product or material flow velocity. We determine it by adding the process time and storage time.
14. PFA and flowchart are the same. Is this statement true or false? Why?
    – False. The PFA includes much more detail than a flow chart and breaks down the steps differently.
15. What did you learn from this chapter?

Chapter 3 Questions and Answers

1. What is a WFA?
   - Workflow analysis (WFA) that is the second step in our analysis process and involves a switch from being the product to being the person(s) doing the work.
2. Why is it important to separate the operator from the product?
   - The separation is important to facilitate the WFA of the operator from the product.
3. Why is it important to separate an operator from a machine?
   - One of the main Lean principles is to separate man from machine. When we follow the product, we get the machine time compared to following the operator where we get the time to unload, load, and cycle the machine. It is important to keep these times separate. If an operator is standing there watching the machine, it is considered idle time. Machine time is not included in the labor time. This is part of the principle of separating man from machine work.
4. What are the first things we look for in an operator analysis?
   - The first thing we always look for when reviewing videos is anything unsafe or that results in poor ergonomic positions.
5. Why do we analyze to the second?
   - If you take steps larger than a second, you can end up combining steps that mix up different codes, which affects true content of the work and eventually impacts the standard work, which is derived from this analysis. If the steps are too big (i.e., too much time per step), we will not know exactly where the split is within that step.
6. What role does ergonomics play with Lean? Are they opposed to Lean principles?
   - Occupational ergonomics is the science of improving employee performance and well-being through the design of job tasks, equipment, and the overall work environment. When coupled with a continuous improvement mindset, it is a relentless effort to design the workplace for what people do well, and design against (mistake proof where possible) what people do not do well.
   - The risk factors ergonomics addresses are conditions in the workplace, which increase one's chance of developing a musculoskeletal disorder (MSD). The three categories of MSD risk factors are as follows:
     - Posture: Extreme postures stress joints and occlude blood flow.
     - Force: Tasks with forceful exertions place higher loads on joints and connective tissues.
     - Frequency: Extreme frequencies can contribute to fatigue debt. Also, the longer the period of continuous work, the longer the recovery time needed. These also lead to conditions that may not be discovered until much later in life like tendonitis, carpal tunnel, and arthritis.
   - When these risk factors surpass known thresholds, the probability of injury increases, and exposure to them should be limited or totally avoided. However, avoidance of injury is not the sole benefit of risk reduction as job tasks with elevated MSD risks are also more likely to take more time and present more opportunities for error, thereby influencing quality, delivery, and safety metrics. For this reason, workplaces should be assessed for MSD risk and the results of these assessments viewed by operational leaders as opportunities to improve the performance of their entire system.
7. What is the importance of motion study?
   - The tool to ultimately expose movement waste is Frank Gilbreth's motion study. Motion study involves analyzing what we do to the fraction of a second. This was all part of the scientific management movement of the Industrial Revolution in the early twentieth century.

8. How is motion study different from time study?
   - Motion study reviews the operator motions in detail and time studies time the specific time an operator takes to accomplish an operation, independent of the analysis of the motion.
9. How do you calculate TLT? Why is it important? What else can you calculate from TLT?
   - The TLT is calculated by adding together the time for each step. The TLT is the total labor time and is obtained by adding VA and NVA time together.
   - It is important because we need it to determine other calculations.
   - It can be used to compute number of people required and cycle time.
10. What is a spaghetti diagram? How does it differ from a point-to-point diagram?
    - A spaghetti diagram is different from a point-to-point diagram. The point-to-point diagram follows the product from point to point through the process, where the spaghetti diagram follows the operator or staff person doing the work and is generally performed by following the operator for one complete cycle of their work. This can be done by following the operator on the floor, or in the office or by mapping it off the video.
11. What does ERSC stand for? Why is it important?
    - ERSC stands for eliminating, rearranging, simplifying, and combining. The omit process is crucial to the analysis process and it should be done with the operator(s) present. If we can omit the step, we reduce the time to zero. If we can't completely omit it, we change the time for the step to a new estimated time. It is critical to have the employees participate in the process so they can help contribute their ideas and understand how we arrived at the new times for the overall work. In this way, they are included in determining their standard work, which will be the resulting process after the steps are reviewed.
12. What role does WFA play with standard work?
    - WFA is very important to standard work. The workflow analysis is entered into the computer so we can preserve the information and make it easier to develop the standard work in a more readable form. We can also easily calculate how much time is spent on each step and summarize the data.
13. What makes a step value added for the operator?
    - A step is value added for the operator if:
      - Customer cares,
      - Physically changes the product (form, fit, shape, size, or function).
      - Done right the first time.
14. What are the three types of NVA work?
    - We break non-value added (NVA) steps up into three main categories:
      - Required work
      - Unnecessary work
      - Idle time
15. What are the two things an operator can do?
    - The two things an operator can do are:
      - Value added
      - Non-value added
    - The definition for value added is as follows:
      - Customer cares,
      - Physically changes the product (form, fit, shape, size, or function).
      - Done right the first time.

16. What environments do operators work in?
    - Operators essentially work in four environments:
      - Assembly
      - Machining
      - Transactional
      - Some combination of assembly, machine, and/or transactional
17. Should an operator ever be idle?
    - Operators should never be idle.
18. What is a world-class goal for the operator? Should be quantified in each environment.
    - Our goal with Lean and the operator is to consistently measure and strive toward world-class benchmarks and the impetus to drive toward continually improving the process. Our goal should always be to reduce the number of operators in the process and yet continually develop them to move them to other positions. We should always be working to reduce both direct and indirect labor and convert staff jobs to line jobs wherever possible and then stop distinguishing direct from indirect.
19. Why do we separate out material handling? What is the test for material handling?
    - We separate material handling to engage employees in redesigning their workstations and eliminating excess motions to provide safe and ergonomically designed jobs for our shop floor and administrative team members, we realize increased productivity, morale, and job satisfaction, which usually leads to higher profits. Tests are: is this step something we can hand off to a water spider (material handler) to do for the line, or could the operator have put the part directly on the assembly or used the tool immediately after he/she picked it up?
20. When can we eliminate inspection?
    - We can eliminate the need for the inspection by using mistake proofing or by using 100% inspection by a machine (optical recognition).
21. Why should we work to eliminate inspection?
    - Inspection is a non-value-added step in the process, ultimately adding costs to the customer and/or reducing margin.
22. What is a spaghetti diagram, how is it created, and why do we create one?
    - The spaghetti diagram follows the operator or staff person doing the work and is generally performed by following the operator for one complete cycle of their work. This can be done by following the operator on the floor, or in the office, or by mapping it off the video. It is constructed by hand drawing a map of the area or taking an existing CAD layout of the area and then putting in a line for each step the operator takes, even if they backtrack or do the same walk pattern over and over, and calculating their overall distance traveled. Ideally, when the new cell is implemented, the operator should only travel within the path of their standard work on the line.
23. What are 4 pieces of Lean do we obtain from a work flow analysis?
    - TLT for one piece or small lot
    - Percent value added for the operator
    - Percent required work for the operator
    - Percent idle time for the operator
    - Standard work for the supervisor
    - Number of operators required
    - Capacity planning when coupled with PFA analysis

    – Ergonomics/safety/fatigue opportunities
    – Work standards
    – Motion study
    – Standard WIP quantity
    – Ten cycle analysis
    – Line Balancing
    – Operator work zones
    – Scheduling flexibility/# shifts and overtime required
    – Operator walk patterns
    – Operator buy-in and morale
    – SWIP for the operators
    – Total inventory required when coupled with PFA
    – Paperwork required and how the paperwork travels in the cell
    – Level loading
    – Proper tool and material presentation
    – Baton zones (bumping)
    – Job breakdown—standard work for the operator
    – Training videos
    – Key points and reasons for key points for each step
    – Operator cycle times for each step in the process
    – Percent of overhead versus direct labor
    – Mistake proofing opportunities
    – Opportunities to reduce variation
24. What did you learn from this chapter?

Chapter 4 Questions and Answers

1. What does SMED stand for?
    – SMED stands for single-minute exchange of dies
2. What does OTED stand for?
    – OTED stands for one-touch exchange of dies. The implication here is we can change-over in less than 100 seconds or we can changeover multiple machines with the touch of one button.
3. Describe OSED.
    – OSED stands for one-shot (cycle) exchange of dies, which means the entire cell is changed over within one cycle time externally, thus zero internal setup time.
4. What are the four parts of a setup?
    – The four parts we utilize for setup reduction are:
      • Preparation (P) and organization
      • Mounting (M) and removing
      • Calibration (C), centering dimensioning, aligning, measurement, and testing
      • Trial (T) runs and adjustments
5. Explain external versus internal work.
    – Another concept is internal time versus external time. In a pit stop example, anything done while the car is in the pit is considered internal time. Examples would be changing

the tires or refueling. In a machining operation, this translates into anything that can only be done when the machine is stopped.

- Anything that can be done while the race car is going around the track is considered external time. For example, we can get the tires ready and properly located in the pit area ahead of time. For machining this implies gathering all the tools ahead of time and dies are preset so the operator never has to leave the machine while setting it up.

6. Where else can it apply other than traditional setups?
   - It can apply to changing over from one part to the next part i.e., unload, load, cycle.
7. Give an example of something we don't normally think of as a setup.
   - Preparing hospital rooms for a new patient is an example of a setup. There are many tasks involved to include removal of soiled linens, adding, or removing equipment, removing trash and biohazards, sterilization, etc.
8. Why is standard work important in a setup?
   - Standard work is critical to improving setups and achieving SMED. Standard work is the most efficient method to produce a product or perform a service at a balanced flow to achieve the desired output rate, which should be matched ideally to customer demand. The standard work process breaks down all work into sequenced elements that are carefully organized and followed repeatedly.
9. What is an external checklist? How is it used? Does it ever change?
   - The external checklists are the steps needed outside of the main process and are implemented "offline." It is used to ensure the primary process continues without interruption. The external process should change (improve) as the continuous process continues as there could be a case when the external process could pace the internal processes.
10. What pieces of Lean do we obtain from a setup?
    - Enabler for one-piece or one-patient flow or smaller batch sizes
    - Immediately increases capacity
    - Improved operator utilization
    - Reduces labor costs
    - Increases overall system reliability and predictability
    - Enabler for chaku chaku
    - Enabler for level loading
    - Increased man-to-machine ratio
    - Enabler for mixed model and ability to supply in sets
    - Provides quick response to demand changes
    - Less reliance on forecasting
    - Capital asset utilization rate increases (if demand is there)
    - Reduces material handling
    - Reduced inventories
    - Smaller layout footprint
    - Results in standardization
    - Improved operator safety
    - Improved patient/product quality
    - Integrates mistake proofing
11. What is world class for a setup?
12. How should we analyze potential savings from implementing SMED processes?
    Once we know which steps can be omitted or improved, we can take the labor time associated with those steps and convert it to dollars and develop a quick return on

investment (ROI) to justify the improvement noting safety and ergonomic improvements should just be implemented regardless of ROI. However, labor savings are not fully realized until such time as the personnel are removed from the area and put to work on something else.

13. Why is SMED important to the Lean implementation journey?
    – SMED is important to the Lean implementation journey and offers many advantages to the organization and associated customers, to include:
      • Organization is much easier to do business with.
      • Free up space that can be used for more manufacturing.
      • Increased machine utilization and capacity for more business and customers.
      • Overall cost of parts decreases and profit increases.
      • No excess inventory to count.
      • Offer customers a price break on their product(s).

14. What did you learn from this chapter?

Chapter 5 Questions and Answers

1. What is the change equation? Why is it important?
   – The change equation is a critical tool and the equation is Dissatisfaction × Vision × First Steps must be greater than resistance to change. Change management is a large part of Lean; it is an essential part of becoming Lean. As you move from accepting new ideas and then transitioning ideas into reality, one should not underestimate the importance of this component to successfully disseminate, deploy, and sustain Lean. When implementing Lean consider 50% is a task and 50% is people. The first 50% is applying the Lean tools to any process, which is the scientific management part of Lean. The other 50% is the people piece or change management. There must be a balance between these two pieces. The change acceleration process (CAP) model was popularized by GE and used at AlliedSignal (now Honeywell). The model is

$$\text{Quality} \times \text{Acceptance} = \text{Effectiveness or } Q \times A = E.$$

This model looks at the message content (quality) of the change, the message being communicated, and assesses the potential level of resistance (acceptance) for the change (soft skills) in order to create a shared need for the change (effectiveness).

2. What is the CAP process?
   – Creating a shared need
   – Shaping a shared vision
   – Mobilizing commitment
   – Making change last
   – Monitoring progress
   – Changing systems and structures

3. Is it important to understand the personality traits of Lean team members? Describe why.
   – Is it very important to understand the personality traits of Lean team members for Lean to take hold, permeate, and sustain with the organization in a significant manner it requires leadership at all levels? Leaders must act as change agents and support their change agents in their efforts. Identifying leaders and individuals within the organization

that exhibit the behaviors of good change agents can develop and can facilitate your change initiatives. It is not unusual to see totally unexpected leaders emerge from the "woodwork" that thrive in this new Lean environment.

4. What process should be used to implement suggestions for establishing quick wins?
   – When evaluating ideas, the best approach for a quick win is to score them as low cost or high cost (see Figure 5.16, in the main book). Select the dollar value of what is considered high cost and rank the ideas accordingly. Then look at which ideas provide low benefit and which provide high benefit. The low cost, high benefit items should be worked first for the quick win. It is best to determine benefit as either pertaining to improving something that will result in increasing your end customer satisfaction or helps to meet a Hoshin or strategic planning goal or objective. Rank each idea accordingly.

   Quick wins = low cost + high benefit solutions. Implement them now! Do not wait.

   There are many quick win examples in an office environment. A simple example is invoicing customers. Some firms allow the invoices to accumulate and send out a batch each month. A better approach is to process the invoice as soon as the good or service is delivered to the customer and preferably trigger the invoice directly from the manufacturing line. Thus, approach would be more efficient, improve cash collection, and cost very little to implement.

5. Concrete heads can cause problems during a Lean implementation. How do we identify a concrete head? How do we deal with them?
   – It is important to identify and determine the best course of action to take when encountering concrete heads. If not addressed, they may negatively impact the ability of the organization to achieve Lean success. People are a company's most valuable resource. This is especially important to consider when implementing a culture change to Lean thinking. On the team, 10% lead, 80% follow, and 10% are the draggers (concrete heads) that impede the change process. Do not spend too much time with the 10% concrete heads who will be either converted or weeded out. Concentrate on helping the top 10% to drive the process and support the 80% followers.

6. Describe how to empower a Lean team for success.
   – Engaging frontline staff in problem-solving and supporting them in the initiatives requires managers to be able to empower and delegate activities they may not have in the past for a variety of reasons. Delegating is not something we learn in school. How do we overcome delegation challenges? It is done through empowerment.
     • To help with this, we use a tool called the empowerment or freedom scale. The scale is composed of the following five levels:
       ■ Told what to do
       ■ Ask what to do
       ■ Recommend, then take action
       ■ Take action, notify at once
       ■ Take action, notify periodically

   These levels represent the comfort levels between a manager/supervisor and their direct reports or team they are championing. The scale can be utilized for individual tasks, job descriptions, and team projects. Ideally, we want a highly empowered team that will take action and notify periodically. This process will take some time to develop; however, the results are powerful.

7. Why do firms need to change and what processes can be used to accelerate changes?
   - Change is usually driven by a leader, who is not satisfied with the status quo, has the desire to transform the company to a top performing firm, but must create the need and vision.

V = Vision

V is for vision and is important in the change equation because vision helps to chart a course (i.e., road map). People must understand the vision and the change required to support the vision, including the how, when, and what their contribution will be as well as their role in the change. This will make the change easier to sell and become adopted thus reducing the resistance to change. Communicate, communicate, and communicate. It is critical when you begin deploying Lean that team members communicate clearly as to why a Lean transformation is needed.

N = Next steps

N stands for next steps. Once we know we have a compelling need to change and know and understand the vision, we need to determine the next steps (not just the first) to get to the vision. These steps come from assessing where we are currently relative to the vision. If the road map of how we are going to achieve the vision is communicated and people gain an understanding of it, this will help diminish the resistance to change.

S = Sustain

The final letter, S, stands for sustain, which we have added to the original equation. Once we have implemented our steps, we must sustain ongoing improvement that is the most difficult step of all. Sustaining is the true test of whether there was a compelling enough reason to change and a sign if the other letters were implemented properly.

8. Name five characteristics of a good reward system.
   - Attributes to take into consideration as you develop or review your current reward system.[21]
     - Availability: The extent to which a particular reward is available for distribution within the organization.
       - Eligibility: Whether classes of employees (e.g., hourly, nonexempt) are eligible to receive a particular reward.
     - Visibility: The degree to which a reward is visible to the recipient and to other organization members.
   - Performance contingency: The extent to which the receipt of a reward, and the size of the reward, are based upon the recipient's performance.
   - Flexibility: The extent to which a reward can be tailored to the needs of individual employees.
     - Timeliness: Whether a reward can be distributed soon after the decision is made to distribute it, as opposed to being delayed by calendar dates, employee anniversary dates, or one-over-one approvals.
   - Reversibility:
     - Whether the reward, once given, can be reclaimed.
   - Whether the decision to give the reward can be reversed so the reward need not be given again.

9. What is the quick wins formula, and how would we use the formula in a manufacturing environment? Can we use the formula in an office environment? If so, provide an example.

$$\text{Quick wins} = \text{low cost} + \text{high benefit solutions}$$

It can be used in any environment.

10. What are the different types of closing statements? Why are they important?
    - The direct close
    - The indirect close
    - The positive-negative close
    - The assumed close

    Objections should be viewed as good. They are not a no. We just need to be persuasive and overcome them.

11. What is the danger with complacency? How do you know if a person or company is complacent?
    - Complacency is the arch enemy of Lean. We must be vigilant never to be content with the status quo or feel we have improved enough or cannot improve any more. There is always room for improvement and a better way to do something. We may not know what it is yet, but we know it exists. A person (or company) is complacent if they resist change. Excuses and roadblocks support the status quo and make change difficult.

12. What makes a good idea system? Why has the United States struggled with idea systems?
    - Small ideas lead to big ideas. We then look to see if they are transferable within a similar system and if they can be utilized in a dissimilar system in some other way? Can we take these ideas and?
      • Transfer them to other sites/plants
      • Further them and generate new ideas
      • Apply the ideas to another area or process
      • Utilize them for people development and discriminator for advancement
      • Understand which team members are not suggesting ideas and why

    Small ideas (especially if they are implemented by in-house personnel) are the best ideas because they cannot be easily copied by other companies unless they have identical processes and equipment to yours. For example, poka-yoke on machines, speeds and feeds, total productive maintenance changes, etc. are difficult for someone else to copy. In the United States, suggestion systems struggle as there is a major emphasis on meeting quarterly financial targets with no real benefit to working on suggestion systems. The stock market rewards firms that exceed revenue and margin targets, without any recognition of continuous improvement processes. Organizations must make implementing ideas part of every managers' job and align the organization to support idea development and implementation. In essence, the employee reward should be the implemented idea not some dollar amount. When eliciting suggestions or ideas, it is critical it is done without judgment or emotion.

13. What is the problem with a suggestion box system?

    Suggestion box systems normally use up significant amounts of time in the review, return on investment (ROI) analysis, and approval cycles and often employees may not hear back on their suggestion. 90% of suggestion box type systems fail.

14. What are the three stages of the suggestion system?

    The three stages of the suggestion system are:
    - Encouragement. In the first stage, management should make every effort to help the workers provide suggestions for the betterment of the worker's job and the organization. This will help the workers evaluate the way they are doing their jobs.
    - Education. In the second stage, management should stress employee education so employees can provide better suggestions. For the workers to provide better suggestions, they should be educated and trained to analyze problems.

    – Efficiency. Only in the third stage, after the workers are both interested and educated, should management be concerned with the economic impact of the suggestions.

15. If an employee gives you an idea, what is the most important thing you need to do?

    – The priority is to take the idea and work to implement in a Lean approach. Lean leaders must find a way to drive Lean improvements and implement employee ideas every day. If you implement on idea, they will give you another! Only the CEO can create this compelling need to change for the organization as a whole thus not only do we go through the change equation but the CEO must develop a way to continuously repeat the change equation cycle in order to create a systemic way to drive continuous improvement every day.

16. What are some of the barriers to change?

    – Cultural barriers result in entrenched habits, behaviors, and attitudes. Most cultural barriers can only be modified, replaced, or removed by a realistic cultural behavioral assessment by the senior leadership team. Senior leaders must be able and willing to take the time to critically assess their organization's strengths and weaknesses. Process barriers are best removed by using cross-functional teams and championed by senior leadership. These barriers normally cross departments and are very difficult to remove. These are good candidates for Lean system-wide kaizen projects or in some cases point kaizen events. These barriers take some change to the overall reward and recognition system. Processes are typically much more difficult to implement than shop floor activities. Technical barriers are those specific to machines or the industry and can normally be removed by individuals or cross-functional teams.

17. What is the importance of WIIFM?

    – Change can be a difficult adjustment for many individuals. We developed this tool knowing each employee is going to ask, "What's In It For Me" (WIIFM) and how is it going to affect me and my future in this company? When challenged with a new initiative, it is important to answer these questions, and they must be addressed from multiple perspectives. Management must be ready with the answers to address both positive and negative impacts from the employees' perspective. If we do not answer the tough questions, employees will fill in any gaps not clearly communicated with the worst-case scenario, often creating, or spreading rumors that will run rampant in the office and potentially on the Internet.

18. What should you script prior to making a change?

    – Script answers to the above questions prior to starting the Lean journey:
- What is the change we are making?
- Why are we making the change?
- How will it affect the employees? Now and in the future?
- How will it affect the company? Now and in the future?
- What is in it for the employee if we make the change?
- What is in it for the company if we make the change?
- Share as much of the implementation plan as possible to provide when, where and how the change will be implemented. People feel much more secure knowing there is a plan in place and that they have a future role in the company.

19. What is the difference between a skeptic and a cynic?

Sometimes resistance to change is good. We say, "Skeptics are good, cynics are bad." Skeptics keep you honest by asking very good questions. Cynics on the other hand will never go along with the change and become concrete heads/blockers during the culture transition. It helps to surface problems and valid objections to the anticipated change.

20. Should you look at change as a threat or an opportunity? Why?

    Change is an opportunity. Team members, who view change as a threat, only focus on the negative, which many times result in a self-fulfilling prophecy. The person is moved, or let go, because they simply could not adjust to the change. This is part of what is called the expectations theory where everything fits their expectation or paradigm, making them believe, the change would not succeed; therefore, they would not succeed. Those who embrace change and see it as a positive not only succeed but also have fun doing it and they tend to advance in their organizations. Some people are just naturally early adopters for change while others wait and sit back to see what will happen.

21. What did you learn from this chapter?

Appendix B - Acronyms

5Ws	when, where, what, who, why
5W2Hs	when, where, what, who, why, how, how much
5 whys	asking why five times in a row in order to get to the root cause
AGV	automatic guided vehicle
AI	artificial intelligence
AP	accounts payable
ASL	approved supplier list
AT	actual time
AT&T	American Telephone and Telegraph
BASICS®	lean implementation model for converting batch to flow: baseline, analyze (assess), suggest solutions, implement, check, and sustain
BFT	business fundamental table
BIG	Business Improvement Group LLC based in Towson, MD
BOM	bill of material
BPD	business process development
BRIEF	Baseline Risk Identification of Ergonomic Factors
BVA	business value added
C	Cold
CAD	computer-aided design
CAP	change acceleration process
CEO	chief executive officer
CM	centimeters
COGS	cost of goods sold
CQI	continuous quality improvement
CTP	cost to produce
CTQ	critical to quality
CV	coefficient of variation
CWQC	company-wide quality control
CYA	cover your ass
DBH	day by hour
DFA	design for assembly
DFM	design for manufacturing
DFMA˚	Design for Manufacturing and Assembly
DIRFT	do it right the first time
DL	direct labor
DMAIC	design, measure, analyze, improve, control

DMEDI	design, measure, explore, develop, implement
DOE	design of experiments
DPMO	defects per million opportunities
EBIT	earnings before interest and taxes
EBITDA	earnings before interest taxes depreciation, and amortization
ECR	engineering change request
ED	emergency department (emergency room)
EDD	earliest due date
EDI	electronic data interchange
EHS	environmental, health, and safety
ERP	enterprise resource (requirements) planning
ERSC	eliminate, rearrange, simplify, or combine
EHS	Environmental Health and Safety
ETDBW	easy to do business with
EV	earned value
EVA	economic value added
FC	full change
FG	finished goods
FIFO	first in, first out, replaced by EDD, earliest due date
FISH	first in still here
FMEA	failure modes and effects analysis
FPY	first pass yield
FT	feet
FTT	first time through (thru)
FWA	full work analysis
GE	General Electric
GM	general manager
GMS	global manufacturing system
GPI	global process improvement
H	hot
H	hour or hours
HBS	Harvard Business School
HEPA	high-efficiency particle absorption
HPWT	high-performance work teams
HR	human resources
HS&E	health safety and environmental
ICE	SMED formula, identify, convert, eliminate
i.e.	that is
IL	indirect labor
IN	inches
INFO	information
INSP	inspection
ISO	International Organization for Standardization
IS	information systems
IT	information technology (computing/networking)
IT	idle time
ITCS	intelligent tracking control system

JB	job breakdown
JEI	job easiness index
JI	job instruction
JIC	just in case
JIT	just in time
JM	job methodology
JUSE	Japanese Union of Scientists and Engineers
KPI	key process indicators
KPO	Kaizen Promotion Office
KSA	knowledge, skill, or ability
LB	pound or pounds
LBDS	lean business delivery system
LCL	lower control limit
LEI	Lean Enterprise Institute
LIFO	last in, first out
LMAO	laughed my butt off
LMP	lean maturity path
LP	lean practitioner
LP1	lean practitioner level 1
LP 2–5	lean practitioner level 2 through level 5
LRB	lean review board
Max	maximum
MBD	month by day
MBTI	Myers-Briggs Type Inventory—personality styles
MH	man hours
Min	minute or minutes
Min	minimum
MM	materials manager
MPS	master production schedule
MRB	material review board
MSA	measurement systems analysis
MSD	musculoskeletal disorder
MSE	manufacturing support equipment
MSE	measurement system evaluation
MT	meter
MTD	month to date
MVA	market value added
NIH	not invented here
NOPAT	net operating profit after taxes
NOW	not our way
NRE	Nonrecurring engineering
NTED	no touch exchange of dies
NVA	non-value added
NVN	non-value added but necessary
OCED	one cycle exchange of die
OE	order entry
OEE	overall equipment effectiveness

OEE	overall engineering effectiveness scale
OPBSF	one-piece balanced synchronized flow
OPER	operator
OPF	one-piece flow
OPI	office of process improvement
OPS	operations
OR	operating room
ORG	organization
OSED	one-shot exchange of dies
OTD	on-time delivery
OTED	one-touch exchange of dies
OTP	on-time performance
PC	production control
PCDCA	plan–control–do–check–act
PDCA	plan–do–check–act
PDSA	plan–do–study–act
PEST	political, economic, social, and technological
PFA	process flow analysis (following the product)
PFEP	plan for every part
PI	process improvement
PI	performance improvement
PIT	process improvement team
P/N	part number
PM	preventative maintenance
PO	purchase order
POU	point of use
POUB	point of use billing
PPCS	part production capacity sheet
PPF	product process flow, synonymous with PFA
PPM	parts per million
PPV	purchase price variance
Prep	preparation
PSI	pounds per square inch
PWI	perceived weirdness indicator scale (1–10) developed by Charlie Protzman
QC	quality control
QCD	quality, cost, and deliver
+QDIP	safety, quality, delivery, inventory, productivity
QTY	quantity
RC	running change
RCCA	root cause corrective action
RCCM	root cause counter measure
Rchange	resistance to change
REQ	requisition depending on the context
Reqmt	requirements
RF	radio frequency
RFQ	request for quote
RFID	radio-frequency identification

RM	raw materials
ROA	return on assets
ROI	return on investment
RONA	return on net assets
RR	railroad
RTC	resistance to change
RW	required work
S	second or seconds
SASL	signal acquisition source locator
SIPOC	suppliers–inputs–process–outputs–customer
SJS	standard job sheet
SMART	specific, measurable, attainable (achievable), realistic (relevant), timely
SMED	single-minute exchange of dies
SMG	strategic materials group
SOP	standard operating procedure
SORS	standard operation routine sheet, same as SWCS
SPACER	safety, purpose, agenda, code of conduct, expectations, roles
SPC	statistical process control
SPEC	specification
SQC	statistical quality control
ST	storage time
STRAP	strategic plan
SWCS	standard work combination sheet, same as SORS
SWIP	standard work in process
SWOT	strengths, weaknesses, opportunities, threats
TBP	Toyota Business Practice
TCWQC	total company-wide quality control
TH	throughput time
TIPS	transport, inspect, process, store
TL	team leader
TLA	three letter acronym
TLT	total labor time
TM	team member
TOC	theory of constraints
TPM	total productive maintenance
TPS	Toyota production system
TQ	total quality
TQM	total quality management
TT	takt time
UAI	use as is
UCL	upper control limit
UHF	ultrahigh frequency
USW	United Steelworkers
VA	value added
VMI	vendor-managed inventory
VOC	voice of the customer
VOP	Value of the Person

VS	value stream
VSL	value stream leader
VSM	value stream map
W	warm
WACC	weighted average cost of capital
WADITW	we've always done it that way
WE	Western Electric
WFA	Workflow analysis, following the operator
WIIFM	what's in it for me
WIP	work in process
WMSD	work-related musculoskeletal disorder
WOW	ways of working
YTD	year to date

Appendix C - Glossary

5 whys: Method of evaluating a problem or question by asking *why* five times. The purpose is to get to the root cause of the problem and not to address the symptoms. By asking why and answering each time, the root cause becomes more evident.

5 Ws: Asking why something happened—when, where, what, why, or who did the task.

5W2H: Same as the five Ws but adding how and how much.

5Ss: Method of creating a self-sustaining culture that perpetuates a neat, clean, and efficient workplace:

- **Shine:** Keep things clean. Floors swept, machines and furniture clean, all areas neat and tidy.
- **Sort:** Clearly distinguish between what is needed and kept and what is unneeded and thrown out.
- **Standardize:** Maintain and improve the first three *Ss* in addition to personal orderliness and neatness. Minimums and maximums can be added here.
- **Store:** Organize the way that necessary things are kept, making it easier for anyone to find, use, and return them to their proper location.
- **Sustain:** Achieve the discipline or habit of properly maintaining the correct procedures.

Absorption costing: Inventory valuation technique where variable costs and a portion of fixed costs are assigned to a unit of production (or sometimes labor or square footage). The fixed costs are usually allocated based on labor hours, machine hours, or material costs.

Activity-based costing: Developed in the late 1980s by Robert Kaplan and Robin Cooper of Harvard Business School. Activity-based costing is primarily concerned with the cost of indirect activities within a company and their relationships to the manufacture of specific products. The basic technique of activity-based costing is to analyze the indirect costs within an organization and to discover the activities that cause those costs.

Affinity diagram: One of the seven management tools to assist general planning. It organizes disparate language information by placing it on cards and grouping the cards which go together in a creative way. Header cards are used to summarize each group of cards. It organizes information and data.

Allocation: A material requirement planning (MRP) term where a work order has been released to the stockroom; however, the parts have not been picked for production. The system allocates (assigns) those parts to the work order; thus, they are no longer available for new work orders.

Andon: Andon means management by sight—visual management. Japanese translation means light. A flashing light or display in an area to communicate a given condition. An andon can be an electronic board or signal light. A visual indicator can be accompanied by a unique sound as well.

Assembly: A group of parts, raw material, subassemblies, or a combination of both, put together by labor to construct a finished product. An assembly could be an end item (finished good) or a higher level assembly determined by the levels in the bill of material.

Backflush: MRP term used to deduct all component parts from an assembly or subassembly by exploding the bill of material by the number of items produced. Backflushing can occur when the work order is generated or when the unit is shipped.

Backlog: All customer orders received but not yet shipped.

Balance on hand (BOH): The inventory levels between component parts.

Balancing operations: This is the equal distribution of labor time among the number of workers on the line. If there are four workers and 4 minutes of labor time in one unit then each worker should have 1 minute of work.

Batch manufacturing: A production strategy commonly employed in job shops and other instances where there is discrete manufacturing of a nonrepetitive nature. In batch manufacturing, order lots are maintained throughout the production process to minimize changeovers and achieve economies of scale. In batch manufacturing environments, resources are usually departmentalized by specialty and very seldom dedicated to any particular product family.

Benchmarking: Method of establishing internal expectations for excellence based upon direct comparison to the very best at what they do. Benchmarking is not necessarily a comparison with a direct competitor.

Bill of material: A list of all components and manufactured parts that comprise a finished product. The list may have different levels denoting various subassemblies required to build the final product.

Bin: A storage container used to hold parts. Bins range in various sizes from small to very large containers and can be made of plastic, wood, metal, cardboard, etc.

Bin location file: An electronic listing of storage locations for each bin. Generally, locations are designated to the work area, rack, and shelf, and location on the shelf, that is, 1—A—2 defines assembly area 1, rack A, and shelf 2 position on the shelf.

Blanket order: An order generally issued for a year or longer for a particular part number or group of specific part numbers. The blanket order defines the price, terms, and conditions for the supplier, thus allowing an authorized representative of the purchasing team to issue a release against the blanket order to the supplier.

Blanket order release: An authorization to ship from the customer to the supplier a specified quantity from the blanket order.

Block diagram: A diagram where the processes are represented in order of assembly by blocks denoting the process name, cycle time, utilities required, standard work in process (SWIP), etc.

Bottleneck: Generally referred to as the slowest person or machine. However, only machines can be true bottlenecks as we can always add labor. A true bottleneck runs 24 hours a day and still cannot keep up with customer demand.

Breadman: Centralized floor stock systems where the suppliers normally own and manage the material until it is used.

Budget: A plan that represents an estimate of future costs against the expected revenue or allocated funds to spend.

Buffer: Any material in storage waiting further processing.

Buffer stock: Inventory kept to cover yield losses due to poor quality.

Capacity: The total available possible output of a system within current constraints. The capability of a worker or machine within a specified time period.

Carrying costs: The cost to carry inventory, which is usually determined by the cost of capital and cost of maintaining the space (warehouse) and utilities, taxes, insurance, etc.

Catch ball: Communications back, forth, up, down, and horizontally across the organization, which must travel from person to person several times to be clearly understood and reach agreement (consensus). This process is referred to as *catch ball*.

Cause and effect diagram: A problem-solving statistical tool that indicates causes and effects and how they interrelate.

CEDAC: Anachronism for cause and effect diagram with the addition of cards. Problem-solving technique developed by Ryuji Fukuda. A method for defining the effect of a problem and a target effect statement. Through the development of a CEDAC diagram, facts and improvements will be identified that allow action.

Cellular layout: Generally denotes a family of product produced in a layout, which has the machines and workstations in order of assembly. Does not necessarily imply the parts that are produced in one-piece flow.

Chaku-Chaku: Japanese term for *load-load*. Refers to a production line that has been raised to a level of efficiency that requires simply the loading of parts by the operator without any effort required for unloading or transporting material.

Checkpoint: Control item with a means that requires immediate judgment and handling. It must be checked on a daily basis.

CNC: Acronym for computerized machining—stands for computer numerical control.

Consigned inventory: Normally finished goods stored at a customer site but still owned by the supplier.

Constraint: Anything that prevents a process from achieving a higher level of output or performance. Constraints can be physical like material or machines or transactional like policies or procedures.

Continuous flow production: Production in which products flow continuously without interruption.

Continuous improvement (kaizen): A philosophy by which individuals within an organization seek ways to always do things better, usually based on an understanding and control of variation. A pledge to, every day, do or make something better than it was before.

Contribution margin: Equal to sales revenue less variable costs leaving how much remains to be put toward fixed costs.

Control chart: A problem-solving statistical tool that indicates whether the system is in, or out, of control and whether the problem is a result of special causes or common system problems.

Control item: A control item is an item selected as a subject of control for maintenance of a desired condition. It is a yardstick that measures or judges the setting of a target level, the content of the work, the process, and the result of each stage of breakthrough and improvement in control during management activity.

Control point: Control item with a target. A control point is used to analyze data and take action accordingly.

Cost cutting: Eliminating costs in the traditional way, that is, reducing expenses, laying people off, requiring people to supply their own pens, making salary workers work much more overtime, etc.

Cost of capital: The cost of maintaining a dollar of capital invested for a certain period. Normally over a year.

Cost reduction: Reducing costs by eliminating the waste in processes.

Correlation: A statistical relationship between two sets of data such that when one brings about some change in the other it is explained and is statistically significant.

Cp process capability: Process capability is the measured, inherent reproducibility of the product turned out by a process. The most widely adopted formula for process capability (Cp) is

$$\text{Process capability } (Cp) = 6\sigma = \text{total tolerance} \div 6$$

where σ is the standard deviation of the process under a state of statistical control. The most commonly used measure for process capability within ASA is a process capability index (Cpk), which is

$$Cpk = \text{lesser of Cpu or Cpl}$$

where

$$Cpu = (\text{upper specification} - \text{process mean}) \div 3$$

and

$$Cpl = (\text{process mean} - \text{lower specification}) \div 3$$

Interpretation of the index is generally as follows:

Cpk > 1.33	More than adequate
Cpk ≤ 1.33 but > 1.00	Adequate, but must be monitored as it approaches 1.00
Cpk ≤ 1.00 but > 0.67	Not adequate for the job
Cpk ≤ 0.67	Totally inadequate

CPIM: APICS—acronym for certified purchasing and inventory manager. Rigorous course material required with five modules of testing to be certified.

CPM: Acronym stands for certified purchasing manager—this is a NAPM (national association of purchasing managers) certification for purchasing professionals. Requires passing rigorous testing and experience criteria.

Cross-functional management: Cross-functional management is the overseeing of horizontal interdivisional activities. It is used so that all aspects of the organization are well managed and have consistent, integrated quality efforts pertaining to scheduling, delivery, plans, etc.

Cross-training: Training an employee in many different jobs within or across cells.

Customer relations: A realization of the role the customer plays in the continuation of your business. A conscious decision to listen to and provide products and services for those who make your business an ongoing concern.

Customer service: Any specifications required to meet the customer demands, needs, or requests for information and service. Everyone in the company should be a customer service representative.

Cycle: Completion of one whole series of processes by a part or person.

Cycle time: Available time divided by the factory capacity demand, the time each unit is coming off the end of the assembly line or the time each operator must hit, or the total labor time divided by the number of operators.

Cumulative: The progressive total of all the pieces.

Cumulative time: Is equivalent to adding up the total times as you progress. For instance, if step 1 is 5 seconds and step 2 is 10 seconds, the cumulative time is 15 seconds.

Daily control: The systems by which workers identify simply and clearly understand what they must do to fulfill their job function in a way that will enable the organization to run smoothly. These items are usually concerned with the normal operation of a business. Also a system in which these required actions are monitored by the employees themselves.

Data: Any portrayal of alphabetic or numerical information to which some meaning can be ascribed. Data can be found in a series of numbers or in an answer to a question asked of a person.

Data box: Term apportioned to a box in a value stream map that underlies a process box and contains elements such as process cycle time, number of persons, change over time, lot size, etc.

Demand flow: Material only moves to a work center when that work center is out of work. Subject of the book *Quantum Leap* by the World Wide Flow College of Denver. Layouts are typically a conveyor down the middle of the line with subassembly lines feeding in both sides.

Deming cycle: A continuously rotating wheel of plan, do, check, act.

Demonstrated capacity: Term to depict capacity arrived at by nonscientific means. Generally, it is arrived at by feel or observing actual output without determining what the process could generate if all the waste was removed.

Deviation: The absolute difference between a number and the mean of a data set.

Direct labor: Labor attributable specifically to the product.

Direct material: Raw material or supplied materials that when combined become part of the final product.

Distribution: Term generally refers to a supply chain of intermediaries.

Distributor: A company that generally does not manufacture material but is a middle man. They normally hold some finished goods but not always. Sometimes they may make some modifications to the finished goods.

Dock to stock: Process where suppliers are certified by the company's supplier quality engineers or purchasing and quality professionals that result in the supplier's products bypassing inspection or sometimes receiving to go directly to the stock room or shop floor where it is used.

Download: Transfer of information from a central computer (cloud) to a tablet, PC, phone, or other type of device.

Downstream operation: Task that is subsequent to the operation currently being executed or planned.

Downtime: Time when a scheduled resource is not operating.

Earned hours: Standard hours credited for actual production during the period determined by some agreed upon rate.

Economic order quantity: Model used to determine the optimum batch size for product running through an operation or a line. It is equal to the square root of two times the annual demand times average cost of order preparation divided by the annual inventory carrying cost percentage times unit cost.

Economy of scale: Larger volumes of products realize lower cost of production due to allocating fixed costs against a larger output size.

EDI: Acronym stands for electronic data interchange which is the ability for computer systems between supplier and customer to talk to each other without human involvement. In some cases, this requires programing of an interface between computers so they can talk to each other.

Effectiveness: Is the ability to achieve stated goals or objectives, judged in terms of metrics that are based on both output and impact. It is (a) the degree to which an activity or initiative is successful in achieving a specified goal and (b) the degree to which activities of a unit achieve the unit's mission or goal.

Efficiency: Production without waste. Efficiency is based on the *energy* one spends to complete the product or service as well as timing. For example, we all know of the *learning curve*. The more one performs a new task, the better they become each time the task is practiced. As one becomes more efficient, they definitely reduce stress and gain accuracy, capability, and consistency of action. A person has achieved efficiency when they are getting more done with the same or better accuracy in a shorter period of time, with less energy and better results.

Eight dimensions on quality: Critical dimensions or categories of quality identified by David Garvin of the Harvard Business School that can serve as a framework for strategic analysis. They are performance, features, reliability, conformance, durability, serviceability, esthetics, and perceived quality.

Elimination of waste: A philosophy that states that all activities undertaken need to be evaluated to determine if they are necessary, enhancing the value of the goods and services being provided and what the customer wants. Determining if the systems that have been established are serving their users or are the users serving the system.

Ending inventory: Inventory present at the end of a period. Sometimes validated by taking a physical inventory.

EPE: Acronym stands for every part every—this denotes batch size of lots running through the process.

Ergonomics: The study of humans interacting with the environment or workplace.

ERP: Acronym for enterprise resource planning system. It is a business management software to integrate all business phases to include marketing/sales, planning, engineering, operations and customer support the third generation of MRP systems usually used to link company plants locally, nationally, or globally. SAP, ORACLE, and BPCS are examples of these types of systems.

Excess inventory: More inventory than required to do any task.

Expedite: To push, rush, or walk a product (or information, signatures, etc.) through the process or system.

Expeditor: One who expedites.

External setup time: Time utilized and steps that can be done preparing for changeovers while the machine is still running. Example—prepping for a racing car pit stop like getting tires in place, having fuel ready, etc. Focus of changeovers or setups moving internal elements to external elements.

Fabrication: The process of transforming metals into a final product or subassembly usually by machine. Generally, a term to distinguish activities done in a machine shop versus manually assembling components into a final product.

Facility: The physical plant or office (transactional areas).

Failure analysis: The process of determining the root cause of a failure usually generating a report of some type.

Family: A group of products (or information) that shares similar processes.

FIFO: First in, first out inventory management system.

Flex fence: Purchasing term used in contracts to mitigate demand risk by having the supply chain capable of flexing production plus or minus 10%, 20%, or 30%. This is accomplished by identifying long lead items and developing plans to stock some of those parts at the buyer's expense.

Flexible workforce: A workforce totally cross-trained, capable, and allowed to work in all positions.

Floater: Cross-trained workers moved around throughout the day to different positions depending on the takt time or cycle time and the staffing requirements for the day.

Floor stock: Generally less expensive C-type parts stored centrally on the floor and owned by the company.

Flow: Smooth, uninterrupted movement of material or information.

Flow chart: A problem-solving tool that illustrates a process. It shows the way things actually go through a process, the way they should go, and the difference.

Flow production: Describes how goods, services, or information are processed. It is, at its best, one piece at a time. This can be a part, a document, invoice, or customer order. It rejects the concept of batch, lot, or mass producing. It vertically integrates all operations or functions as operationally or sequentially performed. It also encompasses pull or demand processing. Goods are not pushed through the process but pulled or demanded by succeeding operations from preceding operations. Often referred to as *one-piece-flow*.

FMEA: Failure mode and effects analysis. A structured approach to assess the magnitude of potential failures and identify the sources of each potential failure. Each potential failure is studied to identify the most effective corrective action. FMEA is the process of mitigating risk by looking at a process to determine what is likely to go wrong, the probability of it going wrong, the severity if it does go wrong, and the countermeasures to be taken in the event it does go wrong.

FOB: Free on board—logistics term used to designate where title passes to the buyer.

Focused factory: A plant or department focused on a single or family of products. Where everything can be done within the four walls. Does not necessarily mean cellular or one-piece flow.

Forecast: An attempt to look into the future in order to predict demand. Companies use techniques that range from historical statistical techniques to systematic wild ass guesses (SWAGs). The longer the forecast horizon, the less accurate the forecast.

FTE: Acronym standing for full-time equivalent. The formula is to take the total number of hours being worked by one or multiple people and divide by 2,080 hours (per year) and come up with the equivalent of one person's worth of labor per year.

Functional: Organized by department.

Functional layout: Layouts where the same or similar equipment is grouped together. These layouts support batch production.

GAAP: Acronym for generally accepted accounting principles.

Gain sharing: Method of compensating employees based on the overall productivity of the company. The goal is to give the employee a stake in the company and share based on productivity. Measures and participatory schemes vary by company and philosophy. There are many different methods of gain sharing. Normally differentiated from profit sharing, which is based on formulas relating only to company profits.

Grievance: Term refers to complaint (contract violation) filed by an employee (normally union based) against someone who is union or nonunion in the company.

Hanedashi: Device or means for automatic removal of a workpiece from one operation or process, which provides proper state and orientation for the next operation or process. In manufacturing, a means for automatic unloading and orientation for the next operation or process. In manufacturing, a means for automatic unloading and orientation for the next operation, generally a very simple device. Crucial for a *Chaku-Chaku* line.

Heijunka: Japanese term for level loading production. Necessary to support Kanban-based systems.

Histogram: A chart that takes measurement data and displays its distribution, generally in a bar graph format. For example, a histogram can be used to reveal the amount of variation that any process has within it based upon the data available.

Hoshin: Type of corporate planning, strategy, and execution in a setting where everyone participates in coming up with goals through a process called catchball and everyone down to the shop floor knows what they are doing is directly supporting the top three to five company goals.

Housekeeping: Keeping an orderly and clean environment.

Idle time: When a person is standing around with nothing to do, visible by arms crossed. Also known as pure waste.

Indirect costs: Traditional accounting costs that are not directly related or accounted to the product. Also known as overhead costs.

Indirect labor: Traditional accounting of labor required to support production without directly working on the product.

Indirect materials: Traditional accounting of materials used to support production but not directly used on the product.

Information: Data presented to an individual or machine.

Information systems: Term used to designate manual or computer-based systems, which convey information throughout the department or organization as a whole. Term used in value stream mapping for boxes located at the top of the map with lines to the process (information) boxes with which they interact.

Input: Work or information fed to the beginning of a system or process.

Inspection: The act of multiple (two or more) checks on material or information to see if it is correct. Can also refer to a department of humans that checks incoming materials (receiving inspection), WIP (in-process inspection), or final inspection before the product leaves the plant.

Internal setup time: Term used to designate time when machine or process is down (not running). Example is time when the racing car is in the pit stop having tires replaced and fuel added, etc.

Interrelationship diagram: A tool that assists in general planning. This tool takes a central idea, issue, or problem and maps out the logical or sequential links among related items.

It is a creative process that shows every idea can be logically linked with more than one idea at a time. It allows for *multidirectional* rather than *linear* thinking to be used.

Inventory: Purchased materials used to assemble any level of the product or to support production. Inventory can be in various stages from raw materials to finished goods.

Inventory turnover or turns: The number of times inventory cycles or turns over during the year. Generally calculated by dividing average cost of sales divided by the average inventory (normally three months). This can be a historical or forward-looking methodology. Can also be calculated by dividing days of supply into the number of working or calendar days.

Ishikawa diagram: Referred to as a fishbone used to graphically display cause and effect and to get to the root cause.

Item number: Normally a part number or stock number for a part.

Jidoka: Automation with a human touch or mind, autonomation. Automatic machinery that will operate itself but always incorporates the following devices: a mechanism to detect abnormalities or defects and a mechanism to stop the machine or line when defects or abnormalities occur.

Job costing: Where costs are collected and allocated to a certain job or charge number. Can be based on actual or standard costs.

Job description: List of roles and responsibilities for a particular job.

Job rotation: Schedule of movement from machine to machine or process to process. Used to support and encourage cross-training.

Job shop: Term used for factories that have high mix and low volume typically nonrepeatable or customized products.

Just-in-time manufacturing: A strategy that exposes the waste in an operation, makes continuous improvement a reality, and provides the opportunity to promote total employee involvement. Concentrates on making what is needed, when it is needed, no sooner, no later.

Kaizen (Kai = change; zen = good): The process improvement that involves a series of continual improvements over time. These improvements may take the form of a process innovation (event) or small incremental improvements.

Kanban: Japanese for a sign board. Designates a pull production means of communicating need for product or service. Originally developed as a means to communicate between operations in different locations. It was intended to communicate a change in demand or supply. In application, it is generally used to trigger the movement of material to or through a process.

Kit: Collection of components used to support a sub- or final assembly of a product.

Kitting: Process of collecting the components used to support a sub- or final assembly of a product.

Knowledge worker: A worker, who acquires information from every task, analyzes and validates the information, and stores it for future use.

Labor cost: Cost of labor, can be direct or indirect. In Lean, we look at total labor cost versus indirect or direct associated with traditional cost accounting systems.

Layout: Physical arrangement of machines and materials or offices.

LCL: Lower control limit, used on control charts.

Lead time: The time to manufacture and deliver a product or service. This term is used in many (often contradictory) contexts. To avoid confusion, lead time is defined as the average total lapse time for execution of the product delivery process from order receipt to delivery to the customer under normal operating conditions. In industries that operate in a build-to-order environment, lead times flex based on the influences of seasonal demand loads. In environments where production is scheduled in repeating, fixed-time segments or cycles, the lead time is usually determined by the length of the production cycle (i.e., days, weeks, months, etc.).

Lead time or throughput time: Time it takes to get through the entire process or time quoted to customers to receive their orders (from order to cash).

Lean production: The activity of creating processes that are highly responsive and flexible to customer demand requirements. Successful Lean production is evident when processes are capable of consistently delivering the highest quality (defect-free) products and services, at the right location and at the right time, in response to customer demand and doing this in the most cost-effective manner possible.

Learning curve: A planning technique used to predict improvement based on experience. Uses log charts to trend the data.

Level load: Process of leveling or equally distributing demand or products across a cell or plant. Also known as heijunka.

LIFO: Last in, first out inventory management.

Limit switch: Various electronic devices used to trigger an action when a particular limit is reached. Used to control machines or count parts, used to turn on or off machines, used often for poka yoke, etc.

Little's Law: Throughput time divided by cycle time = amount of inventory in the system.

Logistics: The art and science of shipping materials, distribution, warehousing, and supply chain management.

Lot: Refers to a group of parts or information generally batched together through the process.

Lot size: Number of parts in a batch to be produced.

LTA: Acronym for long-term agreement. An agreement negotiated with a supplier for a longer term and more complex than a simple blanket (pricing) agreement, normally three to five years with other conditions centering on the supplier's improvement, quality and delivery certification, and price reduction goals.

Machine hours: Total hours a machine is running. Can be value-added or non-value-added time normally used for capacity planning. May or may not include setup time or unplanned downtime.

Machine utilization: The amount of time a machine is available versus the amount of time the machine is being used. Includes setup and run time compared to available time. It used to be the *be all and end all* for traditional cost accounting measures. With Lean, it is not as important unless it is a true bottleneck machine.

Make or buy: Study of costs of purchasing a part versus purchasing the raw materials and making it in house.

Make to order: A product that is not started until after the customer orders it. In some cases, a Kanban or inventory of parts produced to a certain level may then be modified to fit the customer requirements.

Manufacturing resources planning (MRP II): A second-generation MRP system that provides additional control linkages such as automatic purchase order generation, capacity planning, and accounts payable transactions.

Master schedule: Schedule with customer orders loaded by due date or promised date.

Master scheduler: Person who enters sales orders into the master schedule.

Material requirements planning (MRP): A computerized information system that calculates material requirements based on a master production schedule. This system may be used only for material procurement or to also execute the material plan through shop floor control.

MBO: Management by objectives—a system where goals are handed down from manager to employee where the employee participates in the process.

Means (measure): A way to accomplish a target.

Min max: Refers to a type of inventory system where once the minimum level is reached or a reorder point is reached, a quantity is reordered, which brings the quantity back up to the maximum level. Some computer MRP systems (Oracle) have this as an option to manage inventory.

Milk run: Term used to identify the path water spider uses to replenish materials for a line.

Mistake proofing: Also known as poka yoke or foolproofing. A system starting with successive checks by humans to inspection devices built into or added to machines to detect and or prevent defects.

Mixed model production: The ability to produce various models with different levels of customization one by one down the production line.

Monthly audit: The self-evaluation of performance against targets. An examination of things that helped or hindered performance in meeting the targets and the corrective actions that will be taken.

MPS: Master production schedule.

MRO: Term used to designate maintenance repair and operating supplies.

MRP: Material requirements planning; a computerized system developed by Olie Wright using lead time offsets, bill of material, and various planning parameters used to predict when to release requisitions or work orders in order to schedule the production floor.

MRPII: Material resource planning; a more advanced MRP system, which ties various systems together within a single company, that is, manufacturing and finance.

MTM: Methods time measurement; system that has studied and determined times for various operations or movements by operators. Generally used with motion study.

Muda: Japanese term for waste.

Multiskilled or process workers: Description for individuals at any level of the organization who are diverse in skill and training. Capable of performing a number of different tasks providing the organization with additional flexibility.

Mura: Japanese term for uneven.

Muri: Japanese term for overburden.

Nemawashi: Refers to the process of gaining consensus and support prior to implementing a strategy.

Net sales: Total sales less returns and allowances.

Noise: Randomness within a process.

Nominal group technique: Process of soliciting information from everyone in the group.

Non-value added: Designation for a step that does not meet one of the three value-added criteria.

Non-value added but necessary (sometimes called business value added): Any step that is necessary but the customer is not willing to pay for it but it is done right the first time.

Normal distribution: Statistical term where most data falls close to the mean (± 1 sigma), less fall away from the mean (± 2 sigma), and even less fall even further away (± 3 sigma), where the distribution when graphed looks like a bell-shaped curve.

NTED: No-touch exchange of dies.

Objective: What you are trying to achieve with a given plan. The desired end result. The reason for employing a strategy and developing targets.

Obsolete: Loss of product value due to engineering, product life decisions, or technological changes.

Offset: Time entered into MRP systems to designate how long it takes to get through a part of the system, that is, purchasing time entered as two days. MRP uses this information to develop a timeline to predict when to release the order or purchase requirement. When added up, it equals the total lead time of the product in the system.

OJT: Acronym for on-the-job training.

One-year plan: A statement of objective of an organizational event for a year.

Operating system: Refers to the type of system computer is using, that is, DOS, windows, etc.

Operation: A series of tasks grouped together such that the sum of the individual task times is equal to the takt time (cycle time to meet product demand requirements). It is important to distinguish between operations and activities. Operations are used to balance work content in a flow manufacturing process to achieve a particular daily output rate equal to customer demand. An operation defines the amount of work content performed by each operator to achieve a balanced flow and linear output rate.

Opportunity cost: Return on capital, which could have been achieved had it been used for something else more productive.

Order policy: Term used in MRP to decide lot sizing requirements.

Organization structure: The fashion in which resources are assigned to tasks. Includes cross-functional management and vertical work teams. Also includes the development of multiskilled workers through the assignment of technical and administrative personnel to nontraditional roles.

Organizational development: Process that looks at improving the interactions within and between departments across the overall organization. Generally led by a consultant or company change agent.

Organizational tools: These provide a team approach in which people get together to work on problems and also get better at what they are doing. Organizational tools include work groups and quality circles.

OTED: One-touch exchange of dies. Uses a human touch to changeover one or more machines at the same time.

Overhead: Costs not directly tied to the product. Normally refers to all personnel who support the production process whether it is physical or transactional.

Overtime: Work beyond the traditional 40 hours usually results in a premium paid per hour.

Pareto chart: A vertical bar graph showing the bars in order to size from left to right. Helps focus on the vital few problems rather than the trivial many. An extension of the Pareto principle that suggests the significant items in a given group normally constitute a relatively small portion of the items in the total group. Conversely, a majority of the items in the total will, even in aggregate, be relatively minor in significance (i.e., the 80/20 rule).

Participative management: Employees collaborate with managers to work on improvements to the process. Basis for QC circles.

Pay for performance: Pay is tied to overall output by a team.

Perpetual inventory system: System designed to always have the correct amount of inventory in the system.

PFA: Process flow analysis, looks at the flow of just the product through the process using TIPS.

Phantom: A bill of material (BOM) or non-production work order used to determine if there are any parts shortages. How to create the phantom varies depending on the type of MRP or

ERP system. In general, a work order is created and then backed out of the system prior to MRP running again.

Physical layout: A means of impacting workflow and productivity through the physical placement of machinery or furniture. Production machinery should be grouped in a cellular arrangement based upon product requirements, not process type. In addition to this, in most instances, there is an advantage in having the workflow in counterclockwise fashion. Similarly, in an office environment, furniture should be arranged such that there is an efficient flow of information or services rather than strictly defined departments.

PDCA cycle: Plan-Do-Check-Act. The PDCA system, sometimes referred to as the Deming cycle, is the most important item for control in policy deployment. In this cycle, you make a plan that is based on policy (plan); you take action accordingly (do); you check the result (check); and if the plan is not fulfilled, you analyze the cause and take further action by going back to the plan (action).

Piece rate: Form of worker compensation based on individual output targets that vary by employee and process.

Pilot: Trying something out for one or several pieces in a controlled environment to test a hypothesis.

Plan: The means to achieve a target.

Planned downtime: Downtime that is scheduled for a machine or line.

Planner/buyer: Combines planning and buyer jobs.

Planner/buyer/scheduler: Combines planning, buying, and scheduling jobs.

Poka yoke: Japanese expression meaning *common or simple, mistake proof.* A method of designing processes, either production or administrative, which will by their nature prevent errors. This may involve designing fixtures that will not accept a defective part or something as simple as having a credit memo be a different color than a debit memo. It requires that thought be put into the design of any system to anticipate *what* can go wrong and build in measures to prevent them.

Policy: The company objectives are to be achieved through the cooperation of all levels of managers and employees. A policy consists of targets, plans, and target values.

Policy deployment: Hoshin Kanri—policy deployment orchestrates continuous improvement in a way that fosters individual initiative and alignment. It is a process of implementing the policies of an organization directly through line managers and indirectly through cross-functional organization. It is a means of internalizing company policies throughout the organization, from highest to lowest level. Top managers will articulate its annual goals that are then deployed down through lower levels of management. The abstract goals of top management become more concrete and specific as they are deployed down through the organization. Policy deployment is process oriented. It is concerned with developing a process by which results become predictable. If the goal is not realized, it is necessary to review and see if the implementation was faulty. It is most important to determine what went wrong in the process that prevented the goal from being realized. The Japanese name for policy deployment is Hoshin Kanri. In Japanese, Hoshin means *shining metal, compass,* or *pointing in the direction.* Kanri means *control.* Hoshin Kanri is a method devised to capture and concretize strategic goals as well as flashes of insight about the future and to develop the means to bring these into reality. It is one of the major systems that make world-class quality management possible. It helps control the direction of the company by orchestrating change within a company. The system includes tools for continuous improvement, breakthroughs, and implementation. The key to Hoshin planning is it brings the total organization into the strategic planning process, both top down and bottom up. It ensures the direction, goals, and objectives of the company are rationally developed, well defined, clearly communicated, monitored, and adapted based on system feedback. It provides focus for the organization.

POU: Point of use, designates location where product or tooling or information is used.

Preventative maintenance: Term given to duties carried out on machines in order to prevent a breakdown or unplanned stoppage.

Prioritization matrices: This tool prioritizes tasks, issues, product/service characteristics, etc., based on known weighted criteria using a combination of tree and matrix diagram techniques. Above all, they are tools for decision-making.

Problem-solving tools: These tools find the root cause of problems. They are tools for thinking about problems, managing by fact, and documenting hunches. The tools include check sheet, line chart, Pareto chart, flow chart, histogram, control chart, and scatter diagram. In Japan, these are referred to as the seven QC tools.

Process: A series of activities that collectively accomplish a distinct objective. Processes are cross-functional and cut across departmental responsibility boundaries. Processes can be value added or non-value added.

Process capability: See CPK.

Process control chart: Chart that represents tracking the sequence of data points over a number of or 100% samplings. It serves as a basis to define common cause versus special cause variation and to predict when a part or machine is likely to fail.

Process decision program chart: The process decision program chart (PDPC) is a method that maps out conceivable events and contingencies that can occur in any implementation plan. It, in time, identifies possible countermeasures in response to these problems. This tool is used to plan each possible chain of events that need to occur when the problem or goal is an unfamiliar one.

Process hierarchy: A hierarchical decomposition from core business processes to the task level. The number of levels in a hierarchy is determined by the breadth and size of the organization. A large enterprise process hierarchy may include core business processes, processes, subprocesses, process segments, activities, and tasks.

Process management: This involves focusing on the process rather than the results. A variety of tools may be used for process management, including the seven QC tools.

Process segment: A series of activities that define a subset of a process.

Product delivery process: The stream of activities required to produce a product or service. This activity stream encompasses both planning and execution activities to include demand planning, order management, materials procurement, production, and distribution.

Production control: Employee that tracks status of daily production; normally used in batch environments but sometimes in Lean environments.

Production schedule: Orders lined up in order of priority based on due date, promised date, or some other planning parameters.

Productivity: Productivity is the *amount* of products produced in a certain amount of time with a certain amount of labor. The products could be physical products or transactional such as processing an invoice or Internet blogs. Productive means getting things done, outcomes reached, or goals achieved and are measured as output per unit of input (i.e., labor, equipment, and capital).

Prototype: First piece on which new process is tried.

Pull production: In a pull process, materials are staged at the point of consumption. As these materials are consumed, signals are sent back to previous steps in the production process to pull forward sufficient materials to replenish only those materials that have been consumed.

Push production: In a push process, production is initiated by the issuance of production orders that are offset in time from the actual demand to allow time for production and delivery. The idea is to maintain zero inventory and have materials complete each step of the production process just as they are needed at subsequent (downstream) activities.

+QDIP: Acronym stands for safety, quality, delivery, inventory, and production. Ideally, parameters are set by the employees on the shop floor or in the workshop.

Quality: Refers to the ability of the final product to meet both the customers required specification and unspecified specifications.

Quality circles: Quality circles are an organizational tool that provides a team approach in which people get together to work on problems and to improve productivity. Their primary objective is to foster teamwork and encourage employee by involvement employing the problem-solving approach.

Quality function deployment: A product development system that identifies the wants of a customer and gets that information to all the right people so the organization can effectively exceed competition in meeting the customer's most important wants. It translates customer wants into appropriate technical requirements for each stage of product development and production.

Quality management: The systems, organizations, and tools that make it possible to plan, manufacture, and deliver a quality product or service. This does not imply inspection or even traditional quality control. Rather, it involves the entire process involved in bringing goods and services to the customer.

Queuing theory: Applies to manufacturing orders, people, or information that is waiting in line for the next process. Based on Little's law.

Queue time: Amount of time an order, people, or information is waiting for the next process.

Quick changeover: Method of increasing the amount of productive time available for a piece of machinery by minimizing the time needed to change from one model to another. This greatly increases the flexibility of the operation and allows it to respond more quickly to changes in demand. It also has the benefit of allowing an organization to greatly reduce the amount of inventory that it must carry because of improved response time.

Rate-based order management: This order management system employs a finite capacity loading scheme to promise orders based upon the agreed demand bound limits. These minimum and maximum demand bounds reflect potential response capacity limits for production and materials procurement.

Rate-based planning: A procedure that establishes a controlled level of flexibility in the product delivery process in order to be robust to anticipated variations in demand. This flexibility is achieved by establishing minimum and maximum bounds around future demand forecasts. The idea is that both the production facility and the material supply channels will echelon sufficient capacity to accommodate demand swings that do not exceed the established demand bounds. As future demand forecasts move closer to the production window, updated demand bounds are periodically broadcasted to the material suppliers. At the point of order receipt and delivery promising (within sales or customer service), demand bounding limits are enforced to insure that the rate-based production plan remains feasible.

Regression analysis: Statistical technique that determines or estimates the amount of correlation explained between two or more variable sets of data.

ROI: Return on investment, generally compares investment versus the return to determine the payback that is often stated in years and expressed as a percentage of earnings.

RONA: Return on net assets.

Root cause: The ultimate reason for an event or condition.

Run chart: A statistical problem-solving tool that shows whether key indicators are going up or down and if the indicators are good or bad.

Safety: Ensuring that the work environment is free of hazards and obstacles of which could cause harm.

Scanlon plan: A system of group incentives that measures the plant-wide results of all efforts using the ratio of labor costs to sales value added by production. If there is an increase in production sales value with no change in pricing, mix, or labor costs, productivity has increased and unit costs have decreased.

Scatter diagram: One of the seven QC tools. The scatter diagram shows the relationship between two variables.

Scheduled (planned) downtime: Planned shutdown of equipment to perform maintenance or other tasks or lack of customer demand.

Self-diagnosis: As a basis for continuous improvement, each manager uses problem-solving activity to see why he or she is succeeding or failing to meet targets. This diagnosis should focus on identifying personal and organizational obstacles to the planned performance and on the development of alternate approaches based on this new information.

Self-directed work team: Normally, a small group of employees that can plan, organize, and manage their daily responsibilities with no direct supervision. They can normally hire, fire, or demote team members.

Setup: The changing over of a machine or also the loading and unloading of parts on a machine.

Setup time: The amount of time it takes to changeover a machine from the last good part to and including the first good part.

Setup parts: Preparation, mounting and removing, calibration, trial runs, and adjustments.

Seven new tools: Sometimes called the seven management tools. These are affinity and relationship diagrams for general planning; tree systems, matrix, and prioritization matrices for intermediate planning; and activity network diagrams and process decision program charts for detailed planning.

Seven QC tools: Problem-solving statistical tools needed for customer-driven master plan. They are cause and effect diagram, flow chart, Pareto chart, run chart, histogram, control chart, and scatter diagram.

Seven wastes: Seven types of waste have been identified for business. They are as follows:

1. Waste from overproduction of goods or services
2. Waste from waiting or idle time
3. Waste from transportation (unnecessary)
4. Waste from the process itself (inefficiency)
5. Waste of unnecessary stock on hand

6. Waste of motion and effort
7. Waste from producing defective goods

The eighth waste: Waste of talent and knowledge

Shojinka: Means labor flexibility. The term means employees staffing the line can flex up or down based on the incoming demand, which requires employees to be cross-trained and multi-process/machine capable. It also means continually optimizing the number of workers based on demand. This principle is central to baton zone line balancing (bumping).

Shoninka: Means *manpower savings*. This corresponds to the improvement of work procedures, machines, or equipment to free whole units of labor (i.e., one person) from a production line consisting of one or more workers.

Shoryokuka[1]: Shoryokuka means *labor savings* and indicates partial improvement of manual labor by adding small machines or devices to aid the job. This results in some small amount of labor savings but not an entire person as in shoninka. Again this becomes a goal of all follow-up point kaizen events.

Simultaneous/concurrent engineering: The practice of designing a product (or service), its production process, and its delivery mechanism all at the same time. The process requires considerable up-front planning as well as the dedication of resources early in the development cycle. The payoff is in the form of shorter development time from concept to market, lower overall development cost, and lower product or service cost based upon higher accuracy at introduction and less potential for redesign. Examples of this include the Toyota Lexus 200 and the Ford Taurus.

SMED: Single-minute exchange of dies, 9 minutes 59 seconds or less setup time.

Smoothing/production smoothing: The statistical method of converting weekly or monthly schedules to level-loaded daily schedules.

SPC: Acronym for statistical process control.

Standard deviation: Statistical measurement of process variation (σ) which measures the dispersion of sample observations around a process mean.

Standard work: Standard work is a tool that defines the interaction of man and his environment when processing something. In producing a part, it is the interaction of man and machine, whereas in processing an invoice, it is the interaction of man and the supplier and the accounting system. It details the motion of the operator and the sequence of action. It provides a routine for consistency of an operation and a basis for improvement. Furthermore, the concept of standard work is it is a verb, not a noun. It details the best process we currently know and understand. Tomorrow it should be better (continuous improvement), and the standard work should be revised to incorporate the improvement. There can be no improvement without a basis (standard work).

Standard work has three central elements:

1. Cycle time (not takt time)
2. Standard operations
3. SWIP

Standard work (as a tool): Establishes a routine/habit/pattern for repetitive tasks, makes managing such as scheduling and resource allocation easier, establishes the relationship between man and environment, provides a basis for improvement by defining the normal and highlighting the abnormal, and prohibits backsliding.

Standard work in process: The amount of material or a given product that must be in process at any time to insure maximum efficiency of the operation.

Standardization: The system of documenting and updating procedures to make sure everyone knows clearly and simply what is expected of them (measured by daily control). Essential for application of PDCA cycle.

Statistical methods/tools: Statistical methods allow employees to manage by facts and analyze problems through understanding variability and data. The seven QC tools are examples of statistical tools.

Store, storage: Any time a product (part, information, or person) is waiting in the process.

Strategy: The business process that involves goals setting, defining specific actions to achieve the business goals, and allocating the resources to execute the actions.

Subprocess: A series of interrelated process segments that forms a subset of a total process.

Supplier partnerships: An acknowledgment that suppliers are an integral part of any business. A partnership implies a long-term relationship that involves the supplier in both product development and process development. It also requires a commitment on the part of the supplier to pursue continuous improvement and world-class quality.

System: A system is the infrastructure that enables the processes to provide customer value. Business systems comprise market, customer, competition, organizational culture, environmental and technological influences, regulatory issues, physical resources, procedures, information flows, and knowledge sets. It is through physical processes that business systems transform inputs to outputs and, thereby, deliver products and services of value in the marketplace.

Takt time: The frequency with which the customer wants a product or how frequently a sold unit must be produced. The number is derived by taking the amount of time available in a day and dividing it by the number of sold units that need to be produced. Takt time is usually expressed in seconds.

Target: The desired goal that serves as a yardstick for evaluating the degree to which a *policy* is achieved. It is controlled by a *control point, control item,* or *target item.*

Target costing: Method for establishing cost objective for a product or service during the design phase. The target cost is determined by the following formula:

$$\text{Sales price} - \text{target profit} = \text{target cost}$$

Target/means matrix: Shows the relationship between targets and means and to identify control items and control methods.

Target value: Normally a numeric definition of successful target attainment. It is not always possible to have a numeric target, and you must never separate the target from the plan.

Theory of constraints: A management philosophy first put forth in the book *The Goal* by Eliyahu Goldratt to identify bottlenecks in the process. In the book, he follows a young boy scout named Herbie. We call bottlenecks *Herbies* today in some cases. His approach was to identify the constraint, exploit the constraint, subordinate all non-constraints, elevate the constraint, and if the constraint is broken in step 4, then go back to step 1.

Throughput time: A measure of the actual throughput time for a product to move through a flow process once the work begins. Many people incorrectly label this measure as manufacturing lead time but it is actually a small subset and often has little to do with the total time from order inception to fulfillment.

TIPS: Acronym for parts of process flow analysis—transport inspect process store.

Total density: One of the eight Lean wastes is the *waste of motion*. One of the first things we advise when trying to identify wasted motions is do not confuse motion with work. In offices, this concept is revised slightly to the following: *do not confuse effort with results.*[2] Total density = work divided by motion.[3] Not all motion is work. It is important to separate needed motions versus wasted motions.

Total employee involvement (TEI): A philosophy that advocates the harnessing of the collective knowledge of an organization through the involvement of its people. When supported by the management, it is a means of improving quality, delivery, profitability, and morale in an organization. It provides all employees with a greater sense of ownership in the success of the company and provides them with more control in addressing issues that face the organization. TEI does not allow top management to abdicate its obligation to properly plan and set objectives. It does, however, provide more resources and flexibility in meeting those objectives.

Total labor time: The sum of labor value-added and labor non-value-added times.

Total productive maintenance: TPM is productive maintenance conducted by all employees. It is equipment maintenance performed on a companywide basis. It has five goals:

1. Maximize equipment effectiveness (improve overall efficiency).
2. Develop a system of productive maintenance for the life of the equipment.
3. Involve all departments that plan, design, use, or maintain equipment in implementing TPM (engineering and design, production, and maintenance).
4. Actively involve all employees—from top management to shop-floor workers.
5. Promote TPM through motivational management (autonomous small group activities).

The word total in *total productive maintenance* has three meanings related to three important features of TPM: total effectiveness (pursuit of economic efficiency or profitability), total PM (maintenance prevention and activity to improve maintainability as well as preventative maintenance), and total participation (autonomous maintenance by operators and small group activities in every department and at every level).

Transport: Any travel a part or information does throughout the process.

Tree diagram: The tree diagram systematically breaks down plans into component parts and systematically maps out the full range of tasks/methods needed to achieve a goal. It can either be used as a cause-finding problem-solver or a task-generating planning tool.

Value added: Must meet three criteria from the AMA video *Time The Next Dimension of Quality*: customer cares, physically changes the thing going through the process, and done right the first time. Value added was expanded for hospitals to physically or emotionally change the patient for the better in addition to the other two criteria.

Value-added work content ratio: The steps that actually transform and increase the value of the product or test requirements legislated by industrial licensing agencies. The value-added work content ratio is formed by simply dividing the sum of all value-added work steps by the product lead time for the total process. This ratio can also be used to evaluate waste only in the manufacturing process segment by dividing the numerator by the manufacturing flow time.

Vertical teams: Vertical teams are groups of people who come together to meet and address problems or challenges. These teams are made up of the most appropriate people for the issue, regardless of their levels or jobs within the organization.

Vision: A long-term plan or direction that is based on a careful assessment of the most important directions for the organization.

Visual management: The use of visual media in the organization and general administration of a business. This would include the use of color, signs, and a clear span of sight in a work area. These visuals should clearly designate what things are and where they belong. They should provide immediate feedback as to the work being done and its pace. Visual management should provide access to information needed in the operation of a business. This would include charts and graphs that allow the business status to be determined through their review. This review should be capable of being performed at a glance. To facilitate this, it is necessary to be able to manage by fact and let the data speak for it.

Water spider: New role for material handler. Water spiders can be a low-skill or high-skill job. The water spider job is to replenish empty bins on the line daily, plays a vital role in mixed model parts sequencing, should stay 15 minutes or more ahead of the line, can be utilized as a floater, can be utilized to release parts orders from suppliers, and should have standard work and walk patterns/milk runs.

Work groups: Work groups are an organizational tool providing a team approach in which people work together on problems to improve productivity.

World-class quality management: The commitment by all employees. It is a philosophy/operating methodology totally committed to quality and customer satisfaction. It focuses on continuous process improvement in all processes. It advocates the use of analytical tools and scientific methods and data. It establishes priorities and manages by fact. World-class quality management has perfection (world class) as its goal. We should benchmark to be better than the competition by a large margin, the best. To obtain this status, all employees must be involved, everyone, everywhere, at all times. The result will be products and services that consistently meet or exceed the customers' expectations both internal and external. This group is always passionate with respect to improving the customer experience.

Yo-i-don[4]: It means ready set go. It is used to balance multiple processes and operators to a required cycle time using andon. This means each station or line is station balanced to one cycle time. When each operator completes their work, they press the andon button. Once the count-down or count-up clock reaches the prescribed cycle time, any station not completed, immediately turns the andon light to red. At this point, the supervisor and other team members will come to help that station.

Yokoten[5]: It is a process critical for creating a true learning organization. Sharing best practices (successes) is critical across the entire organization. In kanji, yoko means beside, side, or width and ten has several meanings but here it would mean to cultivate or comment. Yokoten is a means of *horizontal or sideways transfer of knowledge*, that is, peer-to-peer across the company. People are encouraged to Gemba, to see the kaizen improvement made for them, and see if they can apply the idea or an improved idea in their area. At Honeywell, this is referred to as horizontal linking mechanisms (HLMs).

Notes

1. *Lean Lexicon*, John Shook, LEI, 2004.
2. Source unknown.
3. Kanban JIT at Toyota—Ohno, Japan Management Association.
4. Monden Yasuhiro, *Toyota Production System*, 3rd edition.
5. http://eudict.com/?lang=japeng&word=ten.

Index

Printed in the United States
by Baker & Taylor Publisher Services